what happens when women

say yes to god

and walk in faith

LYSA TERKEURST

HARVEST HOUSE PUBLISHERS
EUGENE, OREGON

Cover by Faceout Studio, Lindy Martin

Cover Photo © Borja Andreu, Zabrotskaya Larysa, janniwet / Shutterstock

Interior design by KUHN Design Group

For bulk, special sales, or ministry purchases, please call 1-800-547-8979.
Email: Customerservice@hhpbooks.com

M This is a federally registered trademark of the Hawkins Children's LLC. Harvest House Publishers, Inc., is the exclusive licensee of this trademark.

What Happens When Women Say Yes to God and Walk in Faith
Copyright © 2005, 2007 by Lysa TerKeurst
Published by Harvest House Publishers
Eugene, Oregon 97408
www.harvesthousepublishers.com

ISBN 978-0-7369-8583-3 (pbk)
ISBN 978-0-7369-8584-0 (eBook)

Library of Congress Control Number: 2021949968

Printed in the United States of America

22 23 24 25 26 27 28 29 30 / VP / 10 9 8 7 6 5 4 3

To my two beautiful sons, Jackson and Mark.
Through you, God has made my feet walk paths
that I never knew could be so amazing.
From the first night you called me "Mom,"
my heart and life have never been the same.
I lovingly dedicate the words penned here to you.

CONTENTS

What Happens When Women Say Yes to God

What Happens When Women Walk in Faith

what happens when women

say yes to god

INTRODUCTION

I believe God gives every woman a dream. Not the same dream, of course, but a dream that is especially tailored for her talents and His purposes. Each woman receives a dream that only she is destined to fulfill.

But just as the Israelites were promised a land flowing with milk and honey only if they had the faith to move ahead and take the promised land, as women with dreams we'll also face obstacles that will try to keep us from God's best for us. The Israelites had to overcome giants in the land. Those giants struck fear in the heart of those to whom the promise was given. Some drew back as a result. Discouragement set in. Fatigue, impatience, unbelief…all of these were common to those men and women who spent 40 years in the desert because they simply couldn't walk in faith toward the destiny God had called them to.

I meet many women who know in their hearts that God has great things for them. But with every step, they meet obstacles. Giants are in their promised land. And they experience those same feelings of discouragement, fatigue, and unbelief. I also understand these struggles on a deeply personal level. In the past several years, I've experienced betrayal and broken promises in a few of my closest relationships.

The books in this volume—*What Happens When Women Say Yes to God* and *What Happens When Women Walk in Faith*—were written at the very beginning of my writing and ministry journey. Many changes have happened in my life since then, and just like the Israelites, I've faced giants in the promised land. But through it all, God has remained faithful. I still believe what I wrote all those years ago:

Death does not mean defeat.
New life is just around the corner.

Let me ask you this: What dream has God has given you? Maybe you can't quite put it into words except to say that you know that God wants to use you. But how that's going to happen…you're not quite sure.

Not knowing exactly how God wants to use you is okay. When a woman begins to walk in faith toward God, He will give the dream. For me, the dream has resulted in speaking, writing, and the birth of Proverbs 31 Ministries. Your dream—the way God wants to use you—may be totally different. But though the dreams we have are different, I've discovered that the path is very similar for most women. And walking that path by faith, choosing to say *Yes!* even when you can't see the end of the road, is what this book is all about.

So get ready, my friend. Put your most comfortable walking shoes on. You've got a basic understanding of where we're headed, and now it's time to go. At the end of each chapter you'll find a Bible study. You'll find it helpful to get a notebook to record your answers and thoughts along the way. Take time to read the Scriptures, think about the questions, and record your responses in your notebook. Are you excited? I am. Because I really believe that walking with God takes us to amazing places!

Now, let's turn the page together.

ONE

A SOUL THAT LONGS FOR MORE

Whatever God says do, do it.

It all started the day God told me to give away my Bible.

I was exhausted from traveling and speaking. All I wanted to do was to get to my assigned seat on the plane and settle in for a long winter's nap. Imagine my absolute delight at being the only person seated in my row. I was just about to close my eyes when two last-minute passengers made their way to my row and took their seats.

Reluctantly, I decided to forgo my nap. The last thing I needed was to fall asleep and snore or, worse yet, wake up with my head resting on the guy's shoulder beside me. No, I didn't need another most embarrassing moment, so I pulled a manuscript out of my bag and started reading.

"What are you working on?" the guy asked. I told him I was a writer and I was working on a book titled *Leading Women to the Heart of God*. He smiled and said he thought God was a very interesting topic. I agreed and asked him a few questions about his beliefs. Before long, I found myself reaching into my bag and pulling out my Bible, walking him through some key verses that dealt with the issues he was facing. He kept asking questions, and I kept praying God would give me answers.

All of a sudden, I felt God tugging at my heart to give this man my Bible. Now, this was not just any Bible. This was my everyday, highlighted, underlined, written in, and tearstained Bible. My kids had even drawn pictures in this Bible. I started to argue with God in my head, but His message was clear. I was to give away my Bible.

I emptied it of some old church bulletins and other papers, took a deep breath, sighed, and placed it in the man's hands. "I'd like for you to have my Bible," I said. Astonished, he started to hand it back to me, saying he couldn't possibly accept such a gift. "God told me to give it to you," I insisted. "Sometimes the God of the universe pauses in the midst of all His creation to touch the heart of one person. Today, He paused for you."

The man took my Bible and made two promises. First, he said he would read it, and, second, someday he would pass it on, doing for someone else what I'd done for him.

Before I knew it, the plane landed and we were saying our goodbyes. As I stepped into the aisle preparing to disembark, the woman on the other side of the businessman reached out and grabbed my arm. She'd been staring out the window the entire time we were flying, and I thought she'd been ignoring us. But her tearstained face told a different story. In a tone so hushed I could barely hear her, she whispered, "Thank you. What you shared today has changed my life." I put my hand on hers and whispered back, "You're welcome." Then a knot caught in my throat as tears welled up in my eyes. I didn't have another Bible to give away, so I gave her one of my books and hugged her goodbye. It has been said that we are to tell the whole world about Jesus, using words only if necessary. I saw this powerful truth come to life. Though I never spoke to this lady about Jesus, she saw Him through my obedience. How humbling. How profound.

As I got off the plane that day, I could barely hold back my tears. Three people's hearts were radically changed. I believe the businessman came to know Jesus as his Lord and Savior. I believe the same is true for the lady. But my heart was changed in a dramatic way as well. While on the one hand I was overjoyed at what God had done, I was also brokenhearted by the flood of thoughts that came to mind recounting times I'd told God no. How tragic to miss God's divine appointments. I just kept wondering, *How many times have I told You no, God? How many times because I was too tired, too insecure, too uncertain, too busy, or too selfish have I walked right past Your divine appointment for me and missed experiencing You?* I lifted up my heart to the Lord and whispered, "Please forgive me for all those noes. Right now I say yes, Lord. I say yes to You before I even know what You might ask me to do. I simply want You to see a yes-heart in me."

Several minutes after exiting the plane, I was weaving in and out of the crowds, trying to find my connecting gate, when I spotted the businessman again. He stopped me to tell me he had been praying to God and thanking Him for what happened on the plane. We swapped business cards, and, though we lived several states apart, I knew we would stay in touch.

About a month later he called to tell me his life had totally changed. He'd taken a week off from work to read the Bible, and he'd already shared his testimony with numerous people. When he said this to me, my mouth dropped open. I couldn't bring myself to tell him that I'd never taken a week off from work to read the Bible. God was definitely pursuing this man in a serious way! When I asked him what his favorite verse was, he said it was Proverbs 3:5-6: "Trust in the LORD with all your heart; and lean not on your own understanding; in all your ways acknowledge him, and he will make your paths straight." I thought to myself, *Wow! Look at how God has already answered that for my new friend.*

He also told me that after reading the Scriptures he knew he needed to get involved in a church, so he'd decided to visit a large church in his town. On his way there he passed another church, and a strong feeling came over him to turn his car around and go back to that church. So he did. When he got to his seat in the sanctuary, he opened up his bulletin and gasped. Inside the bulletin he saw my picture and an announcement that I was to be the speaker at an upcoming women's conference. He said he felt as though, once again, God had paused just for him.

That day on the plane, when God impressed on my heart to give this man my Bible, I did not know what would happen. This man might have thrown my Bible into the nearest airport trash can, for all I knew. Normally, I would have come up with a hundred reasons not to give my Bible away, but that day something changed in me. That day, for the first time, I truly heard the call of a woman who says yes to God: "Whatever God says do, do it."

A FRESH INVITATION

When I said yes that day, I caught a glimpse of eternity. I saw how beautiful it is when God says to do something and it is done. And I thought, *Why wait for heaven? Why not say yes to God on this side of eternity?*

Oh, dear friend, the call to become a woman who says yes to God is the fresh invitation your soul is looking for. We all feel a tug at our heart and a stirring in our soul for more, but we are often afraid to venture past our comfort zone. Outside our comfort zone, though, is where we experience the true awesomeness of God.

I think at this point it is important for me to paint an accurate picture of what my life looks like on a daily basis. Lest you imagine me as this woman dressed in sackcloth who is perfectly calm, amazingly organized, incredibly disciplined, and who spends hours upon hours on her knees in solemn solitude before the Lord, let me assure you that's not how it is. I am a wife and busy mom of five who can often be found rushing from one carpool to the next. My to-do list rarely gets fully accomplished. My emotions have been known to run wild, and my patience can easily run thin. I get pushed to the limit by everyday aggravations, such as a summer's worth of pictures getting erased from my digital camera by a child who wasn't even supposed to be handling the camera. And a dog that I love dearly who insists on running away. And some important paperwork that should be in a file that has mysteriously sprouted wings and flown the coop!

Can you relate? Great! You are a woman perfectly equipped to say yes to Him. Notice that I did not say you are a perfect woman. But if you are in the thick of living with all that life throws at you and you simply whisper yes, you are equipped. "Yes, Lord. I want Your patience to invade my desire to fly off the handle." "Yes, Lord. I want Your perspective to keep my emotions in check."

"Yes, Lord. I want Your provision so things don't seem so overwhelming." "Yes, Lord. I want Your courage to do what I feel You calling me to do." "Yes, Lord. I want and need more of You in every moment."

You don't need perfect circumstances to be a woman who says yes to God. You don't need the perfect religious attitude or all the answers to religious questions. You simply have to surrender all that's clamoring for attention in your heart with the answer God is longing to hear spill from your lips: "Yes, God."

Each day when I wake up I pray a very simple prayer even before my feet hit the floor. *God, I want to see You. God, I want to hear You. God, I want to know You. God, I want to follow hard after You. And even before I know what I will face today, I say yes to You.* This simple act of surrender each morning will prepare your eyes to see Him, your ears to hear Him, your mind to perceive Him, and your heart to receive Him. This is how to live expecting to experience God.

You see, we have become so familiar with God yet so unaware of Him. We make the mysterious mundane. We construct careful reasons for our rules and sensible whys for our behavior. All the while our soul is longing for a richer experience—one that allows us to escape the limits of sight, sound, touch, taste, and smell and journey to a place of wild, wonder, and passion.

Women who say yes to God will see life like few others. They are drawn in and embraced by a love like no other. They don't have to wait until the next time they're in church to experience God because they sense God's presence all around them, all through their day. Instead of merely walking through the motions of life, they pursue the adventure of the moment-by-moment divine lessons and appointments God has in store for them. They expect to see God, to hear from Him, and to be absolutely filled by His peace and joy—and, therefore, they do and they are.

A woman who says yes to God isn't afraid to be honest with God. Just last week I woke up feeling drained and overwhelmed. I couldn't quite put my finger on the source of my anxiety, but I couldn't shake it, either. As I prayed my normal prayer of wanting to see and hear God, I told Him honestly that I really needed to see evidence of Him in my day. Later on I was in my kitchen washing dishes, preparing dinner, and talking with one of my sons. My attention was focused on my son while my hands were just going through the motions of my tasks. Suddenly I felt God's strong impression on my heart to look down in the sink before I reached for another dish. As I did, I saw a very sharp butcher knife sticking blade up from inside a glass. Immediately, I knew God's presence was there. I closed my eyes and thanked Him. More than just for sparing my hand from serious injury, I thanked Him for caring enough to be so real in my life.

A holy God in the middle of life's mundane activities will change your life. But you might not always feel happy about the changes. I can't let you think that being a woman who says yes to God means everything will suddenly be happily ever after. As I am writing this, I must tell you about an experience I had today where I simply wanted to throw my hands in the air, throw my computer out the window, and cry out to God, "You have hurt my feelings and I'm just a little unnerved and upset!"

I am on a retreat at a friend's lake house where I have three days during which I'd hoped to accomplish a lot of writing. I am under a tight deadline for this project and really needed to make a big dent in the task before me. Yesterday went great. I wrote almost 2,000 words and the friends with me loved what I'd written. I went to bed excited about all I'd accomplished so far. Visions of a completed manuscript and my editor's praises danced in my dreams all night long. I woke up this morning ready to tackle another huge chunk of writing, but first I wanted to admire yesterday's accomplishment. I opened up my documents section and the manuscript was nowhere to be found.

Refusing to panic, I asked for my friends' help. They felt confident we could locate the document I'd saved three times the night before. After two hours of searching, one of my friends gently looked at me and verbalized the truth we'd all come to know. "It's gone, Lysa. You are going to have to start over."

Wait just a minute, I thought. *I have said yes to God today and had a great quiet time. I just know He can and will help me find this.* But for whatever reason, my document was gone and God had chosen not to bring it back. Tears filled my eyes as bitterness started to creep in my heart. Why would God allow this? My friend could sense my despair and gently replied, "Lysa, recently when something like this happened to me, someone told me to look at my loss as a sacrifice of praise to God. It is so hard in today's abundance to give God a true sacrifice, but losing 2,000 words and a whole day's work would qualify. Give this to Him without feeling bitter."

I resisted slapping my well-meaning friend as she then broke into singing, "We bring a sacrifice of praise into the house of the Lord…" By the second stanza I actually found myself joining in with a lighter heart and a resilient spirit. Being a woman who says yes to God means making the choice to trust Him even when you can't understand why He requires some of the things He does. It also means that once you've said yes to God, you refuse to turn back, even when things get hard.

This kind of obedience invites you to embrace a bigger vision for your life. When you look at your everyday circumstances through the lens of God's perspective, everything changes. You come to realize that God uses each circumstance, each person who crosses your path, and each encounter you have with Him as a divine appointment. Each day counts, and every action and reaction matters. God absolutely loves to take ordinary people and do extraordinary things in them, through them, and with them.

A PARTY IN YOUR HONOR

Imagine you're planning a wonderful surprise party for someone you dearly love. You've made the plans, invited all the guests, and decided on an exquisite menu. You can't wait for the big moment when all the guests yell, "Surprise!" and your loved one finally joins in the festivities. You know she'll understand just how cherished and adored she is when she sees everything that's been done in her honor.

Finally, the time for the surprise arrives. All of the guests are waiting in anticipation at the front door. You see your loved one pull into the driveway, and you hear the car engine turn off. As she opens the car door, you see the interior lights come on while she gathers her things. Your heart races as you see her heading up the driveway. Suddenly, she makes an unusual turn and heads to the back door.

You quickly make your way to the back door to redirect her. Your cheerful greeting is met with a half-hearted smile, and your attempts to send her to the front door are brushed aside. She insists she is tired and will look at what you want to show her tomorrow. Only you know that tomorrow the guests will be gone, the leftover food will be stored away, and the party will be over.

How sad for the guest of honor who missed her own surprise party! And how disappointing for the party planner who orchestrated the event.

God must feel the same way when we miss the "surprise parties" (the divine appointments) that await us each day. How it must disappoint Him when we don't hear or don't listen to Him redirecting us to the front door. How it must grieve Him when we walk through our lives oblivious of His activity all around us. How it must break His heart when we brush aside something that not only would make us feel special and noticed by God, but also would allow us to join Him in making life a little sweeter for others.

How many times have we missed our own surprise party?

God reveals Himself and His activity to all of us, but very few really want an encounter with Him. Encounters cause extreme changes in our plans, our perspectives, and our personhood, and most of us hate change. In reality, though, the very act of trying to protect ourselves from change is the very thing that makes our life the boring mess that it sometimes is.

As I've traveled around the country speaking at conferences, I am amazed and saddened by the number of people missing out on the most exciting part of being a Christian—experiencing God. Over and over people tell me they want something more in their Christian life. They want the kind of relationship with God where they recognize His voice, live in expectation of His activity, and embrace a life totally sold out for Him. I suspect that tucked in the corner of your heart is the same desire. And I've discovered that the key to having this kind of incredible adventure is radical obedience.

THE ROAD THAT LEADS TO BLESSING

You may be surprised to discover that radical obedience is not really that radical. It is really biblical obedience—but we've strayed so far from biblical obedience that it now seems radical. In today's society, it is radical to obey God's

Saying yes to God

isn't about perfect performance,

but rather perfect surrender

to the Lord day by day.

commands, listen to the Holy Spirit's convictions, and walk in Jesus' character. But we will never experience the radical blessings God has in store for us without radical obedience. It is the road that leads to blessing. It is what happens when women say yes to God.

And you won't find the full blessing until you give walking in obedience your full attention. Obedience, however, is more than just "not sinning." It is having the overwhelming desire to walk in the center of God's will at every moment. Don't stumble over fearing you won't be perfect or that you are sure to mess up. Saying yes to God isn't about perfect performance, but rather perfect surrender to the Lord day by day. Your obedience becomes radical the minute this desire turns into real action. Radical obedience is hearing from God, feeling His nudges, participating in His activity, and experiencing His blessings in ways few people ever do.

If this is what you want, read on.

SIX SIMPLE WORDS

After hearing about the day I gave away my Bible, people often ask me if I've ever gotten it back. I always chuckle because, to be honest, I don't want to get that Bible back (or any of the Bibles I've given away since then)—at least not for a very long time. I've had this vision of one day being on a plane when I'm old and gray, and the person next to me starts talking. She tells me of the amazing things God has done in her life since the day she received a Bible from a stranger who had received it from another stranger who had received it from another stranger. She'll then reach inside her bag and pull out a worn and tattered book I've held once before. Wow, what a day that will be!

The man I gave the Bible to that day has continued to share his testimony, and I still hear from others whose lives have been changed because of his story. Recently, a lady wrote to tell me that the "Bible man" opened up a business meeting she attended by sharing how God had changed his life.

I just finished visiting with a friend of yours and mine. His name is Ron. Over the years I have seen him struggling with his success and the decisions in his life. Today, Ron is filled with a different spirit. Your actions brought him back in touch with God. He shared his story with the office on how he met you and the effect of your actions. Isn't it strange that we know God is powerful and we know that we should listen, but sometimes we shut Him out? I can't explain the emotion I felt when I heard this story, but I can tell you that I am seeking some way to be more active in spreading God's Word. Bless you and bless Ron for being wonderful messengers.

Don't we all long to see God at work? Evidence of His activity around us, in us, and through us is the greatest adventure there is. The God of the universe wants to use you!

There is but one requirement for this adventure. We have to set our rules and agendas aside—our dos and don'ts, our social graces and proper places—and follow God's command. His one requirement is so simple and yet so profound: Whatever God says do, do it. That's it. That is the entire Bible, Old Testament and New, hundreds of pages, thousands of verses, all wrapped up in six words.

It is the call of the radically obedient woman who makes the choice to say yes to God.

BIBLE STUDY

Did the story about the man on the airplane and giving him the Bible inspire you? How?

What is holding you back from going deeper in your relationship with God?

- Time?
- Intimidation?
- Not feeling like the Bible applies to your everyday life?
- Seems too hard?

Comment on one or more of the above or another thing you sense holding you back.

Psalm 19:7-10 (MSG) says:

> The revelation of GOD is whole and pulls our lives together. The sign-posts of GOD are clear and point out the right road. The life-maps of

GOD are right, showing the way to joy. The directions of GOD are plain and easy on the eyes. GOD's reputation is twenty-four-carat gold, with a lifetime guarantee. The decisions of GOD are accurate down to the nth degree. GOD's Word is better than a diamond, better than a diamond set between emeralds. You'll like it better than strawberries in spring, better than red, ripe strawberries.

List what Psalm 19:7-10 from *The Message* promises about God's Word.

The resolve of the human spirit is truly an amazing thing. We will fight to the death for something we want to protect, truly believe in, or desire. So why would we be lackadaisical about the most eternally significant relationship there is?

Read Deuteronomy 6:5.

- How can you love God with your heart?
- How can you love God with your soul?
- How can you love God with your strength?

Is there something you might need to let go of in order to have the freedom to say yes to God?

- Fear that it may cost you too much?
- Uncertain that you will like what a life sold out to Christ looks like?
- Feeling insecure that you'll be able to go the distance?

Psalm 16:7-9 (NLT) says,

> I will bless the LORD who guides me; even at night my heart instructs me. I know the LORD is always with me. I will not be shaken, for he is right beside me. No wonder my heart is filled with joy, and my mouth shouts his praises! My body rests in safety.

How does this verse give a sure answer for each concern listed above?

Write out a personal prayer of commitment for your new adventure with God.

TWO

HEARING GOD'S VOICE

God wants us to live in expectation of hearing from him.

I received this letter from Neil in the British Isles.

Dear Lysa,

It's winter in the U.K. My wife bought me an exercise bike for my forty-ninth birthday so I could commit to getting my weight down.

While I pedal, I turn on U.C.B. Europe radio [the Christian radio broadcast]. One morning I caught the final part of your story about the Bible man and the plane journey. I just wept right on through. The program repeats in the evening, so I taped it and listened to it again with my wife, and we both wept.

In the 26 years I've claimed to be a Christian, I think my witness has deteriorated. Your message has inspired me to try again. I realize that the time is short and the Lord is coming.

The man who delivers my coal knocked at the door today. He has been sick for several weeks, and he is only 42. I asked him what the problem had been. He has a brain hemorrhage. He went on to tell me that it had made him think about life. I asked him if he had a faith, but he didn't answer. So I shared briefly. It was off the cuff, but next week I'll be "preprayered" for him.

I've decided I will try to hear God's promptings and remember my time is not my own.

Every day, God speaks to us. Sometimes He invites us to draw close and listen as He reveals Himself, His character, and His direction. Other times He calls to us to participate in His purposes—for example, Neil sharing with the man who delivers his coal. Still other times He simply whispers to remind us of His amazing love for us.

Oh, what joy it is to know God speaks to me! But I've found that many believers are missing this vital element in their relationship with Him. As I've talked with people about my own radical obedience journey, they are quick to ask how they might hear from God too. Maybe you have some of these same questions: How do I know if God is speaking to me? How do I discern whether it is His voice speaking or just my own idea? What if I feel God is telling me to do something that doesn't seem to make sense?

There is no magic formula for being able to discern God's voice. We can learn to recognize it the way we recognize the voices of those close to us: by knowing Him. And when we know Him, we can tell if what we're feeling led to do is from Him or not.

Though I hear from God all the time, I've never heard His voice audibly. When God speaks to me, it is a certain impression on my heart that I've come to recognize as Him. I've also learned to ask five key questions to help me determine if what I'm hearing is from God or not:

1. Does what I'm hearing line up with Scripture?

2. Is it consistent with God's character?

3. Is it being confirmed through messages I'm hearing at church or studying in my quiet times?

4. Is it beyond me?

5. Would it please God?

Asking these questions helps me tell the difference between my thoughts and God's impressions.

DOES WHAT I'M HEARING LINE UP WITH SCRIPTURE?

God will not speak to us or tell us to do something that is contrary to His Word. But unless we know Scripture, we will not be able to discern whether what we are hearing is consistent or not with the Word. The apostle Paul wrote, "Do not conform any longer to the pattern of this world, but be transformed by the renewing of your mind. Then you will be able to test and approve what God's will is—his good, pleasing and perfect will" (Romans 12:2). God's Word is the language the Holy Spirit uses to help us understand what God is speaking to our hearts. We must get into God's Word and let God's Word get into us. This will transform our mind and prepare it for whatever God wants to tell us. Then, as Paul wrote, we will be able to test and approve not just God's good will, and not just His pleasing will, but His perfect will.

The good news is that you don't need a seminary degree to read your Bible. If reading God's Word is new for you, choose a translation that is easy to understand with a built-in commentary. A good rule of thumb is "Simply Start and Start Simply." Read a passage of Scripture and ask yourself: Who is this passage speaking to? What is it saying to me? What direction is this passage giving? How might I need to change my way of thinking or acting as a result of this

God will not speak to us or tell us to do something that is contrary to His Word.

verse? What are some other verses that relate to this topic, both in the Old Testament and New Testament?

These questions are just a starting place. I encourage you to get a journal and start recording the verses you study and some of your personal experiences with the things you are learning as you read God's Word.

IS WHAT I'M HEARING CONSISTENT WITH GOD'S CHARACTER?

God's Word also provides rich information regarding His character. As you come across verses revealing aspects of God's nature, make note of them. Just as God always speaks in accordance with His Word, He speaks in accordance with His character. God will not say things that are inconsistent with who He is. The apostle Paul writes, "Those who live according to the sinful nature have their minds set on what that nature desires; but those who live in accordance with the Spirit have their minds set on what the Spirit desires" (Romans 8:5). What is it that God's Spirit desires? Answering this question helps us understand God's character.

We find great insight into God's character in Galatians 5:22-23: "The fruit of the Spirit is love, joy, peace, patience, kindness, goodness, faithfulness, gentleness and self-control." These characteristics in a person's life are the evidence of Christ at work. "The fruit of the Spirit is the spontaneous work of the Holy Spirit in us. The Spirit produces these character traits that are found in the nature of Christ. They are by-products of Christ's control—we can't obtain them by trying to get them without his help. If we want the fruit of the Spirit to grow in us, we must join our lives to his. We must know him, love him, remember him, and imitate him."[1] If the fruit of the Spirit is our imitation of Him, then it must be consistent with God's character.

When you feel God speaking to you, ask yourself: Is what I am hearing consistent with God's love, joy, and peace?

In addition to the fruit of the Spirit, God's character is revealed in a loving relationship with us. As we experience God personally, we come to know new names for Him. When we've experienced His provision, we come to know Him as our Provider. When we've experienced His comfort, we come to know Him as our Comforter. When we've experienced His amazing love, we come to know Him as the Great Lover of our souls. The longer we know Him and the more we experience Him personally, the more we learn about His character.

If what you're hearing is consistent with God's character, ask the next question.

IS WHAT I'M HEARING BEING CONFIRMED THROUGH OTHER MESSAGES?

When God is speaking to me about a particular issue, I cannot escape it. Around every corner there is a sermon or Bible study lesson or speaker's topic or conversation with a friend that is consistent with what I've been hearing from God in my time alone with Him.

Do you spend time alone with God? We shouldn't wait to hear from God just on Sunday mornings or during a weekly Bible study or when a speaker comes to town. These are places to confirm what we've heard in our time alone, where we are personally studying God's Word, learning more about His character, and listening for His voice.

Think about having a conversation with another person. You both speak and you both listen. The same is true with our conversations with the Lord when we're one-on-one with Him. We shouldn't be doing all the talking. God wants us to pour out our hearts to Him, and then He wants to respond to us. Jesus shared this parable:

> The watchman opens the gate for him, and the sheep listen to his voice. He calls his own sheep by name and leads them out. When he has brought out all his own, he goes on ahead of them, and his sheep follow him because they know his voice (John 10:3-4).

Now let's reread this verse with some clarifying remarks added in.

> The watchman [Jesus] opens the gate [a way for us to have direct communication with God] for him, and the sheep [you and I] listen to his voice. He [God] calls his own sheep by name [He speaks to us personally] and leads them out [providing us with direction]. When he has brought out all his own, he goes on ahead of them, and his sheep follow him because they know his voice [they know his voice because they have spent time with him] (John 10:3-4).

Jesus is the one who provides a way for us to be able to talk with God and hear from God. God calls us by name. He wants to have a personal connection with each of us. Think about when you call someone's name. You know that person. You are calling on them so the two of you can connect in some way. This verse is telling us that the way God wants to connect with us is to provide direction for us in life. He has gone before us and sees the dangers and trials we will face. He is telling us the way to go, the perspectives to keep, the things to avoid, and the things to hold fast to. Most of all He is speaking to us because we are His own and He wants a relationship with us. He loves us, adores us, treasures us, and has a good plan for us. He longs for us to know His voice and listen to His voice. The only way to know and trust God in this way is to spend time with Him.

As a parent, I expect the same thing from my children. I know things they don't, and I can perceive dangers they are oblivious to. I want them to listen to me, but not because I want to exert a sense of authority in their life and simply boss them around. No, I want them to listen because I love them, adore them, treasure them, and want only the best for them. Even when they don't understand the why behind my instructions or like the limitations I put in place, I want them to be obedient because they trust me and they love me. The same is true in our relationship with our heavenly Parent.

When we invest in spending time alone with God, He will speak to us, and what we hear from Him in these quiet times will be echoed in other places. Listen for God's voice and then look for the message to be confirmed. If it is, you're ready to ask the fourth question.

IS WHAT I'M HEARING BEYOND ME?

When God leads or prompts us to do something small, we will be able to do it if we're willing. But sometimes God calls us to do something big that we feel we can't do in our own strength—either it is beyond our ability or beyond our natural human desire. It is not something we can strategize and manipulate into being in and of ourselves. It can only happen by God's divine intervention. The beauty of doing things beyond ourselves is that we will know it was by God's doing and His alone. And to Him we give all the glory.

I remember when God called me to write my first book. It seemed so exciting and thrilling to think of accomplishing this huge life goal. I envisioned the cover with my name on it. I delighted in imagining the first time I would walk into a bookstore and quietly say to myself, *I wrote that.* The excitement carried me through writing the first 10,000 words. Everything was clicking right along…until I got a note from my editor after she read my first installment. Her two-page, single-spaced feedback can be summed up in two shocking words, "Start over."

I got down on the floor beside my desk, buried my face into the carpet, and cried. "I can't do this, God. I can't write a whole book. What was I thinking? I'm not an author. I'm an imposter who somehow got lucky enough to fool this publisher with my proposal. But now they've seen the real me and think I'm a fool."

Did you notice an often-repeated word in my cries to God. "I'm not." "I can't." "I'm a fool." It was all about me and my inadequacies until I turned the statements into "God is." "God can." "God has called me; therefore, I am equipped."

If God is calling you to do something you feel is beyond you, you are in good company. God has a history of calling people to things that were beyond themselves. Pastor Rick Warren put it this way:

> Abraham was old, Jacob was insecure, Leah was unattractive, Joseph was abused, Moses stuttered, Gideon was poor, Samson was codependent, Rahab was immoral, David had an affair and all kinds of

family problems, Elijah was suicidal, Jeremiah was depressed, Jonah was reluctant, Naomi was a widow, John the Baptist was eccentric to say the least, Peter was impulsive and hot-tempered, Martha worried a lot, the Samaritan woman had several failed marriages, Zachaeus was unpopular, Thomas had doubts, Paul had poor health, and Timothy was timid. That's quite a group of misfits, but God used each of them in his service. He will use you too.[2]

Don't look at your inabilities and dwell in insecurities. Look at the Almighty God. See this call as the opportunity to watch Him work in you and through you. If you answer yes to the question *Is this beyond me?* chances are God is speaking.

WOULD WHAT I'M
HEARING PLEASE GOD?

It's easy to talk ourselves out of thinking we've heard from God. I think we'll pretty much use any excuse to convince ourselves it's not His voice so we don't need to act. But there's one very important question to ask when we feel prompted to do something, one question that takes away our excuses: Would this please God? You see, if what you are doing pleases God, then even if what you thought you heard from Him wasn't His voice, you still please Him. We should always seek to err on the side of pleasing God. Ask this question, and you'll know what to do.

The more you practice listening for God's voice, the more it becomes a natural part of your daily life. And here's the best news of all: God wants you to hear Him. He wants your faith to grow. He's told us so over and over in Scripture.

This is my prayer: that your love may abound more and more in knowledge and depth of insight (Philippians 1:9).

This is to my Father's glory, that you bear much fruit, showing yourselves to be my disciples (John 15:8).

> We ought always to thank God for you, brothers, and rightly so, because your faith is growing more and more, and the love every one of you has for each other is increasing (2 Thessalonians 1:3).

> For this very reason, make every effort to add to your faith goodness; and to goodness, knowledge (2 Peter 1:5).

> We instructed you how to live in order to please God, as in fact you are living. Now we ask you and urge you in the Lord Jesus to do this more and more (1 Thessalonians 4:1).

My conversations with God are more than a spiritual exercise for me. They are a lifeline. Growing up in my early childhood, I did not have a daddy who was very involved in my life. I was desperate to know that I was loved. I remember watching other little girls with their daddies and wondering what was so wrong with me that my daddy didn't adore me the way theirs did. Maybe it was because I wasn't pretty enough. Maybe I wasn't smart enough. Maybe he had never wanted me.

I was blessed to have another man adopt me as his own when my mom remarried. Charles has been a wonderful father to me who has loved me as his own. However, not having my biological father's love and acceptance left a hole in my heart. Often a little girl's sense of self-worth will be based on her father's love. And her opinion of God will often be based on her opinion of her earthly father.

Both of these were skewed for me. My sense of self-worth was severely lacking. I defined myself as an unwanted, unlovely, throwaway person. I viewed God as a distant, cold ruler who had somehow deemed me unworthy. Many years into my adult life, I came to see a different picture of God. He wooed me and loved me to a place where I finally surrendered my heart to Him. Then a miracle happened…He redefined my identity.

I was no longer a throwaway child. I was a holy and dearly loved daughter of the Most High King. I truly became a brand-new creation. I found the love and acceptance that had been so lacking in my early childhood. That little girl in me craved to spend time with the daddy I had missed out on for so long. He whispered to my heart that I was pretty and special and smart, and, best of all, that I was loved.

As a result of knowing what it feels like to be abandoned as a child, I have always had a tender place in my heart for the orphaned child. But after having three biological daughters of my own, I brushed aside any notion of adopting. That was until one unsuspecting day when God connected my family with two teenage boys from the war-torn country of Liberia, Africa. This meeting changed my family forever as God so clearly whispered to our hearts that they were to become part of our family.

As soon as I heard His whisper, my mind raced through the five-question filter.

1. Does what I'm hearing line up with Scripture?

2. Is it consistent with God's character?

3. Is it being confirmed through messages I'm hearing at church or studying in my quiet times?

4. Is it beyond me?

5. Would it please God?

God is very clear in Scripture that as Christians we are to take care of widows and orphans. Just a few weeks before meeting the boys I recorded the following verse in my journal:

"Religion that God our Father accepts as pure and faultless is this: to look after orphans and widows in their distress and to keep oneself from being polluted by the world" (James 1:27). I had no idea why I was drawn to write this verse in my journal, but God knew. He made sure I was familiar with an answer to my first filter question. Yes, adopting the boys absolutely lined up with Scripture. And in the same verse God answered the second question. God defines part of His character as "God our Father." I saw that God had been a Father to me in my time of need, so I should be willing to be that for someone else in need.

The confirmations were also undeniable. God had been bringing friends into my life who had adopted orphaned children. I never thought it would be something my husband would be open to, and yet God drew his heart to a place of acceptance. My girls begged us to consider adopting and prayed often for big brothers. It seemed everywhere I turned the theme of adopting was staring me in the face. Sermons at church, verses in my quiet times, songs on the radio, and whispers by God to my heart all seemed to be saying the same thing. Yes, adopting these boys was being confirmed.

The fourth question did not require much thought at all. Yes, this was totally beyond me. Having boys was beyond me. I had grown up with all sisters and then had three daughters. I felt very ill-equipped to be a mom of boys—especially teenage boys. Having five kids was beyond me. My schedule was already crazy with three kids. How in the world would I be able to add two more? Financially, this seemed beyond what we could do. Not to mention the host of fears that flooded my brain. What if one of the boys hurt one of my girls or hurt me or had emotional baggage that would take a huge toll on the stability of our family? I would only be willing to do this if I knew beyond a shadow of a doubt that it was God's plan and not my own. Only in His strength would this be possible.

The last question became pivotal in our decision to pursue adopting the boys. More than anything else I desire to please God, but the pull of taking an easier path was incredible with this particular invitation. The tug of believing that my worst fears would surely be waiting on the other side of this step of obedience made me want to run and hide. But the love of God kept my heart stilled, and His constant reassurances kept me on course. We said yes to God, not because we were completely comfortable with adopting, but rather because we completely trusted Him.

His voice was strong and gentle, saying,

> Do not fear. Remember how I faced the devil in the wilderness, and how I conquered with the sword of the Spirit, which is the word of God. You too have your quick answer for every fear that evil may

present—an answer of faith and confidence in Me. Where possible, say it aloud. The spoken word has power. Look on every fear not as a weakness on your part due to illness or worry, but as a very real temptation to be attacked and overthrown. Does the way seem a stony one? Not one stone can impede your progress. Courage. Face the future, but face it only with a brave and happy heart. Do not seek to see it. You are robbing Faith of her sublime sweetness if you do this. Just know that all is well and that Faith, not seeing but believing, is what will bear you to safety over the stormy waters.[3]

We let faith carry us as we faced the future as courageously as we could. We quoted Scripture after Scripture and reminded God that this was His adventure that we were simply saying yes to while trusting Him completely. And you know what we discovered? Sheer joy. Not in the circumstances that we faced necessarily, but in the absolute assurance that we were being obedient to God and walking in the very center of His will.

I can honestly tell you on the other side of this great adoption adventure that I can't imagine my life without my boys. I am so thankful that I followed God's perfect plan instead of being lured away by fear and worry. We've had our boys for three years now, and I'm more convinced than ever that even though they were not born from my body, they were born from my heart. Maybe that was the purpose of that place in my heart that seemed so much like a hole when I was younger, but now I see it as the channel through which God brought my boys home.

Use this five-question filter as a starting place in your conversations with God. Listening for God's voice and communicating with Him has not always come naturally to me. To this day I have to seek it by asking for the desire, discipline, discernment, direction, and delight. I ask for the desire to want God more than anything else. I ask for the discipline to make my relationship with Him top priority. I ask for the discernment to know the difference between my own thoughts and God's voice. I ask for clear direction at each crossroad in my life. I ask for my relationship with God to be characterized by sheer delight rather than a sense of duty. Have you ever asked God for this type of relationship with Him? When you ask for these things boldly and live in expectation of hearing from God, you will. In Jeremiah 29:13 God promises, "You will seek me and find me when you seek me with all your heart." Then respond by saying yes to Him and confidently walking in absolute dependence and glorious obedience.

Yes, indeed. I love being a woman who says yes to God.

BIBLE STUDY

Read Romans 12:1-2 in the NIV. Then, write out a definition for the following:

Living sacrifice:

Pleasing to God:

Do not conform:

The pattern of this world:

Transformed:

Renewing of your mind:

Test and approve God's will:

Now reread these verses and summarize what you can learn from them about discerning God's voice:

List some areas of your life that you currently honor God in:

List some areas that you sense you may need to sacrifice or change:

Are there areas of your life where you've conformed to the world's way of thinking?

How can you renew your mind in this area?

Find two Scripture verses that might be helpful to memorize as you seek to be renewed in this area. Write those here.

What is the promise from these verses for those who actively seek to be transformed and renewed in the way they think?

Write the five questions for discerning God's voice you learned in this chapter:

1.

2.

3.

4.

5.

Remember, this is not the end-all way for hearing God's voice. It is simply a starting place. Which of these questions do you find most challenging? Discuss this in your Bible study group. If you are not doing this as part of a group, find a Christian friend and spend some time discussing this and looking up Scriptures to help you better understand it.

In *The Message*, Romans 9:25-26 says, "Hosea put it well: I'll call nobodies and make them somebodies; I'll call the unloved and make them beloved. In the place where they yelled out, 'You're nobody!' they're calling you 'God's living children.'"

Paul continues,

> How can we sum this up? All those people who didn't seem interested in what God was doing actually embraced what God was doing as he straightened out their lives. And Israel, who seemed so interested in reading and talking about what God was doing, missed it. How could they miss it? Because instead of trusting God, they took over. They were absorbed in what they themselves were doing. They were so absorbed in their "God projects" that they didn't notice God right in front of them, like a huge rock in the middle of the road. And so they stumbled into him and went sprawling. Isaiah (again!) gives us the metaphor for pulling this together: Careful! I've put a huge stone on the road to Mount Zion, a stone you can't get around. But the stone is me! If you're looking for me, you'll find me on the way, not in the way (Romans 9:30-33 MSG).

What a perfect way to end our study—understanding that God wants us to live in expectation of hearing from Him. Sometimes we'll hear Him giving us direction or pointing us to a divine appointment. Other times we'll glean from Him wisdom, correction, or encouragement. But mostly I pray you'll hear His glorious voice proclaiming, "You are somebody! You are my chosen beloved!"

THREE

WHEN OBEDIENCE
BECOMES RADICAL

God wants us to be willing to obey with our whole heart.

I was attending a large conference where the speaker challenged us to pray and ask God to use us in an extraordinary way for His kingdom. Something stirred in my heart, and I started praying. When I got back to the hotel room that evening, I not only continued to pray for God to use me, but I wanted Him to show me what He required. I knew I couldn't climb to new heights in my spiritual journey without going into strict training to prepare. So I knelt beside my hotel bed and asked God to reveal to me what to do.

After I finished praying, I picked up the remote control to click on the evening news, and two words suddenly came to mind: radical obedience. *Radical obedience?* I questioned. *I'm obedient, Lord. I read my Bible, go to church, and try to be a good person.* Then something else came to my mind: *Stop watching TV altogether and put your house up for sale.*

What? I was stunned. *God, how do I know this is You speaking and not just a crazy notion in my head?*

One thing I did know—I was at a crossroads. I could brush these thoughts aside and say I didn't know for sure that this was God speaking to me, or I could heed His direction. I put down the remote and dropped to my knees once again.

I wanted to do whatever He asked me to do, but I wasn't sure I could do this. I didn't doubt God. I doubted my ability to really know if God was speaking to me. I doubted my courage.

As I continued to pray, my mind was flooded with Scriptures that were consistent with what I felt God was calling me to do. Some of those powerful verses were 1 Peter 1:13-16:

> Prepare your mind for action; be self-controlled; set your hope fully on the grace given you when Jesus Christ is revealed. As obedient children, do not conform to the evil desires you had when you lived in ignorance. But just as he who called you is holy, so be holy in all you do; for it is written: "Be holy, because I am holy."

I decided it must be God I was hearing from and I should look for His confirmation over the next couple of weeks.

I also asked God why He'd chosen these two specific actions. After all, I wasn't a TV junkie, and our house didn't have us living beyond our means. As I prayed, I felt God telling me why the TV had to go. I enjoyed sitting down after a tiresome day and being entertained. God showed me that I was vulnerable and empty during those times. It wasn't that what I was watching was bad—it just wasn't God's best. I was filling myself with the world's perspectives and influences, while He wanted to be my strength and fill me with Himself. I knew it would be hard to break this habit, but I was determined to ask God for the strength to do so. I prayed that my desire to please Him would be stronger than my desire for television.

I hope you understand that I'm not saying all television is bad, and I'm not making a case here for all Christians to throw out their sets. What I am saying is that God wanted my obedience in this area for a certain season. I actually had felt His leading to turn off the TV before that night in the hotel room, but I had ignored Him and justified my disobedience to the point where God needed to get my attention. He wanted me to make a choice between my desire and His. I took a sabbatical from television for two and a half years. When I finally felt

God giving me the freedom to turn it back on, something amazing had happened. I was no longer tied to it. I no longer felt the need to record programs I missed. I no longer had any must-see shows. I was able to objectively and carefully discern what would be good to watch and what wouldn't. I found that I was much more picky then I'd ever been before and a lot less willing to make compromises on what was questionable. God may not ask you to turn off the TV—He may ask you to do something else. The point here is that there may come a time at some point in your life when you will need to decide between your will and His.

One thing you can be assured of is that God has already worked out all the details of what your obedience will accomplish—and it is good. We need not fear what our obedience will cause to happen in our life. We should only fear what our *dis*obedience will cause us to miss. The sooner this truth resonates in your heart, the quicker you can make peace with a command from God that you don't fully understand. We tend to want to see the big picture complete with all the details before stepping out in obedience to God. We long for a cost analysis where we can weigh out what we'd be giving up against what we'd be gaining and then decide if the trade is worth it.

This is how I felt about God's request to sell our home. I kept thinking, *My home is very precious to me. Not for its financial wealth, but for the wealth of memories we have made there. Why would God ask me to let this go?* I thought about the things we would not be able to take with us if the house sold: the door frame where we've measured each of our girls' growth since they were toddlers, the handprint tiles we made when we added a bathroom in the playroom, the Bible we'd buried in the foundation when we built the house. Small as they are, these things made our house our home. I decided I would wait for God's confirmation that we were really supposed to put the house on the market.

When I returned home from the conference, I was nervous about mentioning selling the house to my husband, Art, so I said very little. I just kept looking and listening for God's confirmation. Art had just completed construction on his dream bass pond and several landscaping projects. I asked God to reveal the perfect time to share my heart with my husband. A few days later we were

We need not fear what
our obedience will cause to
happen in our life.
We should only fear
what our disobedience
will cause us to miss.

both in our bedroom reading when Art looked up from his book and told me of the devotion he'd just studied.

"It had to do with the fact that sometimes we work so hard to make a heaven on earth that our hearts are pulled away from our real home with God," he said. Then he looked me straight in the eyes and added, "Lysa, I think we should sell our house."

I was shocked. But with tears in my eyes and God's confirmation in my heart, I told him I'd call a Realtor that very day.

When we got to the meeting with the real estate agent, she asked all kinds of questions about the house and our land. When the pond was mentioned, Art's eyes sparkled and he went into great detail about all he'd done to make it the perfect bass pond. He talked on and on about it, and even went so far as to say that while we wanted to be obedient to God in putting the house on the market, we really didn't want to try to aggressively sell it.

We left the meeting and headed home. When we reached the part of our driveway that curves around the pond, we were stunned by what we saw—82 dead fish floating in the water. We had never seen even one dead fish in our pond, so seeing 82 stopped us in our tracks. What followed was a scene I'll never forget. Art got out of the car and, with tears streaming down his cheeks, knelt beside the pond and asked for God's forgiveness. God had made His request clear, and we had given Him a half-hearted response.

A WHOLE AND PURIFIED HEART

God is not interested in half of our heart. He wants it all, and He wants to remove the things that stand in the way of that.

> "See, I will send my messenger, who will prepare the way before me. Then suddenly the Lord you are seeking will come to his temple; the messenger of the covenant, whom you desire, will come," says the Lord Almighty. But who can endure the day of his coming? Who can stand when he appears? For he will be like a refiner's

fire or a launderer's soap. He will sit as a refiner and purifier of silver; he will purify the Levites and refine them like gold and silver (Malachi 3:1-3).

The messenger in this passage refers to John the Baptist. He would go before Jesus and prepare for Jesus' first coming. Now we are the messengers who are called to prepare people for Jesus' second coming. God wants to purify our whole heart so we are prepared and mature for our calling.

God turns up the heat from the refiner's fire so our impurities will rise to the top where they can be skimmed off and discarded. I appreciate the insight the *Life Application Study Bible* sheds on this passage:

> Without this heating and melting, there could be no purifying. As the impurities are skimmed off the top, the reflection of the worker appears in the smooth, pure surface. As we are purified by God, his reflection in our lives will become more and more clear to those around us. God says leaders (here the Levites) should be especially open to his purification process.[1]

The Bible also tells us that the Levites' inheritance would not be land but rather God Himself (Numbers 18:20). God wants us to desire Him above all else.

I didn't want to give God any more half-hearted answers. I was determined that when He spoke to my heart, He would never again have to shout. By asking Art and me to put our home up for sale, God was skimming greed from our hearts. Art and I were holding what God had given us with a closed fist. God wanted to teach us that when we tightly hold on to the things of this world, we not only lose the desire to give, but we lose the ability to receive more as well.

Did you catch that? If we hold all that we treasure with our hands open and our palms facing upward, we are telling God we recognize it is His and we offer it up freely to Him. God may or may not remove what we've offered Him, but He will continue to fill our open hands with blessings—His amazing blessings and not the cheap counterfeits of the world!

OFFERING IT ALL TO GOD

No one understands the concept of offering it all to God better than Abraham (Genesis 22). When God commanded Abraham to lay his only son on the altar of obedience, I am sure Abraham fully expected to plunge the dagger through Isaac. It would be an end...the death of a dream. Yet, Abraham was willing to give up the son he loved to the God who loved him more, and God blessed him. God poured His compassion and mercy into Abraham's open hands, and He spared Isaac. But even more than that, God lavished the evidence of His presence upon Abraham, and Abraham walked away having experienced God in a way few ever do. God wants to know if we're willing to give up what we love to Him who loves us more. He desires for us to open our fists and trust Him with absolutely everything.

As I opened my fist about our home, I felt God piercing a little dark corner of my heart. My selfishness couldn't reflect God's generous heart. But as I let His light in, His reflection became clearer in my life. Then something amazing came about. Just as God provided a ram instead of taking Isaac, God did not allow our house to sell. For more than a year the Realtor's lockbox stayed on our front door as a beautiful reminder that we are managers and not owners of this home. Interestingly enough, the week we brought our boys home the box disappeared. Maybe the Realtor finally came and got it, or maybe God removed it to get our attention. But isn't the timing interesting?

I'm so thankful I made the connection between these two events so I could weather the transition of going from three to five children in a more settled way. I've always been a bit particular with my home. I like it to smell nice, sound quiet, and have a sense of order about it. Having three little girls who like to play quietly fit so nicely into my scope of how things should be. Then suddenly we had five children and things stopped being just so. It's not that any one of us is particularly messy or loud; it's just the nature of seven people living under the same roof.

There have been times where I admit to feeling bitterness and resentment creep into my heart toward my kids...all my kids. Every time I would clean something that ended up dirty just minutes later, I felt a little pang in my heart.

Every time I went to look for an item in its assigned place and it had mysteriously disappeared, I felt this pang twist and grow. Every time I discovered something broken or destroyed, it felt as though the pang had grown into a choking vine in my throat. I found myself snapping at the kids and blaming them for anything and everything that went wrong at home.

I was in the middle of one of my aggravated dissertations one day when one of my sons stopped me and asked me the strangest question. "Mom, will you teach me to dance?"

I was mad and in no mood to dance. My thoughts were racing. *Dance? Dance? I am trying to teach you to put things back where they belong and stop messing up my house, and you want to dance?* Then my attention turned fully to him as he lifted out his hands, signaling he wanted to dance as if I were wearing a princess ball gown and he were wearing a tux. His gaze was so sincere that suddenly the missing scissors I had been so frustrated by no longer gnawed at my attention. Here was this beautiful young man awkwardly lifting up his arms and asking me to dance. This boy, who just months before had been stuck in a forgotten orphanage on the other side of the world with no hope and no reason to dance, was standing in my kitchen asking me to show him how.

I took his hand, wrapped my arm around his shoulder, and taught him to step and glide and twirl and dip. The world seemed to melt away as I realized what a privilege this experience was. How selfish of me to call our home "my house." How ungrateful I must have seemed to God. I could have a neat and tidy house where things never got lost, misplaced, or broken if there were no others living there but me. But my heart never wanted just a house. My heart longs for a home full of people who I love. As we stopped dancing, I lifted up a prayer of thanksgiving to God. I praised Him for teaching me to finally let go of my house so I could have a real home.

I no longer see things like this in my life as mere coincidence and brush them aside. I ponder these events and encounters. I pray over them. I pursue God and ask Him what I'm supposed to learn through the experience.

I suspect you have moments like this where God's fingerprints are all over them. Live in expectation of experiencing God and hearing His voice. Record these times in a journal. Look for answers to the prayers you've prayed and understanding from the steps of obedience God has called you to take. See how God weaves everything together in deep, wonderful, and wondrous ways.

ABIDING IN THE SWEET SECRET PLACE

Can I let you in on something? There is a place I escape to that allows my soul to breathe and rest and reflect. It is the place where I can drop the "yuck" the world hands me and trade it in for the fullness of God. It is a place that God reassures me, confirms that He has everything under control, and gives me a new filter through which I can process life. The Bible calls it the remaining place. I call it my sweet secret place.

John 15:4 says, "Remain in me, and I will remain in you. No branch can bear fruit by itself; it must remain in the vine. Neither can you bear fruit unless you remain in me." Let's be honest. It's hard for a well-meaning soul that desires radical obedience to God to live in a body made of flesh. Our flesh is pulled by the distractions of the world, lured to sell our soul for temporary pleasures, and conned by Satan's evil schemes. Other people rub us the wrong way, and we instantly want to give them a piece of our mind. Worldly wealth screams that if only you could do more to have more, then ultimate happiness could be yours. And our right to be right seems to supersede the sacrificial call of God. All the while God invites our souls to break away from the world and remain in Him.

To remain in Him and enter the secret place, I simply have to close my eyes and make the choice to be with God.

Sometimes it's because I'm in a desperate place. I pray, *"God, I am here and I need You right now. I'm feeling attacked, invaded, pressed, and stressed. Meet me here and help me process what I'm facing using Your truth. Nothing more and nothing less. I don't want this thing I'm facing to be processed through my selfish and insecure flesh. I will surely act in a displeasing and dishonoring way if I'm left to face this on my own. Block my flesh's natural reaction and fill me with Your Spirit. You handle this for me. You speak what needs to be spoken and give power to hold my tongue for what needs to be left in silence."*

Other times I need to be with God because I'm feeling pulled into something I know is not part of His best plan for me. I see something new I can't afford. How easy it is to justify our way to the checkout line, whip out a credit card, and decide to deal with the consequences later. Or maybe it is a relationship we know is not in God's will. Or a particular eating habit we know is not healthy for us.

Whatever it is, we don't have to be rendered powerless by this pull. We can pray, "God, I know You are more powerful than this pull I am feeling. I know this thing I think I want so much will only provide temporary pleasure. I know the consequences of making this choice will rob my joy and peace in the near future. Through Your power I am making the choice to walk away. I will find my delight in You and look forward to feeling Your fullness replace the emptiness this desire is creating."

Still other times I simply know I need a fresh filling of God's Spirit in me. I go to this secret place and simply talk to God. Then I listen for His voice. Sometimes He provides direction and instruction on something that needs to be done. Other times I sense Him warning me of something coming. Still other times He simply lavishes me with His love.

I love saying yes to God and going to the secret place with Him. God clearly tells us in John 15:4 that this is the only way to bear fruit in our lives. It is the only way to experience what Galatians 5:22-23 explains this fruit to be: love, joy, peace, patience, kindness, goodness, faithfulness, gentleness, and self-control. Oh, how I want these to be the character of my heart and the legacy of my life.

Obedience is the key that unlocks this secret place with God. John 15:10 goes on to explain this, "If you obey my commands, you will remain in my love." The more we say yes to God, the more we will live in expectation of seeing Him. The more we expect to see God, the more we will. The more you experience Him, the more you'll trust Him. The more you trust Him, the more you'll open up your hands in absolute obedience.

Obedience becomes radical when we say, "Yes, God, whatever You want," and mean it. We release our grip on all that we love and offer it back to Him, who loves us more. And it is into these upturned hands that God will pour out His blessings—His abundant, unexpected, radical blessings. Soon, saying yes to God will no longer be a discipline of your heart but rather the delight of your life.

BIBLE STUDY

Read Titus 2:11-12.

What are we to say no to?

Define this in the realm of your everyday life.

Titus 2:11-12 in *The Message* says,

> God's readiness to give and forgive is now public. Salvation's available for everyone! We're being shown how to turn our backs on a godless, indulgent life, and how to take on a God-filled, God-honoring life. This new life is starting right now, and is whetting our appetites for the glorious day when our great God and Savior, Jesus Christ, appears. He offered himself as a sacrifice to free us from a dark, rebellious life into this good, pure life, making us a people he can be proud of, energetic in goodness.

Is turning our backs on the godless, indulgent life taking away from our lives or adding to it?

....

What is it taking away? What is it adding?

....

Is there something that stirred in your heart as you read this chapter that God might be leading you to give up either permanently or for a season?

....

What is holding you back from doing this?

Comment on this statement from the chapter:

> "We need not fear what our obedience will cause to happen in our life. We should only fear what our *dis*obedience will cause us to miss."

Read Isaiah 41:13. Are we to give things up in our own strength? Are we walking this new path of deeper obedience alone?

How refreshing and comforting to know that God doesn't point us down this path of obedience and then simply stand back to watch us struggle. No, He takes our hand and leads us, whispers reassurances, and gives us back so much more than we give up.

In the chapter we read John 15:4. Record that verse here.

List the fruits found in the secret abiding place.

....

Of all these fruits, list three that you want to focus on when you escape to the secret place with God this week.

1.

2.

3.

....

Now, look up Scriptures that give direction and instruction on pursuing these fruits and record them below.

Lastly, journal your thoughts below about this statement: "Soon, saying yes to God will no longer be a discipline of your heart but rather the delight of your life."

FOUR

YOU NEVER KNOW HOW GOD WILL USE YOU UNTIL YOU LET HIM

God must be Lord of all if He is our Lord at all.

I received an amazing letter from Christine in Colorado:

> Ever since I became a Christian in high school, the mark of my faith had always been radical obedience to Christ. I loved the church and everything about it, and I was always striving to follow Jesus beyond the everyday practicalities of faith. I was always certain there had to be more to Christianity than just Bible study, fellowship times, and prayer, and I found true joy in being involved in the lives around me.
>
> In the aftermath of September 11, though, I found myself with new questions, seeking God's true direction. I found myself disillusioned with the church and disenchanted with my faith. I heard you speak on radical obedience at a women's conference, and it was as though my heart was being called back to the roots of radical obedience.

As I celebrated my birthday the other week, I really had a chance to reflect on where God has been taking me over the past year. Has it ever been a wild ride! He has torn down all the things I had held so dearly about the church and about Christianity. And in the process, I am finding the Jesus I knew when I first became a Christian—the Jesus of social justice, mercy, and compassion. The Jesus who did not walk blindly through the earth and not feel the suffering of those around Him. He and the disciples were not tame and safe and nice. They were not a social club with watered down grace and entry requirements that have nothing to do with the sacred. They did not trade that which was eternal for that which was material.

At the same time, God has reawakened a heart of compassion and mercy in me. I am more aware than ever of the needs of others, and I have found great joy in working with social projects and even acts of compassion in everyday life. I see so much brokenness, so much pain in the lives of the women around me, and so often their cries are unheard and their needs go unnoticed as they walk alone through the trials of life. I have really been trying to reach out more to those around me and to draw them closer to the only One who holds the answers to life's questions.

Whether I'm writing an encouraging note to a discouraged friend or lending a helping hand to a mother who is overwhelmed with the responsibilities of her life, I've discovered it's so simple to bring the light of God into the midst of our everyday world. It is in the small acts of life that He can be reflected so beautifully—taking a meal to a new mother, welcoming a new neighbor with an invitation for dinner, or even just smiling at strangers as we pass them on the street. As I pause to help others, I am reminded that, just like Jesus, we are called to notice the people around us and to bring a touch of hope into their lives.

Looking back at where I've been, I can see now that I had gotten off track. I was caught up in the social club mentality that so often permeates the church, and I had lost sight of what was really important. Yet, out of my brokenness, I have seen the true call of Christ...a call to love our neighbors in ways that may seem radical in our selfish, sin-soaked culture. It has been a definite reawakening for me, a challenge to throw off the status quo and to really make a difference in my world. I am convinced that this is a picture of the true church...not a forced sort of family bonding because we all sit in the same building on Sunday, but a true family built out of genuine love for one another. And in those relationships, Christ's love is so evident and so full.

In following the path of radical obedience, I have tasted the mystery of the sacred fellowship that comes when two or more are gathered in His name, and it has added a richness to my life that I would never again want to live without. It is a richness that goes beyond the tradition of the church to a holy existence before a dangerous and untamed God. It is an invitation to live tremblingly joyful before the God of radical obedience and radical *grace, the God that I want to know and serve all the days of my life.*

Christine has discovered the joy of a heart wholly committed to God. She has discovered that there is no end to what God can do with you—if you let Him.

WHERE TRUE CHANGE COMES FROM

How did Christine do it? What changed her walk of faith from ordinary to extraordinary?

Perhaps the better question to ask is who changed her walk of faith from ordinary to extraordinary? When we answer that question, we find the true source of radical obedience, and our soul transcends the muck and mire that keeps us from all God has for us.

Radical obedience is not just following a list of right things to do. Nonbelievers can do that and call it "good." Radical obedience is choosing to exchange what is "right" for God's righteousness. Only the pursuit of God's righteousness leads to His best. And it's there we find the source: "God made him who had no sin to be sin for us, so that in him we might become the righteousness of God" (2 Corinthians 5:21).

The answer is simple and complicated all at the same time: It's Jesus. He is our source. He should be the only object of our pursuit. When we accept Jesus Christ as Lord of our life, we exchange our worthless sin for the immeasurable worth of His righteousness.

The apostle Peter put it this way: "But in your hearts set apart Christ as Lord" (1 Peter 3:15). He must be Lord of all if He is our Lord at all. Many people know Christ as their Savior, but the woman who says yes to God longs to know Him as Lord. A person pursuing obedience is able to pause and touch those that He says need our time, in spite of busy schedules. The obedient soul redefines who she is through God's eyes, and any hesitation to do what He asks fades away. This radically obedient woman realizes she is righteous and will find God's best when she pursues right choices that bring glory to Him.

When we accept Jesus Christ as Lord of our life, we exchange our worthless sin for the immeasurable worth of His righteousness.

THE LOVE THAT COMPELS US

Yes, becoming women who say yes to God starts with Jesus, and it is His amazing love that compels us:

> Christ's love compels us, because we are convinced that one died for all, and therefore all died. And he died for all, that those who live should no longer live for themselves but for him who died for them and was raised again. So from now on we regard no one from a worldly point of view. Though we once regarded Christ in this way, we do so no longer. Therefore, if anyone is in Christ, he is a new creation; the old has gone, the new has come! All this is from God, who reconciled us to himself through Christ and gave us the ministry of reconciliation (2 Corinthians 5:14-18).

The love of Christ compels us to choose obedience. Being obedient is not our way of earning God's favor; it is not the path to a more prosperous life. God's favor is with those who love His Son, and our promise of prosperity lies in what we have waiting for us in our eternal home.

Jesus, whose amazing love compels us, said, "If you hold to my teaching, you are really my disciples. Then you will know the truth and the truth will set you free" (John 8:31-32). The truth is the name of Jesus that causes us to pause and redefine ourselves. The truth is the love that compels us to embrace the calling to be Jesus' ambassador. The truth is the freedom to soar above this life and learn to live beyond ourselves and our circumstances.

The real question now becomes do we really want this freedom, this life of ministry that now lies before us? Do we really want to be interrupted in the middle of our busy lives to see God, hear God, and pursue God? Do we really want to be compelled by the love of Christ? Do we really want a Lord of all of our life?

Yes, Jesus, we do.

THE POWER TO OBEY

If Christ is the very source of radical obedience, and it is His love that compels us, then it is His power that enables us to do what we're called to do.

Know this: Satan will do everything he can to convince you to say no to God. Satan's very name means "one who separates." He wants to separate you from God's best by offering what seems "very good" from a worldly perspective. He wants you to deny Christ's power in you. He wants to distract you from God's radical purpose for you.

The apostle John warned us of Satan's strategic plan,

> Do not love the world or anything in the world. If anyone loves the world, the love of the Father is not in him. For everything in the world—the cravings of sinful man, the lust of his eyes and the boasting of what he has and does—comes not from the Father but from the world (1 John 2:15-16).

The *Life Application Bible* offers this insight:

> Some people think that worldliness is limited to external behavior—the people we associate with, the places we go, the activities we enjoy. Worldliness is also internal because it begins in the heart and is characterized by three attitudes: 1. the cravings of the sinful man—preoccupation with gratifying physical desires; 2. the lust of his eyes—craving and accumulating things, bowing down to the god of materialism; and 3. boasting of what he has and does—obsession of one's status or importance...By contrast, God values self-control, a spirit of generosity, and a commitment to humble service. It is possible to give the impression of avoiding worldly pleasures while still harboring worldly attitudes in your heart.[1]

It all started way back in paradise with our fruit-loving friend, Eve. She had God's best and traded it all because Satan convinced her that worldly good was more appealing and worth the swap: "When the woman saw that the fruit of the tree was good for food [physical need: the cravings of sinful man] and pleasing to the eye [psychological need: lust of the eyes], and also desirable for gaining wisdom [emotional need: boasting of what he has and does], she took some and ate it [sin separated man from God's best]" (Genesis 3:6). The rest of Genesis 3 covers the shame, hiding, blaming, punishment, and banishment from the Garden.

Well, take heart! This story doesn't end in Genesis 3. Jesus came, and everything changed. He faced temptation just like Eve: "Then Jesus was led by the Spirit into the desert to be tempted by the devil" (Matthew 4:1). And He was tempted in the same three ways that Eve was tempted, only Jesus' temptations were magnified a hundredfold. Eve was in a lush garden with delicious food, an incredible companion, and all the comforts of paradise. Jesus had been in a desert for 40 days where He went without food, companionship, or comfort of any sort. Satan tempted Him with food that was outside of God's plan for someone who was fasting (physical need: the cravings of sinful man), an opportunity to prove Himself (emotional need: boasting of what he has and does), and the riches of the world (psychological need: lust of the eyes). Jesus withstood the temptations because instead of taking His eyes off of God, He intentionally focused on God and refuted each of Satan's temptations by quoting God's Word.

Satan has no new tricks up his sleeve. He still has nothing better to tempt us with than worldly things. Physical, emotional, and psychological pleasures that fall outside the will of God are still what Satan is using to pull the hearts of God's people away.

For me, the most amazing part of looking at Eve's temptation in relation to Jesus' temptation is what happens next in each of their lives. Eve turns away from God and says yes to worldly distractions. The next chapter of her life is tragic. Eve has two sons, one of whom kills the other. Jesus turns to God and says yes to His divine plan. The next chapter of His life is triumphant. Jesus begins His ministry here on earth. Something will happen next in our life as well. Will the next page in your life be filled with doubts and distractions? Or will it be filled with discovering the blessing of answering God's call on your life?

NO MATTER WHAT

There are some things God wants us to get settled in our heart. Do we want to chase after the world's emptiness instead of His fullness? Or do we want our lives to be characterized by perfect love instead of perfect performance? Many people half-heartedly claim to be Christians, believing that because we will never be perfect this side of eternity we have an excuse to pursue that which pleases our human longings. Why not push the limits, live for the now, and worry about eternity later? The problem is that we miss the whole point of our existence, the very purpose for which we were created. God made us for the relationship of His perfect love. While we are not capable of perfect performance this side of eternity, we are capable of perfect love. We can settle in our hearts that we will choose God's love and the pursuit of a love relationship with Him above all else, no matter what comes our way.

The day my husband and I made this decision we were in the hospital with our middle daughter, who was six weeks old. She had seemed a perfectly healthy baby until an allergic reaction to the protein in my breast milk landed us in the intensive care unit. The doctors told us on the fourth day of our visit that Ashley needed emergency surgery, and they did not expect her to survive. They gave us five minutes to tell our baby goodbye.

My heart was shattered. I so desperately wanted to scoop her up and run out of the hospital. I wanted to somehow breathe my life into hers. I wanted to take her place. I could handle my own death so much easier than the death of my child. Art prayed over Ashley, we both said our goodbyes, and then with tears streaming down our faces, we let her go.

Art took me outside to the hospital parking lot, where I collapsed into his arms. He gently cupped my face in his hands and reminded me that Ashley was God's child to give and His to take back. "Lysa, God loves Ashley even more than we do," he gently told me. "We must trust His plan."

Art then asked me to do something, and it changed my whole perspective on my relationship with God: "We have to get it settled in our hearts that we will love God no matter the outcome of Ashley's surgery," he said.

At first I resented Art's desire that we love God in this way. I feared it might give Him the impression it was okay to take Ashley. With all my being I wanted to hold on to my child and refuse God. Yet, though I was heartbroken, I also felt God's compassion. I felt Him drawing me close and pouring out His tender mercy. God knew firsthand the pain we were feeling because He'd felt it Himself. I knew that, ultimately, I had no ability to control my child's future. With tears pouring from our eyes, Art and I released our sweet Ashley to the Lord and promised to love Him no matter what.

It was as if the more I fell into God's arms, the less the pain of the moment seared my heart. Feeling the power of God took away the fear of the unknown. I stopped thinking about the what-ifs and let my soul simply say, *Okay. God, in this minute I choose rest with You. I will not let my mind go to the minutes that are coming. I will simply be in this moment and face it with peace.*

That day we settled our love for God not just for this situation but for all time. Though we did not feel at all happy, a gentle covering of unexplainable joy settled over our hearts. Knowing that the One who loved Ashley even more than we did was taking care of her, and that His plan for her was perfect, brought peace in the middle of heartbreak.

The end of this chapter of Ashley's life was miraculous and wonderful. Though the doctors couldn't explain how, she made a full recovery. Who can understand why God answers prayer the way He does? We just know we're grateful. And we can also know that no matter God's answer, our hearts were settled to trust and love Him. This kind of radical obedience brings about a depth of relationship with God you can't get any other way.

Nothing in life is certain. Circumstances roll in and out like the ocean's tide. The unknown can sometimes seem so frightening as we ponder all the tragic possibilities that we know can and do happen to people. We catch ourselves wondering what the next page of life might hold. We can't stop or control the things that roll our way any more than we can stop the water's edge. But we can make the minute-by-minute choice to let our souls rest in God.

Rest knowing all is so safe in My Hands. Rest is Trust. Ceaseless activity is distrust. Without the knowledge that I am working for you, you do not rest. Inaction then would be the outcome of despair. My Hand is not shortened that it cannot save. Know that, repeat it, rely on it, welcome the knowledge, delight in it. Such a truth is as a hope flung to a drowning man. Every repetition of it is one pull nearer shore and safety.[2]

HERE IS A WOMAN WHO GETS IT!

Recently, I was introduced to a blog written by a woman named Beverly. She is a homeschooling mother battling cancer. As I read the writings of this courageous woman, I couldn't help but say to myself, "Here is a woman who gets it!"

She is a woman fighting for her very life who refuses to get swept up in the bitterness and anxiety that surely come knocking on the door of her heart. She has made the choice to say yes to God every day, in big ways and small. Some of the writings on her blog addressed her cancer. But, surprising to me, most did not. I found her blog entries to be full of her adventures with God. I think what I liked most about the following entry is that it does not wrap up with a sweet little, "Of course, God gave us all the answers and everything turned out just right." She simply found purpose and peace in her choice to experience God.

The parking lot of a Kentucky Fried Chicken. Not exactly where we were planning to spend the first night of our vacation. The day had actually been great. We had spent time at the pool that morning, gone to Wal-Mart for groceries for the week, and then headed down to Pensacola Beach. The beach was wonderful. White sand, beautiful water that was not too robust for my boys, and fairly mild temperatures, considering that it was Florida in July. As we were pulling out of the beach parking lot, our van had stalled. It took Greg a couple of tries to get it going again, but it drove just fine all the way up to the KFC. As I went into the restaurant to get our supper, I called out to Greg not to turn off the engine, just in case there was something wrong. When I returned with our food, the van was not running. It had died when he had parked, and it would not start again.

Thus began our two-and-a-half-hour wait. It was already 8:30, and no one had eaten since lunch.

Now, my wonderful husband is very mechanically minded, and he was sure that he could get it going. Of all things, there was an Auto Zone right next door, and he went in to get something. It didn't work. He then wondered if our gasoline gauge had gone bad and we were out of fuel. So back to the Auto Zone for a can and down the road to a station. That wasn't it. At some point I handed out the biscuits from our dinner, since some of the gang were starting to get cranky. Finally, we accepted a ride back to our motel with one of the employees (in shifts, of course, as we would not all fit in her car). We sat down to our chicken dinner at 11:30 PM, and I have to admit that it had rather lost its appeal by then.

The next day we were able to arrange for a mechanic to take Greg over there to look at it, and he agreed with Greg that it was the fuel pump. He had the van towed to his shop, and we stayed in our room and prayed. How much was this going to cost? Would he be able to fix it? What were we going to do without a vehicle? But we also consoled ourselves. God must have a plan. We fantasized over what it might be. Maybe He wanted us to share Christ with the mechanic, and he would give his heart to the Lord. Maybe we would see God's provision by the mechanic fixing the van for free. We just knew that there would be some obvious sign that this was all in God's plan. In the meantime, our boys were well content at the motel with the pool and cable TV, and we had plenty of food.

Two days later our van was fixed. To our knowledge, the mechanic did not accept the Lord. He charged us full price for the work he did, and he wanted cash at that. In other words, we did not see that the Lord had done anything through our trial with our van. We were poorer, but not wiser. Why, Lord, did You allow this to happen?

It would surely be wonderful if life was so prettily packaged, wouldn't it? Every time we had trouble in our life, we could then see the good that came out of it. Oh, for sure, there are plenty of times where we clearly see the hand of God in difficult circumstances. We look back and marvel at how God brought great things out of challenging situations. But there are plenty of times when God, in His own sovereignty, does not open our eyes to what He is doing. He wants us to trust Him, no matter what is happening.

So what does the Bible say about this? Does it guarantee that we will always see what God is doing? The clear answer is no, it doesn't. We walk by faith, not by sight. Hebrews 11 is often called the hall of fame of faith. It outlines the lives of many who went before us, who stood on God's Word despite incredible odds. Verses 39 and 40 say these words, "These were all commended for their faith, yet none of them received what had been promised. God had planned something better for us so that only together with us would they be made perfect." These people all lived waiting for a Savior. Yet they never saw Him in their lifetimes. But they believed. And we too need to believe, even if we don't always see what God is doing.

One day God may open up our spiritual eyes to see what He was doing during our trial with our van. Maybe He just wanted us to learn to be content despite the circumstances. Maybe He wanted us to know how others feel who are experiencing the same thing we did. Maybe we just need to realize that we are living in a fallen world, and vans break down in a fallen world. I don't know. But I do know that God is God, and that I can trust Him no matter what happens in this world.[3]

As I read about Beverly's experience, I thought about how hard it is to stay godly when things in life go awry. Her story caused me to think about the way I might have reacted in her shoes. Her experience wasn't life threatening, but it was life interrupted. For me, sometimes, it is so much harder to pass the small tests of life than the big ones.

I can picture myself thinking, *This was supposed to be a vacation where we take a break from life being hard and unfair. The van can't break now!* Our flesh pulls at our soul to yell and scream and demand things go the way we planned. We don't want inconvenience. We don't want to be tested. We're not even in the mood to be a witness to the participants in our unexpected drama. We want to get in our van, drive back to the motel, eat our dinner, put the kids to bed, and sit out on the balcony in quiet reflection lulled by the sights and sounds of the ocean. But we have a great enemy to the peace we crave, one who loves to interrupt our lives at the most unsuspecting times. Satan wants to catch us off guard and use our reactions against us. He loves to whisper, "If you can't stay godly and obedient in the small mishaps of life, how do you think you're going to be able to pass the bigger tests and trials?" So, in the quietness of our hearts we ponder our reactions to life's situations. And if we find our attitude wanting, we label ourselves unable.

I don't qualify to be a woman who says yes to God. Look at how I acted: impatient, unkind, emotional, angry, unstable, and irrational.

We label ourselves, close up this book, and put it in the tall stack of other unfinished books. I know because I did this for too long in my life. It wasn't until I settled God's amazing love in my heart that I finally understood what Lamentations 3 refers to when it tells us, "His compassions are new every morning." Actually, God's compassions, or mercies, are available minute-by-minute, step-by-step, decision-by-decision, reaction-by-reaction. We don't have to get bogged down and label ourselves as unable. We just have to ask God for forgiveness and move on.

I am not a woman who should be labeled unable. I am a woman on a journey of learning how to make sure my reactions don't deny Christ's presence in me. I am a woman who says yes to God not because my emotions and reactions are always perfect. No, I say yes to God because He is perfectly able to forgive me, love me, remind me, challenge me, and show me how to weather trials in ways that prove His Spirit resides in me. I remind myself often that people don't care to meet my Jesus until they meet the reality of Jesus in my life.

Job was a man who lived this way. He was tested and tried in ways most of us can't imagine. He experienced everything he ever feared: "If only my anguish could be weighed and all my misery be placed on the scales! It would surely outweigh the sand of the seas" (Job 6:2). Even Job's wife said to him, "Are you still holding on to your integrity? Curse God and die!" (Job 2:9). But Job had settled in his heart to trust God: "You are talking like a foolish woman," he told his wife. "Shall we accept good from God, and not trouble?" (Job 2:10). And because of that radical obedience, Job received a radical blessing in his relationship with the Lord: "My ears had heard of you but now my eyes have seen you" (Job 42:5). Job had known of God, but only through his trials and his obedience did he experience God personally.

The psalmist David discovered this radical blessing—this intimate, deep relationship with God—when he settled in his heart to love God no matter what.

> My life is consumed by anguish and my years by groaning; my strength fails because of my affliction, and my bones grow weak... But I trust in you, O LORD; I say, "You are my God." My times are in your hands; deliver me from my enemies and from those who pursue me. Let your face shine on your servant; save me in your unfailing love...How great is your goodness, which you have stored up for those who fear you, which you bestow in the sight of men on those who take refuge in you...Praise be to the LORD, for he showed his wonderful love to me (Psalm 31:10, 14-16, 19, 21).

With God's amazing love settled in our heart, we have His power to keep our faith steady and to experience lasting hope and joy independent of our situation. It's true—God wants it all. And it's in the exchange of what we want for what God wants that we experience the adventure and freedom and power of saying yes to God. God is using all of your experiences, both good and bad, to develop your character to match your calling.

After all, dear friend, you never know how God will use you until you let Him.

BIBLE STUDY

Read 1 Peter 3:15 and record it here.

How are we to set apart Christ?

What does it mean for Him to be Lord?

Lord over what in our lives?

Read Jeremiah 12:2. Describe the person being referred to in this verse.

Where are we to set apart Christ?

Read Jeremiah 11:7-8. What does it mean to have a stubborn heart?

Read Proverbs 13:25 and write the word that describes the condition of the heart of those who live to make right choices that honor God.

Read Psalm 84. Look at verses 1-2 and verse 10:

> How lovely is your dwelling place, O LORD Almighty! My soul yearns, even faints, for the courts of the LORD; my heart and my flesh cry out for the living God...Better is one day in your courts than a thousand elsewhere; I would rather be a doorkeeper in the house of my God than dwell in the tents of the wicked.

This is a person who has decided to chase not after the world's emptiness, but rather God's fullness. The more you are satisfied with God, the more you crave to spend time with Him. Have you ever felt as though your time with the Lord is empty and simply done as another thing to check off your never-ending chore list?

Write a prayer asking God to make your time with Him more meaningful. Ask God to give you a deep desire for Him.

Read Psalm 84:4. What is a common characteristic for those abiding with the Lord?

Is it a common practice for you to praise the Lord? How could you incorporate more praise in your everyday relationship with God?

According to verse 5, where do we draw our strength from? Where should our hearts be set? What type of pilgrimage are we on?

How does Psalm 84:9, 11 encourage you?

What is surely in store for a woman who says yes to God?

FIVE

WHAT KEEPS US FROM SAYING YES TO GOD

Whatever we worship, we will obey.

I could see it in the cross expression on her face and in the urgency in her stride. The woman approaching me had a few things on her mind.

Sure enough, this woman in my Bible study class thought I was taking my faith a little too seriously and the Bible a little too literally. After she dumped her load of concern on me, she smiled and encouraged me to lighten up. "Honey," she said, "I wouldn't want to see you carry this obedience thing too far."

This, my friend, is a naysayer. If you choose the life of radical obedience, you are going to encounter such people. They don't understand you. They don't want to understand you. And often what you're doing makes them feel convicted. If someone is quick to find fault in something good someone else is doing, that person is usually wrapped up in his or her own self-centered outlook. Naysayers make themselves feel better by tearing others down. Paul warned Timothy about people like this:

> Mark this: There will be terrible times in the last days. People will be lovers of themselves, lovers of money, boastful, proud, abusive,

disobedient to their parents, ungrateful, unholy, without love, unforgiving, slanderous, without self-control, brutal, not lovers of good, treacherous, rash, conceited, lovers of pleasure rather than lovers of God—having a form of godliness but denying its power. Have nothing to do with them (2 Timothy 3:1).

Becoming a woman who unashamedly says yes to God is going to cause you to be different from many of your family members and friends. You will examine life's circumstances with a different outlook. You will perceive things with a different expectation. You will understand that just because life is busy doesn't mean you have to rush about without God. You understand your responsibility is to obey God and He will handle the outcome. When you start to fret or worry, you know how to get swept into God's assurance rather than swept away in fear. You will rely on a strength and power that simply does not make sense to most people.

While not all of your friends and family will be naysayers, some will. The difference naysayers see in you compels them to come against you full force because Christ working through you will sometimes step on the toes of their consciences. While naysayers may talk a good Christian game, they deny Christ in their attitudes and actions toward others. Instead of allowing those feelings of conviction to produce good changes in them, they seek to discourage you in hopes of hushing Christ in you.

It's not easy to keep their negativity from being discouraging, but as my husband always reminds me, "Lysa, consider the source." I ask myself, "Is this person criticizing me active in pursuing a relationship with the Lord? Is this person answering God's call on his life, producing the evidence of Christ's fruit? Does he have my best interest in mind?" The answers are almost always no. So I look for any truth that might be in what this person has said, forgive him for any hurt he may have caused, and let the rest go.

What about when the person causing the hurt and becoming a source of discouragement is a strong believer? Even strong believers pursuing God can get pulled into ungodly attitudes. If only people had flashing signs above their heads that gave warning when they were operating in the flesh instead of the Spirit. A wise friend once gave me a real nugget of truth that I think about often. She warned me as I stepped out and determined to say yes to God in all things, "Never let others' compliments go to your head or their criticisms go to your heart."

Author Rick Warren, in his book *The Purpose Driven Life*, comments on naysayers:

> You will find that people who do not understand your shape for ministry will criticize you and try to get you to conform to what they think you should be doing. Ignore them. Paul often had to deal with critics who misunderstood and maligned his service. His response was always the same: Avoid comparisons, resist exaggerations, and seek only God's commendation.[1]

Rick then goes on to quote John Bunyan as saying, "If my life is fruitless, it doesn't matter who praises me, and if my life is fruitful, it doesn't matter who criticizes me." That's so true! But I know firsthand how hard it is to live in that truth.

THE FOES OF GRACE

Grace for the journey...we all need it. God is the only one we should be living for, and we need His grace to handle the successes and the failures, the applause and the criticism, and everything in between. Sometimes our efforts will be fruitful and other times fruitless. But as long as we please God, it's all for good.

Grace has two fierce foes, though—acceptance and rejection. Imagine, for a moment, a tall, gated wall. Puddles of mud dot the well-worn, barren ground. It is evident that many have lingered here. Two gatekeepers wish to detain you. They wish to take your hand in friendship and have you remain on the outside of the wall. All the while, Jesus is standing on the other side of the wall in an open field full of beauty and adventure. So few have actually made it past the gatekeepers into this field that the blades of grass remain unbroken and the flowers unpicked.

The first gatekeeper is Acceptance. He requires much of me. He seems so enticing with his offerings of compliments and big promises. But though he is fun for a moment, soon my mind is flooded with concerns of being able to continue to impress him. I am quickly overwhelmed with pondering my interactions with others and keeping score on the table of comparison.

The second gatekeeper is Rejection. He also requires much of me. He seems appealing because he gives me permission to excuse myself from following my true calling. Yet he demands that I pull back and shy away from the obedience for which my soul longs. His whispered questions of "What if?" and "What do they think of you?" linger in my mind and influence my actions and reactions.

How do I deny the lure of these two gatekeepers of grace? After all, I've tasted their laced fruit and, though I'm aware of their poison, I also crave their sweetness. In my flesh I desire the praises of Acceptance and the excuses of Rejection. The limelight of Acceptance shines on the pride that has yet to be driven from my heart. The thought that I am really something denies the reality that, but for the grace of Christ, I am nothing. The ease of settling for less is the pull of Rejection. When I listen to him, I shrink back and pull inside myself. I no longer want to press on. I want to quit. The thought that I am really nothing eclipses the reality that, because of the grace of Christ in me, I am a treasured something.

So goes the battle in my heart. Honestly, it sickens me that I even give thought to and feel enticed by these life-draining agents of Satan. Jesus is standing behind these two slick gatekeepers. His arms are open, waiting to embrace and enfold me in the security of His truth. His truth is that I am precious and accepted, no matter what. No matter what choices I make, His love is not based on my performance. His love is based on His perfect surrender at the cross. But, I must choose to accept this love and walk this truth for it to make a difference in how I journey through life.

No matter what choices
I make, His love is not
based on my performance.
His love is based on His
perfect surrender at the cross.

THE GREAT DANCE

Pursuing obedience and saying yes to God has been the most fulfilling adventure I have ever let my heart follow after. However, the journey has not been without bumps and bruises. I would be remiss in this chapter of what keeps us from radical obedience if I did not talk about the great dance between the desire of our flesh and the desire of God's Spirit in us. Our flesh seeks the approval of others, is swayed by Satan's voice of condemnation, and looks for the comfortable way out. God's Spirit in us opposes Satan and the world's way and offers an unexplainable peace that transcends the circumstances around us.

The dance plays out in rather subtle voices in my head. There is the pull between condemnation and conviction. If I'm hearing thoughts of condemnation, these only come from Satan. There is no condemnation from Jesus, only conviction. It's important for us to know the difference. Condemnation leaves us feeling hopeless and worthless. Conviction invites us to make positive changes in our lives.

I also sometimes find myself getting caught up in my own weariness and grumbling over the empty places of my life. These are all the places that chip away at my contentment, that nag me into thinking I'm being cheated out of something somehow. Last year we did a renovation on the house. Things were new and perfect for a couple of days. But it didn't take long with five kids and a dog for the carpet to get stained and the woodwork to get scratched. My car has dings on each of the front doors and a scratch on the driver's side door, and sometimes this bothers me. We won't even talk about what the inside of my kid-toting vehicle looks like! With all of their great qualities, my kids sometimes pout, complain, and whine, and, you guessed it, this bothers me. My husband and I are crazy about each other but still find ways to get on each other's nerves at times, and this bothers me. I struggle with trying to cram too much into too little time and often find myself running late—which really bothers me. When these little things get piled on top of bigger things, I can really get down.

There are things in my life, little and big, that fall short, don't meet my expectations, and cause grumpy feelings inside my heart. Do you ever sense empty places in your life too?

Usually this happens to me when the busyness of life has crowded out my quiet times with Jesus. When I have not spent enough time allowing the Lord to refuel and refill me, I forget that this is not my real home. When my soul gets down, these places can be distracting and difficult. And sometimes the reality is we feel hurt and discouraged.

THE CHOICE TO WORRY OR WORSHIP

When we find ourselves in these hard places, we make the choice to worry or worship. When we worry, we feel we have to come up with justifications and careful explanations for the naysayers. When we worry, we listen to the voices of Acceptance and Rejection. When we worry, we lay awake at night and ponder Satan's lies. When we worry, we have pity parties where the guests of honor are Negative Thinking, Doubt, and Resignation.

But we can make the choice to worship. When we worship in these hard places, we are reminded that none of this is about us—it's all about God. We turn our focus off of ourselves and back onto God Almighty. God can use empty places in your life to draw your heart to Him. He is the great love of your life who will never disappoint. He is building your eternal home that will never get broken, dirty, or need redecorating. He is preparing a place of eternal perfect fellowship where no one will be a naysayer. And heaven won't be limited to human time frames, so no one will ever be late...not even me!

Our hearts were made for perfection in the Garden of Eden, but the minute sin came into the picture, strokes of imperfection began to cast a dingy hue. When we know Christ, however, we know this is not all there is. Realizing that this life is temporary helps me to live beyond this moment and rejoice in what is to come. Each time I feel my heart being pulled down into the pit of ungratefulness and grumbling, I recognize it as a call to draw near to the Lord. I thank Him for the empty places, for they remind me that only He has the ability to fill me completely. In my worship of Him, my soul is safe and comforted and reassured and at peace.

We all worship something. We must choose whom—or what—we will worship. Will it be the opinions of others, our fears, or even our own comfort? Or will it be the One who created our souls to worship? Whatever we worship, we will obey. As we choose to be radically obedient and say yes to the Lord, we must be radical about choosing to worship Him and Him alone.

PEACE LIKE A RIVER

What is the result of choosing to worship God, to obey Him alone? "Peace is the fruit of the obedient, righteous life."[2] If I am ever going to find peace past the naysayers, past the attacks of Satan, and past my own weariness, it will only be because I choose daily to walk in absolute obedience to the moment-by-moment, day-by-day, assignment-by-assignment commands of the Lord.

The prophet Isaiah writes, "If only you had paid attention to my commands, your peace would have been like a river, your righteousness like the waves of the sea" (Isaiah 48:18). Did you catch the treasure hidden here? One of the most radical blessings for the woman saying yes to God is the peace that rushes through the soul of the one who is attentive to the Lord's commands.

God chose such a unique word to describe His peace—a river! A river is not calm and void of activity. It is active and cleansing and confident of the direction it is headed in. It doesn't get caught up with the rocks in its path. It flows over and around them, all the while smoothing their jagged edges and allowing them to add to its beauty rather than take away from it. A river is a wonderful thing to behold. Beth Moore says,

> To have peace like a river is to have security and tranquility while meeting the many bumps and unexpected turns on life's journey. Peace is submission to a trustworthy Authority, not resignation from activity.[3]

Jesus tells us His peace is unlike the world's peace: "Peace I leave with you; my peace I give you. I do not give to you as the world gives. Do not let your hearts be troubled and do not be afraid" (John 14:27). The world's way to peace would have me pull back to make life a little easier for me, my circumstances, and my family. The problem with this is that we were not put here to be all about ourselves—we were put here to be all about God. We are to die to our self-centeredness so we can have more of Christ in our hearts and minds. Jesus clearly tells us to focus on Him, His ways, and His example, and His peace will be with us. The focus of our hearts and minds will shape our decisions and actions that follow: "You [God] will keep in perfect peace him whose mind is steadfast, because he trusts in you" (Isaiah 26:3).

When we focus our minds and fix our attention on Christ, He is magnified and made bigger in our lives. When we focus our minds and fix our attention on life's obstacles, they will be wrongly magnified and made to appear larger than they really are. Our attention is like a magnifying glass—whatever we place it on becomes larger and more consuming of our time and energy. We desire to focus on Christ alone, but sometimes other things seem bigger, and so, without even realizing it, we shift our focus: "For the sinful nature desires what is contrary to the Spirit, and the Spirit what is contrary to the sinful nature. They are in conflict with each other, so that you do not do what you want" (Galatians 5:17). Before we know it, we are drawn into the muck and mire on the outer banks of Jesus' river of peace.

But sometimes it is down on your face in the mud in complete humility (and sometimes even humiliation!) that you will find a sweet and tender truth. It's from this position that you can say, "Jesus, I love You and want You more than anything else. I love You and want You more than the approval of my peers, family and friends, and even the naysayers in my life. I love You and want You more than the comforts and trappings of this world. I love You and choose to believe Your truth over Satan's lies. I love You and choose to worship You and You alone. Jesus, I love You and want to come to You empty-handed and offer my life in complete surrender."

Saying yes to God is a lot more about being than doing. It is choosing who I will worship and then depending on God to give me the strength to follow through. As my soul looks up from life's muck and rights the focus of its attention, I find myself pressing back into the river, where Jesus' peace rushes over me, refreshing, cleansing, and invigorating.

A LITTLE GIRL'S DANCE

My touch has always comforted my youngest daughter, Brooke. I can remember running errands when she was a baby, knowing we should have been home an hour earlier for her nap. But also knowing there were things that had to get done, I pressed on, hoping for the best. She started getting fussy, which made everyone else in the car start to lose patience. One of my older daughters, feeling very wise at five years old, said, "Mom, just tell her to stop crying. Tell her she'll get in big trouble if she doesn't."

Well, that might make a toddler who wouldn't want to miss out on watching *Barney* that afternoon settle down, but it did not work with a baby. She wanted to get out of that car and she wanted to make sure we all knew it. What started as some whines and whimpers soon escalated into a full-blown meltdown complete with tears, wailing, and screaming.

I couldn't do much to comfort her while trying to drive, but I could reach my arm into the back seat and gently pat her leg. It took a few minutes, but eventually she settled down and reached her tiny hand out to hold mine.

All of my kids like a hug, a pat on the shoulder, a hand of comfort on their back, but to Brooke these gentle touches seem to be a lifeline. Maybe touch is her love language. As Gary Chapman puts it in his book *The Five Love Languages*, touch might be the way Brooke will speak and understand love the most. Whatever it is, my touch is important to Brooke.

One day, she had a performance with her praise dance team from school. All the girls looked especially beautiful that day dressed all in white, their hair pulled gently back from their faces, and each had an extra measure of grace in their step. I couldn't wait to see Brooke perform these dances she'd been working on and talking about for weeks. She loves getting up on a stage, so I expected her to be full of smiles and giggles. But just a few minutes before the performance was about to begin a very distraught Brooke made her way to the audience to find me. With tears streaming down her cheeks, she explained that the teacher had moved her from the front row to the back row, and she didn't know the back row's part. I assured her everything would be fine. I whispered, "Honey, just get up there and watch the other girls for cues and follow in step. You know this dance, Brooke. You'll be fine."

She sobbed back, "I won't be fine if I mess up, and I know I'm going to mess up."

That's when it occurred to me. She would need my touch to get through this. But she and I both knew that it would not be possible for my arm to reach all the way up to the stage. So I quickly whispered, "Brooke, lock your eyes with mine, and Mommy will touch you with my smile. Don't look at anyone or anything else. Don't even look at the other girls dancing. It doesn't matter if you mess up. What matters is that you keep your eyes on me the whole time. We'll do this together."

Quietly she asked, "The whole time, Mommy?"

"The whole time, Brooke," I replied as I watched my brave girl walk away to take her place in line.

Several times during the dance, Brooke fell out of step. Her arms would go down when the rest of the back row lifted theirs up. She would go left and bump into the others headed right. She knew her steps weren't perfect, so her eyes brimmed with tears. However, the tears never fell. With her eyes perfectly locked on my smiling face, she danced. She danced when the steps came easy. She danced when her steps got jumbled. She danced even when her emotions begged her to quit. She danced the whole way through. She danced and I smiled.

I smiled when her steps were right on track. I smiled when they weren't. My smile was not based on her performance. My smile was born out of an incredible love for this precious, courageous little girl. As she kept her attention focused solely on my smile and the touch of my gaze, it was as if the world slowly faded away and we were the only ones in the room.

This is the way God wants me to dance through life. Though I can't physically see Him, my soul pictures Him so clearly. In my mind's eye He is there.

The touch of His gaze wraps about me, comforts me, assures me, and makes the world seem strangely dim. As long as my gaze is locked on His, I dance and He smiles. The snickers and jeers of others fade away. Though I hear their razor-sharp intentions, they are unable to pierce my heart and distract my focus. Even my own stumblings don't cause the same feelings of defeat. My steps so often betray the desire of my heart, but it is not my perfect performance that captures His attention. Rather, it is my complete dependence on Him that He notices.

He then whispers, "Hold on to Me and what I say about you. For My words are the truth of who you are and the essence of what you were created to be." I then imagine Him pausing and, with tears in His eyes and a crack in His voice, He adds, "Then you will know the truth, and the truth will set you free" (John 8:32).

His truth frees you from the chains of doubt and despair. His truth frees me from feeling unable and inadequate to try and pursue God in an all-out way. His truth washes over me as I tentatively whisper, "I want to be a woman who says yes to God." And in that moment, with my eyes locked on His, I am.

BIBLE STUDY

When faced with the choice to worry or to worship, which Scripture will be a powerful reminder for you of God's certain help?

Read Matthew 6:26-27. What good will worry do?

Read Matthew 6:30-32. What does God promise for our provision?

Read Matthew 6:34. How can we let go of worries for the future?

Read Mark 13:10-11. While you might not get arrested for preaching the gospel, you may find yourself in a situation where you are worried how to speak. How does this comfort you?

Instead of worrying, the mark of our life should be worship. Worship replaces anxiety brought on by fear with an unexplained peace that can only come from focusing on God.

> My eyes are fixed on you, O Sovereign LORD; in you I take refuge—
> do not give me over to death (Psalm 141:8).

Remember the story I shared about Brooke fixing her eyes on me when she faced fear? What does *fixed* in this verse mean? What does *taking refuge in the Lord* mean? How can we fix our eyes on the Lord?

Read Isaiah 30:21.

What voice is being referred to here?

What direction will this voice give us?

How does this calm your worries?

> Let us fix our eyes on Jesus, the author and perfecter of our faith,
> who for the joy set before him endured the cross, scorning its shame,
> and sat down at the right hand of the throne of God (Hebrews 12:2).

What does it mean that Jesus is the author of our faith? What does it mean that Jesus is the perfecter of our faith? How does this verse comfort and encourage you?

Most people assume that Saint Patrick is from Ireland. Patrick was actually kidnapped as a teen from his native land of Britain and forced to be a slave for six years in Ireland. During his captivity, his job was tending sheep. He spent many hours each day in prayer. By the time he escaped back to Britain, he was no longer a self-centered aristocratic child. He had become a man sold out for the cause of Christ. Several years later, he returned as a missionary to Ireland and lived out his life winning that country to Christ. His life circumstances often could have caused a lot of worry. Instead, he made the choice to worship God and trust His plan. I thought his constant prayer would inspire you:

Christ shield me this day:
Christ with me,
Christ before me,
Christ behind me,
Christ in me,
Christ beneath me,
Christ above me,
Christ on my right,
Christ on my left,
Christ when I lie down,
Christ when I arise,
Christ in the heart of every person who thinks of me,
Christ in every eye that sees me,
Christ in the ear that hears me.

SAINT PATRICK,
FROM HIS BREASTPLATE

SIX

IF IT WERE EASY,
IT WOULDN'T BE
WORTH DOING

Radical obedience is born out of delight, not duty.

I was discouraged. In two months' time my life went from being wonderfully fulfilling and clicking right along to completely topsy–turvy. I felt myself getting caught in a whirlwind of emotions. My computer went on the blink and some very important documents disappeared. A big book deal I was excited about fell through. Our well broke, and we had to go several days without water. A diamond fell out of my wedding ring.

Then, on top of a host of other interruptions and haphazard happenings, my husband blew out his knee and had to have major reconstructive surgery, leaving him bedridden for nearly five weeks. I didn't know whether to laugh or cry. A friend of mine hit the nail on the head when she said, "Lysa, I think when you go with God to a new level, you get a new devil."

I'm not sure about the exact theological accuracy of that statement, I do know that Satan hates the radically obedient soul. He hates it when a person jumps off the fence of complacency and into the center of God's will. There is a spiritual battle raging around us and, because of that, life can be hard. While saying yes to God does bring blessing, it's not easy. If our desire for obedience is born merely out of duty, we may be quick to give up. However, if our desire is born out of delight, out of a love relationship that burns deep in our soul, it won't be extinguished—no matter the cost.

PURPOSE, PERSPECTIVE, PERSISTENCE

One of my favorite love stories in the Bible is that of Jacob and Rachel. Jacob's love for Rachel gave him purpose and perspective, which led to amazing persistence. He served Rachel's father for many years to earn the right to marry Rachel because he loved her that much: "So Jacob served seven years to get Rachel, but they seemed like only a few days to him because of his love for her" (Genesis 29:20).

Do you see what love can do for a person's view of his circumstances? When you are crazy in love with someone, you'll do anything for him—and do it with the highest level of sheer joy. I want to be so crazy in love with Jesus that not only do I serve Him, but I do it with absolute delight.

A real sign of spiritual maturity is looking to God not for comfort and convenience but for purpose and perspective. Comfort and convenience lead to complacency. When trouble comes, the complacent person becomes critical of everyone, including God. On the other hand, purpose and perspective lead to the perseverance that is evident in those living a truly devoted life. The persistent person eagerly looks to handle trials and struggles in a way that honors God and allows personal growth.

Because we love God, we look for and trust in His purpose in everything. The persistent person understands the meaning of Romans 8:28: "We know that in all things God works for the good of those who love him, who have been called according to his purpose." This does not mean that everything that happens to us will be good, but that God will work in and through every situation to bring good from it. And let's not miss the last four words of this verse, where we are reminded that it is all "according to His purpose." God has a purpose, and His plans to accomplish that purpose are perfect. Trusting God's good

A real sign of spiritual maturity is looking to God not for comfort and convenience but for purpose and perspective.

purpose, seeking to understand that He takes all the events from our life and orchestrates good from them, leads to a changed perspective.

SEEING GOD IN EVERYTHING

Our changed perspective helps us see God in everything. I am convinced that Satan wants to keep my perspective in a place where my heart is discouraged and my mind is questioning God. Yet God's Word calls me to a different action: "We also rejoice in our sufferings, because we know that suffering produces perseverance; perseverance, character; and character, hope" (Romans 5:3). God's Word calls me to rejoice! Not that I rejoice in the bad things—I would have to fake that. But I can rejoice in what God is doing in me through difficult times.

When Art hurt his knee, we prayed and prayed this would be a minor injury and surgery wouldn't be required. We just knew God was going to go before us and make the way smooth for this injury. However, when the test results came back, we were facing a worst-case scenario. Not only would Art have to have surgery, but it was one of the worst knee injuries the doctor had ever seen. Simply looking at the circumstances and the doctor's report, we might have been tempted to get pulled into Satan's lies that God had not answered our prayers, that He wasn't trustworthy. However, the truth is that God is faithful and true, and His Word promises us, "He has not despised or disdained the suffering of the afflicted one; he has not hidden his face from him but listened to his cry for help" (Psalm 22:24).

So what do we do with the fact that my very athletic husband is out of commission for several months? What does he do about missing many weeks of work and having his life totally interrupted? What do I do with my feelings of being overwhelmed and frustrated because I need his help with the kids? What do I do with the fact that he can't drive, is in extreme pain, and needs my unconditional love and support—even on the days when I'm too tired to give it?

Okay, God, where are You? I cried out. There were too many details and too much stress. Our everyday life was already too busy, and now this. To be completely honest, I started to get a little frustrated with God. Satan was having a field day.

PROVISION, PROTECTION, PROCESS

What do you do when you feel as though God isn't hearing your cries for help? Or, worse yet, He's saying no?

It hasn't been easy, and God has had to remind me several times, but here's what I do know: God always hears me when I cry out to Him, and when He says no, it's for my provision, my protection, and it's part of the process of growing me more like Christ.

Provision

On one of my "Woe is me, my husband is still in bed and I am still doing everything" days, I took my kids along with a friend's child out to lunch. I was determined to have a good attitude, but with each whiney response and sibling spat I could feel my blood pressure rising. I was at the counter trying to place my order and keep an eye on the kids sitting in the booth across the restaurant when a lady came up and put her hand gently on my shoulder. "I've got your napkins and straws," she said, "and I'll put them on your table." I was shocked. Who was this sweet stranger?

After I made my way back to my table, I found her sitting with her family and went over to thank her. When I did, she told me that when I walked into the restaurant, God told her to help me. She didn't know who I was until I turned around to talk to her at the counter, and she recognized me as the speaker from a women's conference she attended last spring. She then went on to ask me if she could make my family a meal. I told her that my husband had just had surgery and a meal would be great.

I walked back to my booth with tears in my eyes. Just that morning I had cried out to God to fill in the gaps where I was feeling weary and weak. I asked Him to be my portion of all I needed to take care of my family that day. God was answering my prayer! My perspective totally changed. God was working good from Art's surgery. He had said no to us not having to have surgery, but He didn't leave us in that hard spot. He was teaching us about His provision.

How can He be our Ultimate Provider if we aren't ever lacking and in need? I was so touched by this lady's obedience to God's call to reach out to me. I was blown away by the personal and practical way God answered my cries for help despite my bad attitude.

Protection

My husband is an avid runner and can often be seen running the country roads near our home. After his knee injury occurred, he was very disappointed, to say the least, when the doctor told him it could be up to a year before he could run again—and that some people with this type of injury have to give up running altogether. Anytime we have to take a break from something we really enjoy, it's hard. But the thought of forever giving up running seemed too much to swallow.

Then came the call from a friend who knew of a man who was injured playing flag football the same week that Art had been injured, only the doctors were telling him he would never walk again. He was now paralyzed from the waist down. Then another call came from a friend who told me she read in the paper of a man riding his bike on the same roads my husband runs on. This man was struck by a car and killed.

Art and I had been so quick to throw a pity party over our circumstances, but now we were coming to the realization that God had protected him from situations that could have been a lot worse.

I confess I don't always understand the ways of God in these circumstances—why Art would just need surgery while another man lay paralyzed and another man was killed. Many have had to go through severe circumstances and unfathomable pain, and my own family is no exception. We have experienced tragedy. But I know that I know that I know: God has worked good in every one of these situations. As I look back and reflect on our difficult times, I can see how He has protected us.

Part of the Process

Ultimately, our time here on earth is for one single purpose: to grow more and more like Christ. Each of us comes to a place in our Christian journey where we have to make the decision whether we will become part of that process or not. I wrote a poem to express that moment of decision:

> *A man journeyed to a place*
> *Where the road caused him to ponder,*
> *Should he travel the wide, clear road?*
> *Or should he venture up the other?*
>
> *The wide road was more often traveled,*
> *It was level and easy and clear.*
> *The narrow one seemed barely a path,*
> *With very few footprints there.*
>
> *His senses said to choose for ease*
> *And walk where many have wandered.*
> *But the map he held in his hand*
> *Showed the narrow going somewhere grander.*
>
> *In life we will all come to a point*
> *Where a decision must be made.*
> *Will we choose to walk with comfort's guide?*
> *Or journey the narrow path God says?*

We want to live the totally sold-out life for Christ, yet there are other things pulling at us, enticing us, calling out to us—causing our indecision. Brent Curtis and John Eldredge said it well in their book *The Sacred Romance*:

> At some point on our Christian journey, we all stand at the edge of those geographies where our heart has been satisfied by less-wild lovers, whether they be those of competence and order or those of

indulgence. If we listen to our heart again, perhaps for the first time in a while, it tells us how weary it is of the familiar and indulgent. We find ourselves once again at the intersection with the road that is the way of the heart. We look down it once more and see what appears to be a looming abyss between the lovers we have known and the mysterious call of Christ.[1]

In times where the road diverges in front of us, we can either fall away from God or fall toward Him. During Art's long healing process, he made the decision to fall toward God and humbly thank Him for allowing the injury to happen. He chose to look for opportunities every day to rejoice in this trial and make the most of being still and quiet. He dove into God's Word and spent hours praying, reading, and writing notes about all God was teaching him.

Christmas happened to fall right in the middle of Art's recovery. Every Christmas morning we have a special breakfast with Jesus where we give Him a gift from our heart. I wondered what gift Art would have this year. When his turn came, he said he wanted to look for a way to serve another or give to another in Christ's name every day for the next year. By next Christmas he will know that 365 people's lives were made better because of Christ in him. Throughout the following months our dinnertime conversations each night centered around what "God adventures" Daddy had participated in that day. Soon, we were all sharing our own ways that we listened to God. My sweet husband made a choice to rejoice in the process of growing more like Christ, and what a difference it made not only in his life, but in others' lives as well.

I've especially seen a difference in my children. It is a good thing to talk about your faith and make going to church a priority, but when your kids participate in adventures with God and see truth lived out in front of their eyes, He becomes too real to deny. What a joy for me to hear my kids talking about God speaking to them to reach out to someone. How it lights my heart up to hear my kids tell us a story of them making a good decision, though the wrong one seemed more appealing. What comfort there is seeing proof that our kids are pursuing their own relationship rather than just buying into the God thing because of family tradition.

My husband's injury and time spent recovering turned out to be a blessing. What we gained as a family during this time was more than a new perspective; it was a gift from God. This time of looking for ways to serve God like never before prepared our hearts for the night we met our boys in August of that year. We were all so in tune with saying yes to God in the little things that when this big thing came, we faced it head-on. We didn't run away with a trail of good excuses flying about behind us like dust on a dirt road. No, we looked at the opportunity before us, asked for God's will to be done, and leapt into the unknown with nothing but God's sweet confirmations.

Has it been completely easy and without challenge? No. We've had days where my husband and I look at each other in a daze and think, *How did we get here?* How did we get to this place where five (FIVE!) children all need something from us? This place is messy and loud and full of irresponsible choices. This place where things are never where they are supposed to be...the scissors are lost, the remote control misplaced, and the phone sounds garbled and full of static after being dropped in the water.

But this place is also full of life. This place is full of joy. This place is full of five amazing young people whom God fashioned and designed for some glorious purpose. What a privilege it is to be the ones who get to watch what God is doing to draw their hearts to His. Three of my children were born from my womb and two from my heart, but either way, this parenting thing is a beautiful unfolding of an eternal story. Reflecting this thought is a sign that hangs above my bed that reads, "All because two people fell in love." Two people fell in love, not just with each other but also with the God who drew them together.

Look at all that might have been missed had God answered our prayers about Art's knee the way we wanted Him to. We wanted a quick, easy healing where life could carry on. God wanted life interrupted. God wanted our attention. God wanted to give a huge blessing wrapped in a most unlikely package.

The prophet Jeremiah wrote, "Because of the LORD's great love we are not consumed, for his compassions never fail. They are new every morning; great is your faithfulness. I say to myself, 'The Lord is my portion; therefore I will wait for him'" (Lamentations 3:22-24). God is our portion of protection and peace. He's our portion of provision and security. He's our portion of all of the joy and patience we need during the process of growing more like Christ. He is our portion of whatever we need, whenever we need it—if only we'll recall His goodness and ask Him.

It isn't going to be easy. But we have Jesus and His power, and that power is able to completely change our outlook on life. This is how we can find the kind of joy the apostle Peter talks about: "Though you have not seen him, you love him; and even though you do not see him now, you believe in him and are filled with an inexpressible and glorious joy" (1 Peter 1:8). This is a radical blessing for the radically obedient—the ability to have a radically different perspective.

We're human. We know we're not always going to like our circumstances. Just because I am a woman who says yes to God does not mean I always like the things that come my way on any given day. I do not like some of the things my husband does. I sometimes find myself aggravated and annoyed because he processes things differently and looks at the world in a very black-and-white way. Mix this with my emotional views and hormonal responses, and the product is what we affectionately call "growth opportunities." I've faced a lot of things just this week that I don't particularly like. I already mentioned the scissors, remote control, and telephone. In addition, the girls were swinging too roughly on the hammock and it broke. My son burned my favorite pot. Somehow, most of my nice forks are missing. Though we haven't had enough rain lately to keep the grass green, the weeds are thriving. And ants have taken up residence in my kitchen and bathroom. Maybe they are still looking for remnants of a science experiment gone bad, which caused a smell to breed in our home that only creatures born from larvae could be attracted to.

I don't wake up and think, *Joy, joy, joy. I love misplaced and broken things. I love setting my table with stainless steel knives and plastic forks. I love phones with static. I love weeds and ants with messed-up smellers.* No, I wake up and say, "God, I love You and choose to accept the assignments You place before me with an attitude that reflects the truth that You live in me. I know I won't do this perfectly, and I admit my inability to do this in my strength. So, I say yes to You today. I say yes to Your desire to invade my natural flesh responses. I say yes to Your forgiveness when I mess up. I say yes to persevering even when I want to give up. I say yes to Your invitation to be obedient even when other paths seem more appealing. I say yes even as my lips desire to utter a thousand times over, 'I can't.' I say yes to loving You more."

NO MORE "I CAN'TS"

I can't. These two words can seem quite innocent and reflective of some obvious truths. I can't fly through the air like Superman. I can't make my scalp suddenly start growing the silky straight blond hair that the hair model so beautifully tosses across the pages of a magazine ad. I can't grow a tree in my backyard that sprouts dollar bills. These statements are truths born from cold hard facts and not from my own laziness or fear.

Other "I can't" statements are often born from laziness or fear. Assumptions that have been around so long that they feel like truth. Last summer I decided to take an honest assessment of some of these "I can'ts" in my life. As I marched up to each of these giants, I asked myself the question: What would it take to slay this giant in my life? Most of the time, the answer was as simple as a decision. "Decide that you ought to, you can, and you will."

I shared this sentiment with a friend who was struggling with her own "I can't." She had known God was calling her to be a speaker and a writer and had signed up for a conference our ministry offers every year called She Speaks. Then the doubts and fears started to overwhelm her. She wrote to me saying:

Dear Lysa,

I am looking forward to the upcoming conference with a great deal of fear and trembling. I feel like somewhat of an idiot putting myself on the writers' track because I have done so little writing since college. I have been afraid to respond to the appointment schedule because I am fearful of looking like a jerk in front of people I hope to impress. Do you have any suggestions for me? I will have a book proposal, but I feel like a third grader who has been asked to submit a high school term paper. I can hardly tell my friends and family where I am going. They will surely wonder, *Why would she be going to a conference like that?* I walk into Christian bookstores, and I am convinced that it has all been covered.

What is my deal? Last fall I knew without a shadow of a doubt that this was what the Lord wanted me to write. Now I feel as though I am chasing a pipe dream. I have a haunting sense I should just give it up and get back to gardening.

I quickly began a response back to her. It read:

I love your honesty, sweet friend. I also love your heart. Though you are scared, you are walking that narrow road of absolute obedience. God is pleased.

Now to address your questions and fears. First of all, you are not an idiot at all. You have taken a step toward a dream God has placed in your heart. That makes you obedient, not idiotic. I am so proud of you for doing more than 90 percent of all people who lurk in the shadows of their dreams but never get intentional about them.

Before I could continue I felt that gentle nudging in my heart that I've come to recognize as God's voice. He brought to my mind another conversation I'd had with this friend where she's shared with me about her running several times a week with a group of ladies from her neighborhood. She was getting in such good shape and feeling great. I just smiled and nodded while thinking, I could never run that far or be that disciplined.

God brought this past conversation to my mind, I'm convinced, to challenge me. How could I ask her to step out of her comfort zone into a world where I feel very comfortable, that of speaking and writing, if I wasn't willing to do the same? My advice and encouragement would mean so much more to her if I stepped into her comfort zone and pushed through my own fears. It was time to strap on my tennis shoes and run.

Running more than a mile or two was a big "I can't" in my life. But I felt God telling me to go out and run until I couldn't run anymore. Every time my body wanted to stop, I was to pray for my friend. I ran and ran and ran. When I finally stopped, I immediately got in my car and clocked how far I'd gone. I was shocked as the odometer turned to a little more than three miles. I had done it. I threw my hands up in victory and prepared to retire my tennis shoes for eternity.

That is, until a few days later when God nudged my heart again to run. I continued to run several times a week over the next month and prayed for my friend every time my side ached, my breathing became labored, and my legs cried out for me to stop. I pushed through the "I can't." Then, the day before the conference I threw my hands up as I victoriously exclaimed, "I can!" That day I clocked 8.6 miles.

My friend was also victorious that weekend as she attended the conference, met with publishers, and determined to press on with this calling in her life. And you'd better believe that we carved out time early one morning during the conference to run together. In both of our situations there was nothing standing in our way but our own minds repeating the life-draining words that hold too many people back: "I can't."

I can assure you on the other side of every "I can't" excuse is a glorious adventure with God just waiting to happen. And rest assured, the victory is not found in your performance. Rather, it's in your pursuit of taking that first step with God. A joy will be there like you've never known. As we choose to say, "With God, I can," we can expect Him to show up and be our daily portion of everything we need. Don't be afraid of the outcome; that's in God's hands. You just rest in the delight that walking with God this way is what your soul was designed for. The more you experience God, the more you expect to see and hear from Him every day. Obedience stops being a dutiful obligation and starts becoming a delight you crave.

When a woman says yes to God, she discovers a thrilling way to live.

BIBLE STUDY

Write your thoughts on this statement from this chapter:

If our desire for obedience is born merely out of duty, we may be quick to give up. However, if our desire is born out of delight, out of a love relationship that burns deep in our soul, it won't be extinguished—no matter the cost.

What does serving God out of duty look like?

What does serving God out of delight look like?

Psalm 37:3-4 says,

> Trust in the LORD and do good; dwell in the land and enjoy safe pasture. Delight yourself in the LORD and he will give you the desires of your heart.

Where will we find safety?

What will you be given as a result of delighting in the Lord?

How will the desires of our heart change as a result of having a love relationship with God?

Think about a tough situation you've faced recently. Write out a brief recount of this experience and identify the three things we learned when God says no.

Provision

Protection

Process

What are some of the "I can'ts" in your life right now?

Second Corinthians 12:8-10 says,

> Three times I pleaded with the Lord to take it away from me. But he said to me, "My grace is sufficient for you, for my power is made perfect in weakness." Therefore I will boast all the more gladly about my weaknesses, so that Christ's power may rest on me. That is why, for Christ's sake, I delight in weaknesses, in insults, in hardships, in persecutions, in difficulties. For when I am weak, then I am strong.

Do these verses give you an excuse to remain weak and subject to your "I can't"? Or do they tell you where you can draw strength from?

....

How do we tap into the strength of the Lord and use it to help us?

....

Romans 8:14-16 says,

> Those who are led by the Spirit of God are sons of God. For you did not receive a spirit that makes you a slave again to fear, but you received the Spirit of sonship. And by him we cry, "Abba, Father." The Spirit himself testifies with our spirit that we are God's children.

....

What does it look like to be led by the Spirit?

What is the promise of these verses, and how does it encourage you?

SEVEN

KEEPING OUR VISION CLEAR

Our life will follow where we focus our vision.

My husband and I found ourselves blessed with a little extra money once, and I started dreaming of new kitchen curtains. I stood in the kitchen and envisioned beautiful toile fabric cascading down and around my windows. I pleaded with my less-than-enthusiastic-about-the-curtains husband to understand that a woman's home is an expression of who she is, that curtains are important to the overall happiness I feel in my home. I even went so far as to pull out some handy-dandy Scriptures straight from Proverbs 31! I showed Art how this biblical woman made coverings for her bed, and I was sure she made matching window treatments as well.

Art still wasn't convinced. He kept gently telling me he felt led to give the money to ministry.

Ministry! Our whole lives were dedicated to ministry! "Honey," I countered, "I will have so much more to offer if only I feel complete and refreshed in our home. Did I mention that the home is the way a woman expresses her God-given creativity?"

My arguments, however, were not working. Eventually, my countenance turned sour and my words turned cold and flat toward my husband.

"Look, Lysa," Art finally said, exasperated, "if it's that big of a deal, we'll get the curtains."

I had won! You'd think I'd be overcome with joy and glee, but I caught a glimpse of my face in our bathroom mirror. It wasn't happy. It was harsh and pinched. I wasn't about to be deterred, though. I just needed a little makeup and all would be well. I reached underneath my sink where I keep my makeup bag, and it was gone. Then I felt God speak to my heart. He told me no amount of makeup was going to help what was wrong with me, and He would not allow me to find my makeup until I got back on track.

What? I asked Him in disbelief. *Don't You have some terrorists to round up? Or some hardened criminal to convict?* It was ridiculous to think that God would hide my makeup, so I determined to prove how crazy this was by finding my bag. I searched the entire house and both of our cars. I looked high and I looked low, and my makeup was nowhere to be found.

During my great hide-and-seek game, I continued to hear God's still, small voice speaking to me. As He tugged and prodded and convicted, I came to realize that my harsh facial expression was reflective of something ugly in my heart. My desire about what to do with the money had been all about me, me, me! Never once did I stop to pray. Instead, I pushed on with my agenda. Never once did I stop to consider the beautiful thing God was doing in my husband's heart by giving him the desire to share more abundantly. Never once did I take a step back to consider God's bigger picture and plan.

Was there anything wrong with new curtains? No. Was there anything wrong with my heart? Oh, yes. I had closed my heart to what God wanted, to His calling. I had limited my vision to new curtains and, had it stayed there, that's all I may have been blessed with. But if I took hold of His vision, the Lord gently reminded me, how much more would my life be blessed?

That night when Art came in from work, I humbly went before him and told him how wrong it was that I had been so self-centered. With tears in my eyes, I apologized for not stopping long enough to consider what he and God wanted. Art accepted my apology, and suddenly I knew where my makeup was. Even though I had already thoroughly searched Art's car, I asked if he would go look once more. When he did, he found the makeup bag on the passenger floorboard—in plain sight.

GOD'S BIGGER, GRANDER VISION

Why is it that we can be so nearsighted when it comes to God's plans for us? Why do we let what's right in front of us distract us from the bigger, grander vision God has in mind?

To be radically obedient is to keep God's vision clearly in front of us, to be so busy looking at what He wants, looking at Him, that everything else becomes less important. C.S. Lewis describes it as looking at "something beyond":

> I think all Christians would agree with me if I said that though Christianity seems at first to be all about morality, all about duties and guilt and virtue, yet it leads you on, out of all of that, into something beyond. One has a glimpse of a country where they do not talk of those things, except perhaps as a joke. Everyone there is filled with light. But they do not call it goodness. They do not call it anything. They are not thinking of it. They are too busy looking for the source from which it comes.[1]

Oh, Lord, give me the desire to be too busy looking at You to consider anything but Your plan! Strip away my short and narrow vision to see the wonderful adventure of truly being Your follower. Help me to be like Your disciples who followed immediately and fully rather than like the people who simply played games at the foot of Your cross.

How easy it is to obey partially. Obeying just enough to give the right Christian appearance is not the obedience God desires. He looks past all the outside trappings and misguided intentions straight to the heart. He wants our full attention and absolute devotion. Don't mistake this to look like a bunch of Christianese-speaking robots walking around chanting the rules of God. No, women who say yes to God are as unique in their approach to the sold-out life

To be radically obedient is to keep God's vision clearly in front of us, to be so busy looking at what He wants, looking at Him, that everything else becomes less important.

for Christ as pebbles found creekside. We've all been tumbled and smoothed in different ways, but we all have one thing in common…we know we rest in the mighty hand of God. Right now we may simply be an unsuspecting rock, but at any time God could use us to slay the mightiest of giants. We live in anticipation and expectation of God showing up and giving evidence of how very near He always is.

A few months ago I was praying specifically for God to reveal His activity in each of my children's lives. I knew they were Christians, but I wanted to see that they each had their own personal relationship with Him. I wanted God to be less about our family tradition and more about their own experience of Him. In little ways I started to see evidence of God's activity and discipleship springing to life in each of my kids. But the one that really captured my heart and burned a lasting impression in my soul was with my daughter Ashley.

I was speaking at a Ruth Graham and Friends conference out in California. While setting up my book table in the lobby of the church, Ashley called me on my cell phone. Immediately, I sensed the heavy emotion in her tone as she tearfully said, "Mom, I need you to pray for me." I stopped what I was doing and walked outside. I assured her I would absolutely pray for her throughout the weekend but that I'd love to pray with her right that minute. I then inquired about what was troubling her. Her answer stunned me.

She was asking for me to pray that she would have the strength to continue a fast she'd started that morning. Two little boys from her school had recently lost their dad to cancer. She told me that God had clearly spoken to her heart that morning and challenged her to pray and fast for that family all day. She did exactly what God had told her to do, but now her stomach was really hurting and she was having a hard time.

I checked my watch and calculated that it would be around 9 p.m. East Coast time. I encouraged her that sometimes God just intends a fast to be from sunup to sundown and that I was sure He'd be fine with her eating a little something before going to bed. She replied back, "Mom, I know exactly what God told me to do and I want to be obedient. I did not call for you to talk me out of this. I just need for you to pray for me to have the strength to continue."

Just what I'd been praying for. Ashley got it! She was more concerned about keeping God's vision clearly in front of her. She was so busy looking at what He wanted, looking at *Him*, that everything else became less important.

By the time I walked back into that speaking engagement, I looked like a wreck. My hair was windblown, my makeup tear streaked, and my countenance emotional. But my soul was overflowing with the joyful knowledge that my precious daughter was becoming a true disciple, a young woman who says yes to God!

TRUE DISCIPLES VS.
THE GAME PLAYERS

Two New Testament accounts from the life of Jesus contrast the true disciples from the game players. First, we find Simon Peter:

> He [Jesus] saw at the water's edge two boats, left there by the fishermen, who were washing their nets. He got into one of the boats, the one belonging to Simon, and asked him to put out a little from shore. Then he sat down and taught the people from the boat. When he had finished speaking, he said to Simon, "Put out into deep water, and let down the nets for a catch" (Luke 5:2-4).

Did you notice that there were two boats on the shore that day, and Jesus specifically chose Simon Peter's boat? Why? Because Jesus knew Simon Peter had a radically obedient heart and would be willing to do what He asked him—even when it made no sense. I like Peter's response to Jesus' request: "Master, we've worked hard all night and haven't caught anything. But because you say so, I will let down the nets" (verse 5). Do you hear what Peter is saying? "Though I'm tired from working all night, though I don't think You know much about fishing, Jesus, though it makes no sense at all in human terms...because You say so, I will do it."

How many times have I found myself in Peter's position and not responded in obedience the way he did? It saddens my heart to remember the occasions

I've ignored Jesus' call for my radical obedience because I was tired, or because I didn't really believe Jesus would work miraculously in a particular situation, or mostly because the Lord's request made no sense in human terms.

I often wonder now at the blessings I've missed because of my lack of obedience. Look at what happened to Peter because of his obedience:

> When they had [let the nets down], they caught such a large number of fish that their nets began to break. So they signaled their partners in the other boat to come and help them, and they came and filled both boats so full that they began to sink. When Simon Peter saw this, he fell at Jesus' knees and said, "Go away from me, Lord; I am a sinful man!" For he and all his companions were astonished at the catch of fish they had taken, and so were James and John, the sons of Zebedee, Simon's partners (Luke 5:6-10).

But Simon Peter's blessing that day didn't end with a huge catch of fish. His radical obedience to Jesus' simple request ultimately resulted in him discovering the calling on his life.

> Then Jesus said to Simon, "Don't be afraid; from now on you will catch men." So they pulled their boats up on shore, left everything and followed him (Luke 5:10-11).

We have to remember that Simon Peter didn't know that something as mundane as lowering his net into the water would change his life—but it did! And that's how it can be for us. Our calling is revealed as we walk in daily obedience to Christ in the little things.

That's what's remarkable about radical obedience. You don't know where it will lead. You don't know how God will use it. That's what I love about Peter's story. It shows us so much about the radically obedient life.

First, as Peter discovered, our call to obedience may challenge our pride. God hates a prideful attitude (James 4:6). Many times the little steps leading to the bigger steps in our calling will be tests that help whittle the pride out of our heart. Peter, for instance, could have easily questioned Jesus' fishing knowledge...after all, Peter was a professional fisherman and Jesus was a carpenter. But Peter chose to swallow his pride and take the small step of obedience.

Second, God uses our experiences to equip us for our calling. God doesn't waste our experiences in life. I know in my own life God has been able to weave everything together to form a beautiful tapestry of good experiences, bad experiences, hurtful things, joyous things, professional jobs, ministry jobs, and everything else to prepare me for the work He is in the process of revealing to me. The same was true for Simon Peter. Yesterday he was fishing for fish; today he would be fishing for men.

Third, our obedience may inspire others to respond. What a radical blessing! As we respond in obedience, others will catch the vision and respond to God's calling on their own lives. Think of it. It wasn't just Peter's life that changed that day. The lives of his fishing partners, James and John, were never the same either. And it started with Peter saying yes to Jesus.

One caution at this point. We need to be careful not to fall into the trap of thinking that our blessings for radical obedience will profit our accounts and fill our pockets. Yes, Peter got a boatload of fish as a result of his obedience, but notice what he did: "So they pulled their boats up on shore, left everything and followed him" (Luke 5:11). They didn't celebrate their banner fishing day. They didn't consider the fish a just reward for all their hard work. They didn't sell the fish and use the money to buy more boats and hang out a new shingle announcing their expanded fishing fleet. No, they were only thinking of the person who allowed it to happen—and they left it all behind and followed Him. Sounds a lot like that C.S. Lewis quote. "They do not call it anything. They are not thinking of it. They are too busy looking for the source from which it comes."

WHERE WE FOCUS OUR VISION

Now contrast Peter's story with another incident we find recorded in Luke:

Jesus said, "Father, forgive them, for they do not know what they are doing." And they divided up his clothes by casting lots (Luke 23:34).

It's hard to imagine anyone playing games in the shadow of the cross while the Savior of the world looked on in excruciating pain. He was dying for their sins, and they were dying for one good roll of the dice. They didn't even hear His cry for God to forgive them. They missed His offer of eternal significance because they were too distracted by earthly rags. They had no vision beyond the moment. Max Lucado writes of this scene:

> We are not so unlike those soldiers. We, too, play games at the foot of the cross. We compete for members. We scramble for status. We deal out judgments and condemnations. Competition. Selfishness. Personal gain. It's all there...So close to the timber yet so far from the blood.[2]

Are we like Peter? Or are we like these soldiers at the foot of the cross? Our life will follow where we choose to focus our vision. If we are serious about radical obedience, about having a vision that's God inspired, then we must keep our focus on Christ. When Christ speaks, we must listen. When He directs us to act, we must act. When He compels us to give, we must do so freely. When He reminds us to get past trivial matters, we must let our pride fall away. When He invites us to leave the world behind, we must follow Him.

For Peter, it was a net full of fish. For me, it was those kitchen curtains. You'll probably be happy to hear that I did eventually get new kitchen curtains. But they are not the lovely, feminine ones I always thought I wanted.

A few years before we adopted our sons from Africa, Art was invited to participate in the hunting expedition of a lifetime. He and several of his friends traveled to South Africa to hunt wild beasts with bows and arrows. I have to admit, I was not happy about this little adventure, but I knew that Art desperately wanted to go. God softened me by whispering a promise to my heart that if I let Art go on this manly excursion, it would be a big way that I could give

Art the respect he needed from his wife. I sent off my rough-and-tumble husband only to welcome him home two weeks later a changed man.

He brought me back some beautifully written love letters—I could hardly believe he penned them himself. He brought back pictures of the award-winning warthog he'd taken as well as other animals I'd never heard of in my life. Then he proudly announced that several of these stuffed beasts would soon be residing as prize mounts in our home. Needless to say, my lovely floral, toile, and girly plaid decor soon gave way to more of a Survivor theme. Pinks, greens, blues, and yellows gave way to earth tones and our traditional white woodwork was stripped, stained, and even replaced in some areas with cedar and stone accents.

Those lovely toile kitchen curtains that I fought for, agonized over, and felt so deprived in not getting would have been a complete waste. They would either be collecting dust in my attic or be in a trash bag labeled "garage sale" and taking up space in the garage. The rustic brown curtains that adorn my kitchen now are not at all what I envisioned but just the right accent to my now earthy kitchen. I have to admit that I hardly notice my kitchen curtains, but when I do I smile. Not because of their decorator appeal, although I really do like them, but rather because of the funny way that even in something as simple as curtains for your home, you can experience God. That is, if you choose to. Truly, a woman who says yes to God knows that her life will follow where she focuses her vision.

BIBLE STUDY

Think about one of the key points from this chapter: "Her life will follow where she focuses her vision." How does this statement challenge you personally?

Are you sometimes guilty of sacrificing what you want most for what you want right now? For example: I want a great relationship with God, but I want to sleep in more right now. So, once again I sacrifice my time with the Lord for a few more minutes of sleep. Or, I want to lose weight, but I want this piece of chocolate cake more right now. So, once again I satisfy my tastebuds and sacrifice my desire to be healthier. Write your thoughts here.

In this chapter we discovered three truths about obedience.

The first truth: *Our call to obedience may challenge our* _____ (page 125).

> You're cheating on God. If all you want is your own way, flirting with the world every chance you get, you end up enemies of God and his way. And do you suppose God doesn't care? The proverb has it that "he's a fiercely jealous lover." And what he gives in love is far better

than anything else you'll find. It's common knowledge that "God goes against the willful proud; God gives grace to the willing humble" (James 4:4-6 MSG).

....

Define "willful proud" and give an example of something you might be willfully proud about in your life right now.

....

Define "willing humble" and give an example of something you might be willingly humble about in your life right now.

....

The second truth: *God uses our _____ to equip us for our calling* (page 126).

> Do everything readily and cheerfully—no bickering, no second-guessing allowed! Go out into the world uncorrupted, a breath of fresh air in this squalid and polluted society. Provide people with a glimpse of good living and of the living God. Carry the light-giving Message into the night so I'll have good cause to be proud of you on the day that Christ returns. You'll be living proof that I didn't go to all this work for nothing (Philippians 2:14-16 MSG).

How can your life experiences help provide people with glimpses of God?

....

The third truth: *Our obedience may inspire* _____ *to respond* (page 126).

....

Read Luke 5:11. Who responded that day?

....

How does their response inspire you?

EIGHT

GIVING UP WHAT
WAS NEVER OURS

We are managers, not owners, of God's resources.

I was going through a fast-food drive-through one day when I realized I didn't have enough cash on me to pay for the lunch I'd ordered for my daughter Hope and myself. I knew Hope, who had just celebrated her ninth birthday, had received a ten-dollar bill as a gift from her aunt. I asked Hope if I could borrow just a few dollars to make up for my shortage, and I promised I would pay her back. She refused, explaining that she was seeing some of her friends that afternoon and wanted to show them her ten-dollar bill. It just would not be the same to show them a five-dollar bill and a couple of ones. No, she insisted, she had to keep her ten-dollar bill for herself.

I asked her if she trusted that I would pay her back. She said she did, but I might not pay her back with a ten-dollar bill. She did not want two fives. She did not want ten ones. She did not want any combination of bills. She wanted a ten. A ten-dollar bill would, after all, be much more impressive to her friends.

As it was approaching my turn at the drive-through window, I got more aggressive with my offer. I told her I would not only give her the change from her original ten-dollar bill, which was going to be about seven dollars, but that I would also give her another ten-dollar bill later. Even this offer was not enough to release her tight grip on her beloved bill. She did not want a ten-dollar bill later because she might miss showing off to her friends today.

Did my sweet daughter not realize that I had the ability to bless her with many ten-dollar bills? Did she not appreciate the fact that I had just spent the equivalent of more than ten ten-dollar bills on her birthday party? Did she even have a clue as to how many ten-dollar bills I've spent on her over her lifetime? Not to mention the fact that her lunch was part of the reason I was spending this ten-dollar bill at the moment?

Finally, when we were at the window, Hope begrudgingly gave me the money. How it disappointed me that she would not willingly release the ten-dollar bill.

How it must disappoint God when we do this very same thing.

You see, I had special knowledge that Hope did not have. I knew that waiting in our mailbox at home was another birthday card—one from her grandmother that contained a whopping fifty dollars! Her ten-dollar bill would pale in comparison.

Likewise, God has special knowledge in our lives. He has blessings for the radically obedient that make the dime-store stuff we are so intent on holding on to pale in comparison. The question is, do we trust Him? Do we trust that He will bless us? Do we trust that His blessings are infinitely better than what He might first ask us to release?

THE FLOODGATES OF BLESSING

Trust. Isn't that why more of us don't offer all we have to God? We don't trust that He really will throw open the floodgates of blessing in return.

> "Bring the whole tithe into the store-house, that there may be food in my house. Test me in this," says the LORD Almighty, "and see if I will not throw open the floodgates of heaven and pour out so much blessing that you will not have room enough for it" (Malachi 3:10).

Sacrificial giving is one of the few times God asks us to test Him. Yet for many years I found myself unwilling to accept the challenge. I was willing to tithe but not willing to go beyond what I felt comfortable giving. Leaving our comfort zone, however, is the very place God calls us to. He wants us to venture into truly abundant giving. He wants us to get out from under our own selfishness with our possessions and accept His invitation to become radically obedient with what we own. Then, not only will He bless us, but He will lavish blessing upon blessing on us.

I saw this firsthand when I was saving money for a new outfit. I started this "new outfit fund" because of an embarrassing situation I found myself in during a country club speaking engagement. I was wearing what I thought was a very nice outfit. When I showed up at the event, however, I quickly realized that not only was my outfit a little out of style, but my white discount store shoes were the only light-colored foot apparel in the entire building. (Not being a queen of fashion, I was unaware of the rule that white shoes have to wait until after Memorial Day in some parts of the country.) Everyone had on dark-colored shoes, so with every step I took, I felt as though my feet were screaming, "White shoes! Everyone look at my shocking white shoes!"

You'll be happy to know that not even white shoes could stop me from sharing about Jesus with this lovely group of women, but you'd better believe I was determined to update and improve my wardrobe.

It took me a while, but I managed to save up one hundred dollars in my "new outfit fund," so I set a date to go shopping with some of my fashion-savvy friends. Just a few days before I was to go shopping, another dear friend phoned to ask me to pray for her family's financial situation. They could not make ends meet and had many bills they were unable to pay. She mentioned they needed one hundred dollars immediately. While she was only asking me to pray for her and nothing more, I knew God was looking for a response from me that would honor Him. I prayed for my friend and I obeyed God's prompting to give to her the money I'd saved.

The day arrived for my shopping trip, and I must admit that instead of being excited, I felt a pang of dread. I knew that because I had given my money away, what happens when women *say yes to god*

I could only look and not purchase anything. I didn't want my fashion friends to think I was wasting their time, so I decided I would put whatever clothes they picked out for me on hold and pray that God would provide the means to return later and purchase them.

While I was moping about and strategizing, God was at work in my friends' hearts. After trying on three beautiful outfits complete with shoes and accessories, I returned to my dressing room to try and decide which outfit to put on hold. While I dressed, my friends took everything to the checkout counter and treated me to a $700 shopping spree! I was shocked and humbled that God had taken the little gift I'd given to my friend and returned it sevenfold through other friends.

THE LIFE THAT IS TRULY LIFE

The apostle Paul wrote:

> Command those who are rich in this present world not to be arrogant nor to put their hope in wealth, which is so uncertain, but to put their hope in God, who richly provides us with everything for our enjoyment. Command them to do good, to be rich in good deeds, and to be generous and willing to share. In this way they will lay up treasure for themselves as a firm foundation for the coming age, so that they may take hold of the life that is truly life (1 Timothy 6:17-19).

In this country, I think we would agree that most of us are "rich" and this passage applies to us. So, what motivates us to venture out into the area of sacrificial giving—an area that for many of us is a real stretch? There are two radical blessings tucked within Paul's words here. The first, which is also referenced in Matthew 6, speaks of laying up treasures in heaven—sending that which we cannot take with us ahead where we can enjoy it and benefit from it in eternity. If you knew you could immediately enjoy a treasure for one day or enjoy it forever if you waited just a short while, which would you choose? In this light, the eternal route makes so much more sense.

The second blessing goes hand in hand with the first. God is aware of our humanness and our desire for instant gratification. He tends to that as well. Not only are we blessed for eternity when we give, but we are blessed for today too: "So that they may take hold of the life that is truly life."

To live life that is "truly life" is to live abundantly in the here and now.

In his book *The Treasure Principle*, Randy Alcorn wrote:

> The act of giving is a vivid reminder that it's all about God, not about us. It's saying I am not the point, He is the point. He does not exist for me. I exist for Him. God's money has a higher purpose than my affluence. Giving is a joyful surrender to a greater person and a greater agenda. Giving affirms Christ's lordship. It dethrones me and exalts Him. It breaks the chains of mammon that would enslave me. As long as I still have something, I believe I own it. But when I give it away, I relinquish control, power and prestige. At the moment of release the light turns on. The magic spell is broken. My mind clears. I recognize God as owner, myself as servant, and others as intended beneficiaries of what God has entrusted to me.[1]

If we choose to obey and give of our resources in abundance, a feeling of amazing satisfaction will follow. The radical blessing of being able to take hold of a real life—a fulfilled and satisfied life we can't find any other way—will be ours.

JUST GIVE ME FIVE MINUTES

Dane and Kema Kovach are friends of ours who just a few years ago seemed as though they were on the fast track to the American Dream. Dane was an orthodontist with a thriving practice. He was a dedicated family man, leader in our church, and avid outdoorsman. Kema was a terrific mother of four precious adopted children and busy making plans to build their dream home. They had land, architectural drawings, and beautiful decorating plans. Just a few months before they were to break ground, our church started a building campaign that would allow us to move from our temporary high school auditorium home to a real building we could call our own.

During this campaign many amazing stories of sacrifice began to surface within the families of our church. The Kovaches were no exception. God began stirring in Dane's and Kema's hearts individually. Both were nervous about sharing with the other the absolute radical direction they felt God leading them in. Just a few weeks before the commitment ceremony, where the leaders of the church promised the firstfruits of the building offering, they both sheepishly approached a conversation they had to have. Imagine their shock as they realized God was speaking to both of them about sacrificing the money they'd saved for their dream home.

Joyfully, they placed their dreams in God's hands and invested their finances for eternity.

This act set their hearts on fire for God. Never did I see Dane and Kema after that where the joy of the Lord didn't just radiate off them. It wasn't long afterward that Dane went on a mission trip only to return with another shocking revelation from God: Both Dane and Kema felt they were being called to the mission field.

Just before they left, they proudly stood before our congregation and gave some insights from their amazing adventure with God during the years leading up to their departure for Papua New Guinea.

Dane was quick to give an answer to the questions swirling about them during their time of preparation to leave. "When people ask me why I'm doing all this, selling my thriving practice, taking my family of six on the mission field for four years, giving up what most consider the American Dream, I have to point to the overwhelming joy and fulfillment I feel at this point in my life in my relationship with the Lord. I only wish I could place my heart inside the person questioning me and let them experience this joy that I feel for just five minutes."

I have a feeling that if Dane could do this, our world would look like a dramatically different place. Our thinking is so upside down. We fear that giving sacrificially will make our lives empty, when in reality withholding is what leads to emptiness. Giving, releasing, surrendering to God in this way, is what leads to more fulfillment than we ever dreamed possible.

SEEING BEYOND OUR OWN MAILBOX

I must admit that sometimes I am tempted to become consumed with all the ministry opportunities just within the walls of the TerKeurst home. Having five kids can be a delightful but daunting task at times. Yet while my family is my primary ministry, it is not my only ministry.

God has placed the desire in my heart to reach out past my mailbox, past myself, and look for opportunities to live a sacrificial life that touches others for Christ. While God has not called me to the mission field on foreign soil, He has called me to a life of mission work in this place He has me now. Sometimes these "others" I'm called to reach out to are complete strangers whom I touch for a moment and pray God will use me to draw their hearts closer to Him. Other times the opportunities I'm blessed with are with people I know and come in contact with often enough to see God's bigger plan after I play my small role. Such was the case with my dear friend Genia one evening as we gathered with a couple of our close friends for dinner.

Genia and I are part of a small group of very close friends. We call our group "ASAP," which stands for Accountability, Sharing our dreams, Asking the tough questions, and Praying for one another. One night during our meeting, Genia was sharing a tough place she found herself in. As she described her situation, it reminded me of a song on my favorite CD. The Christian artist who sang the song perfectly described what it is like to be caught between life before really living for Christ and life where you sense God leading. This longing to go back and yet the desire to move ahead into a deeper walk with Christ was the place my friend found herself. I knew I had to let Genia hear this song.

After dinner I asked Genia to walk to my car with me to listen to the CD. I was in the process of telling her how I had this CD on continual play in my car

We fear that giving sacrificially will make our lives empty, when in reality withholding is what leads to emptiness.

because I loved it so much when God interrupted my thoughts and told me to give Genia the CD.

As the song played, Genia had tears in her eyes and told me that it perfectly described how she was feeling. I pushed eject, placed the CD in its plastic case, and handed it to her. I told her that God wanted her to have this CD, so now it was hers. Instead of listening to the music as I made my way home that night, I sat in silent prayer for my friend. It was a beautiful ride home.

The next day, Genia called with such excitement in her voice that she could hardly contain herself. She said she had listened to the CD over and over. She had played it for her husband, who agreed it perfectly described their situation. Then she remembered something that brought her to her knees. Three weeks earlier she'd attended a special prayer service where a woman whom Genia did not know came over and prayed with her. The woman told Genia that God loved her, He understood where she was, He promised not to leave her, and that He would give her a song to minister to her. "A song, Lysa, a song!" she exclaimed. "God promised me a song, and He used your hands to deliver it last night."

Tears welled up in my eyes as I realized that what I thought was a simple gift had actually been a well-timed God event for my friend's life! But the blessing didn't end there. Later that same day, the vice president of a large ministry called me on my cell phone. She said God had given her an idea for special retreats to reach women all across the country. She told God that she would write down any names that came to her mind as possible leaders for these retreats. She took out a piece of paper and instantly three names came to mind. She wrote her own name at the top. She then wrote two other names that had really been on her heart: mine and the Christian artist of the CD I had given to Genia.

All I did was give away a CD.

THE BLESSINGS OF A SACRIFICIAL LIFE

Understanding and discovering the beautiful opportunities of sacrificial living is so opposite of what the world tells us, and yet it is the only way to find the happiness and joy our hearts long for. The apostle John put it this way:

> Dear children, let us not love with words or tongue but with actions
> and in truth. This then is how we know that we belong to the truth,
> and how we set our hearts at rest in his presence (1 John 3:18-19).

I am convinced there is a treasure in life that very few find: a heart that is at rest in His presence. And how do we find this heart at rest? Through actions and in truth. I must confess I have moments where my heart is at rest in His presence, but they are broken up by pitfalls and pity parties. Sometimes I just simply want to be selfish. But when I choose selfishness, I may be happy for the moment, but I'm miserable in the long run.

Yet, my Lord, with His incredible patience, doesn't leave me in my misery. I call out to Him in repentance and, just like a connect-the-dots game, Jesus fills in the gaps between the dots to reveal a beautiful picture of Himself in my life. What if there were less and less space between my dots, revealing an even clearer picture of Christ in my life at all times? Oh, that it could be so. If only I could learn to practice the presence of Christ at every moment, in every decision, with all whom I come in contact. Setting my heart at rest in His presence in this way comes with practice and maturity. The more I practice His presence, the more I will experience His presence, and the more mature I will become.

Elizabeth George talks about the process of maturity in a beautiful way:

> The Old Testament term for the word gentleness, *anah*, describes a mature, ripened shock of grain with its head bent low and bowed down. Just think for a moment on the beauty of this word picture. As wheat grows, the young sprouts rise above the rest. Their heads shoot up the highest because no grain has yet formed. In their immaturity, little fruit, if any, has appeared. But, as time passes and maturity sets in, fruit comes forth—so much of it that the burdened stalk bends and its head sinks lower and lower—and the lower the head the greater amount of fruit.[2]

Lord, help me to lower my head past my selfishness and pride, past desiring others to serve me and on to serving others, past wanting more and on to giving more, past me in search of You. Help me to always desire the lowered head, full of Your fruit and consumed with Your presence. Help me to be forever mindful of my ministry at home as well as the ministry opportunities that wait beyond my own mailbox.

God owns it all. We are simply managers of His resources. When we pursue the beautiful opportunities of sacrificial living, we freely acknowledge that truth and then reap the blessings. When we come to understand that we're giving up what was never ours to begin with, we're walking in radical obedience.

BIBLE STUDY

Read Psalm 81:8-16. Now let's break down some of the verses to unearth the rich treasures contained within. First, look at verse 9:

> "You shall have no foreign god among you; you shall not bow down
> to an alien god."

Though our hearts are not often tempted to bow down to statues and gods of other religions, we are often tempted to bow down to other things. Write some things that tempt us to pull our focus off God.

Though we may not physically get on the floor and bow to these things, when we give them so much attention that they take priority over the things of God in our life, it's problematic. Also, when we hold on to these things so tightly that to be asked to release them causes great turmoil in our spirit, that is a sign of trouble. And don't mistake the fact that these things in and of themselves may not even be bad things. They might be good things. But as Jim Collins in his business book called *Good to Great* points out, sometimes the enemy to great is often settling for good. Write a description of what many consider to be the "good life."

Now contrast that with what God would define as "the great life."

Read verse 10 from Psalm 81:

> "I am the LORD your God, who brought you up out of Egypt. Open
> wide your mouth and I will fill it."

There are three key points from this verse. First, a reminder of the fact that the Lord is our God. Why is it important for us to keep that in the forefront of our minds?

Second, He is our God, who has been faithful throughout our journey and delivered us. What does this mean to you personally?

Third, if we open ourselves up to Him fully, He will fill us. What does opening ourselves up to Him fully mean?

What will God fill us with?

Verse 16 says:

> "You would be fed with the finest of wheat; with honey from the rock I would satisfy you."

What does temporary satisfaction look like?

What does real satisfaction look like?

Do you believe God is capable of truly satisfying you?

Verses 11 and 12 warn us about being self-focused, close-fisted, and stubborn-hearted:

> "My people would not listen to me; Israel would not submit to me.
> So I gave them over to their stubborn hearts to follow their own
> devices."

What were the consequences for the Israelites not listening to God, not trusting God, and constantly complaining to God? Find an example in the Old Testament of Israel following their own devices and suffering because of it. If you are having a hard time knowing where to start, look in Numbers 11:1, 4; 14:1-4; or 20:2-3.

List their complaint, their sin, and their consequence.

In this chapter we read,

> "Dear children, let us not love with words or tongue but with actions
> and in truth. This then is how we know that we belong to the truth,
> and how we set our hearts at rest in his presence" (1 John 3:18-19).

How do you plan to apply this verse to your life?

What is the promise in store for the person who applies this truth?

NINE

RADICALLY BLESSED

The blessings of radical obedience are unending.

The other day I was driving down a busy road when I came upon a traffic light that was both green and red at the same time. I slowed, unsure of what I should do, as did other cars coming from all directions. It was a confusing and dangerous situation. Some people stopped, others ran through the light, and still others pulled off to the side of the intersection.

I finally made it through the intersection and thought about this unusual happening. It was as if God were showing me a visual picture of what it's like when a person is indecisive in her obedience to Him. We can't seek to follow God wholeheartedly if part of our heart is being pulled in a different direction. We can't pursue the radically obedient life and still continue to flirt with disobedience in certain areas of our life. We can't be both red and green toward God at the same time. It gets us nowhere. It's confusing. It's dangerous.

This book has been your invitation to become a woman who says yes to God and catches a glimpse of the blessings that are ahead. Now it's time to respond.

Don't be afraid, my friend. I know your mind might be flooded with the same questions that flooded my mind as I was responding to this invitation.

"What if I don't feel able to make such a commitment?"

"What if I say yes and then mess up?"

"What if I have times when I just don't feel like being obedient?"

Let's go back to my husband's sage advice: Consider the source. Who is asking these questions? That's not your voice sowing seeds of doubt; it's Satan's voice. He wants to keep you in doubt and confusion. He wants you to pull off to the side of the intersection and remain ineffective. He wants you to fail to fulfill the purposes God has for you and thwart the positive impact you could make in the lives of so many.

You don't feel able? Good! Christ's power is made perfect through weakness (2 Corinthians 12:9). Ask God for the strength to persevere every day. Ask God for the desire to remain radically obedient and for spiritual eyes to see the radical blessings He will shower upon you.

What if you mess up? Grace! "God opposes the proud but gives grace to the humble. Submit yourselves, then, to God. Resist the devil, and he will flee from you. Come near to God and he will come near to you…humble yourselves before the Lord, and he will lift you up" (James 4:6-8, 10). Please don't think I walk this radical obedience journey with perfection, because I don't. Chances are you won't either. But God doesn't expect perfection from us—He expects a person humble enough to admit her weaknesses and committed enough to press through and press on. He will guide us past the doubts and fears and lift us up to fulfill our calling.

What if you wake up in a bad mood and just don't feel like being obedient? Choose! Obey based on your decision to obey, not on your ever-changing feelings. I don't feel like giving. I don't feel like smiling. I don't feel like listening to God. But here's what God has to say about that: "It is *God* who works in you to will and to act according to his good purpose" (Philippians 2:13, emphasis added). When we ask God to continually give us the desire to remain obedient, He does. He will help us to want to obey Him and will give us His power to do so.

GET READY!

If your answer is no to radical obedience, then let it be no. I just ask you to do one thing while you sit at the red light. Pray that God will give you the desire to say yes. Let me challenge you for the next 30 days to pray and ask God to reveal Himself to you and fill you with a desire for Him like never before. Remember that lasting obedience must be born out of desire, not duty. Choose to be a woman who says yes to God by starting with this simple prayer. It will cost you only a minute of your time each day, but it will bless you for a lifetime!

If your answer to this invitation is yes, then get ready. You have not only signed up for the most incredible journey you can imagine, but you've also just given God the green light to pour out His radical blessings on your life! What I'm writing about here is just a glimpse of how God will bless you. He's capable of so much more!

Deeper Relationship with God

You will begin to live in expectation of hearing from God every day. You will start to better understand His character and seek to be more like Him. You will discover the depth of love that the Father has for you that you never even knew was possible. This will give you a feeling of acceptance and significance that you can't get any other way.

Some people spend their whole lives chasing things they think will make them feel accepted and significant. But the truth is this world only has packages full of empty promises to offer. The new house, the fancier car, the latest gadget, the fastest computer, the sleek fashions, and everything else that seems so enticing won't last. They will all wear out, break down, tear up, and become obsolete. Five, ten, twenty years from now, they won't look so appealing and will have to either be updated or replaced. Fifty years from now, most will be taking up space in a junkyard somewhere.

In contrast, every investment we make in our relationship with God will only serve to reap rich dividends for now and eternity. No time spent experiencing God will ever be a waste.

More Adventurous Life

I've heard it said that life would not be so hard if it weren't so daily. Yet the Bible says that each day is a gift from God that we should rejoice in (Psalm

118:24). Daily adventures with God will add an excitement to your life that will change your whole perspective. No longer is your day just one humdrum task after another, but rather a string of divine appointments and hidden treasures waiting to be discovered.

Seeing life like this opens up God's storehouses of joy. The mark of a truly godly woman is one who reveals the power of God not so much in her doing as in her being. She has opened God's treasure chest of joy and so filled her heart with gratitude and love that just being around her inspires you. She goes about the simplest of tasks, her everyday duties, and even the rough patches of life with such grace that you find yourself wanting to imitate her. She is full of adventure yet not worn out from the journey.

Depth of Inner Peace

In our world of turmoil and uncertainty, there is nothing more precious than peace. When we say yes to God, we know that our life and the lives of those we love rest in the certainty of His never-changing love for us. While we can't control the circumstances we face, we can choose how we react to them. If you've settled in your heart to say yes to God and completely trust Him, then you don't have to worry about the future. You are not in charge of the outcome, you are simply responsible to be obedient. You will be blessed with the peace of knowing that God has a perfect plan and holds everything in His perfect control. What freedom this brings!

Personal Satisfaction

Radically obedient people no longer have to strategize and manipulate things into being. Instead, they are blessed with opportunities that bring them real satisfaction according to God's perfect design for them. When my husband and I adopted our sons from Liberia, I thought the responsibility of adding more children would mean the end of my ministry. But that has not been the case. God has grown the ministry, sent more people to help run it, and blessed us with the most amazing opportunities to tell our adoption story. We've been allowed to freely talk about listening and obeying God on *Good Morning*

America and *The Oprah Winfrey Show*. God has taken our obedience and maximized our ministry's impact.

Better Relationships with People

In every relationship with others, you will find things that you love and things that, to be quite honest, get on your nerves. The radically obedient person is blessed with being able to appreciate another's Christlikeness and to give grace to their humanness. Whether a person is a believer or not, he is still made in God's image, and God is crazy in love with him. When you are committed to radical obedience, you see everyone through God's eyes of love.

Meaning and Purpose to Life

Author Bruce Wilkinson wrote:

> Once the Lord has fed His child through intimate devotions, He begins to call him more pointedly to deeper obedience. At this point, the believer desires more of the Lord so much that he is more than willing to do whatever the Lord requires…Obedience for this individual is no longer a burden, undertaken only because the Bible tells him to do something. Rather, obedience becomes a joy because his closest friend and most compassionate Lord beckons him to be like Him.[1]

Our hearts search for deeper meaning in life, and radically obedient people find it in loving the Lord, loving others He brings in our path, and continually seeking to become more like Jesus.

Eternal Perspective

Life is about so much more than just the here and now, and the radically obedient person lives in light of that perspective. Life isn't about being comfortable and taking the easiest route. It's about living to give our lives away and making a real impact in this world. It's not about serving out of religious duty. It's about delighting in our relationship with God so much that we want to serve out of an overflow of love and gratitude. Our time here is but a small dot on an eternal line. What we do now in this brief moment will determine our destiny for eternity. The radically obedient person is blessed with an eternal perspective.

A RADICALLY
OBEDIENT EXAMPLE

I am drawn to the story of one New Testament woman who was radically obedient—Mary, Lazarus' sister. I am moved by Mary's overwhelming love for Jesus. She was a woman who understood the essence of radical obedience. She knew when to listen and when to act. She knew when to simply sit at the Master's feet and when to pour out all she had in lavish love for her Lord (Matthew 26:6-13).

Jesus had just announced He would be crucified. Mary took what was probably her most costly possession, the perfume from her alabaster jar, and poured it out on Him. Normally, one would pour perfume on a dead body, but Mary anointed Jesus while He was still living. I believe it was so Jesus could carry the scent of her love with Him to the cross.

Mary was scolded by some of the disciples for her act of extravagance (naysayers!), but Jesus was quick to jump to her defense. What others saw as waste, Jesus saw as the purest form of walking out the gospel message. She was willing to love Him without reservation, without concern for what others might think or even concern for herself. Mary showed an unabashed love through this act, and, make no mistake, Jesus was quick to lavish His love right back on her. "I tell you the truth," Jesus said, "wherever the gospel is preached throughout the world, what she has done will also be told, in memory of her" (Matthew 26:13).

Isn't it amazing that such a small act of obedience could have such far-reaching effects? That can happen in our lives as well. Indeed, Mary was radically obedient and radically blessed...and you can be too.

The radically obedient person is blessed with an eternal perspective.

HOW IT ENDS

Well, this whole adventure began with God telling me to give away my Bible, so is it any surprise that it ends the same way? Just last weekend I was flying to the Washington, DC, area for a speaking engagement. The man next to me on the plane was busy working on his computer and did not appear to be in the mood to be interrupted. My heart kept feeling drawn to share the gospel with him, but it didn't seem appropriate to force a conversation. So I prayed.

I prayed that God would prompt him to start talking to me. And talk he did. It wasn't long before he put his computer away and started asking me all kinds of questions about my career. Because I write and speak about Jesus, this was a perfect opportunity to tell him all about my Boss! When we started talking about God, he said he'd been studying the Koran and several other religious writings, but not the Bible. However, he'd called the friend he was traveling to see and asked if they could buy a Bible that weekend to complete his collection.

I almost fell out of my seat. Of all the planes traveling to Washington that day and of all the people who were seated together, God arranged for a man who needed a Bible to sit beside a woman who loves to give Bibles away! I shared with my new friend my passion for giving away Bibles, and I promised I would send him one the next week. He sat stunned. When he finally spoke again, he told me he knew this was more than sheer coincidence. He knew God was reaching out to him.

Oh, my friend, we don't have to seek to create opportunities to say yes to God. God has already gone before us and established them. We simply have to respond.

I pray that the end of this book is not the conclusion of your journey. I sincerely hope this is only the starting place, the point of inspiration and expression for you to live a radically obedient, radically blessed life. What happens when women say yes to God? The world is changed.

BIBLE STUDY

For this concluding Bible study, we are going to do something a little different. God's Word has much to say on the topic of saying yes to God and the amazing blessings that follow. Pick ten of these key verses, look them up for yourself, and discover what God wants you to know about His calling on your life. I've summarized the verses, but it will be so much more powerful to dig into God's Word and record the powerful promises yourself.

Deuteronomy 28:1-14
Obedience opens God's storehouse of blessings.

2 Chronicles 16:9
God will strengthen the heart of the obedient person.

Esther 4:14
God has called you to obedience for such a time as this.

Psalm 15
Obedient people dwell in the presence and peace of God.

Psalm 24
Obedience in what you say, what you do, and what you think leads to holiness and blessings from God.

Isaiah 55:1-3
Obedience brings your soul satisfaction, delight, and new life.

Hosea 10:12
Obedience reaps the fruit of unfailing love and brings showers of righteousness.

Malachi 3:8-10
Being obedient givers will open God's storehouse of blessing.

Malachi 3:16-17
Radically obedient people are treasures to God.

Matthew 26:12-13
Even small acts of obedience have widespread effects.

Romans 1:5
Obedience comes from faith.

Romans 6:15-16
Obedience leads to righteousness.

Romans 8:5-6
Those walking in obedience have their minds set on God's desires.

2 Corinthians 9:6
The extent that we sow in obedience will determine
the extent we will reap in blessings.

2 Corinthians 9:13
Men will praise God for the obedience that accompanies our faith.

Ephesians 4:24
We were created to be like God. We walk this
out in obedience leading to holiness.

Philippians 2:13
It is God working in us that prompts us to be
obedient and fulfill His good purpose.

Philippians 4:9
What you have learned, heard, or seen from God, walk it
out in obedience and you will be blessed with peace.

2 Timothy 2:20-21
God is able to use the obedient person for His noblest purposes.

Hebrews 11
A list of radically obedient, radically blessed people.

1 Peter 1:13-14
Prepare your mind for obedience, which leads to holiness.

1 Peter 2:21-22
Those who walk in obedience walk in Jesus' footsteps.

1 John 2:3-6
Obedience makes God's love complete in us
and enables us to walk as Jesus did.

what happens when women

walk in faith

INTRODUCTION

In the following chapters, I want to talk to you about the five phases I've identified in the Bible common to people who have stepped out with God in pursuit of their dream. Throughout this book we'll see how different biblical characters weathered those five phases, and we'll learn how to recognize these phases in our own faith walk. I'll also be sharing with you many of my own adventures as I've progressed through these stages time and time again. I hope that as you better understand these phases of faith, you'll avoid the discouragement and defeat so many of us have gotten bogged down in along the way. You'll be able to press through, walk confidently, and avoid doubting God.

The five phases of faith go hand in hand with five fundamental truths of God:

1. God has a plan for me.

2. God is with me.

3. God will make a way.

4. God isn't surprised by death.

5. God brings dreams to life.

Keeping these five vital truths in mind will sustain you as you pass through the five phases of faith. As you'll soon discover, Satan will oppose you as you begin to fulfill your dream. He will suggest some lies that are in direct opposition to the five truths above:

1. God couldn't care less about you.

2. God is too busy with the important people to be bothered by insignificant you.

3. God isn't to be trusted.

4. Death means defeat.

5. Dreams only happen by chance.

These are the lies that Satan will use to kill your dream. The better we understand the difference between truth and lies, the freer we are to walk with God through the phases of faith and not get sidetracked.

These are the five phases of faith you'll pass through to achieve your dream:

1. Leaving: In order to go to a new level of faith with God, you've got to leave the old behind.

2. Famine: In this new place, you'll realize your comfort zone is gone, and you'll learn to depend on God like never before.

3. Believing: You've always wanted to really believe God, but now your experience of Him becomes too real to deny.

4. Death: Coming to the end of your ability to make things happen seems like death to you. But to God, this is the only way to new life with Him.

5. Resurrection: In a way only He could, God makes your dream come true. Only then do you understand that real joy isn't in the dream itself but rather in the richer faith you acquired along the way.

PHASE ONE

Leaving

ONE

THE MAP

I felt so insignificant. So small. I made my way up to the speaker in the front of the room. She was surrounded by women of all ages. Some just wanted to give her a tearful hug. Others held her book in their hands, looking for a note of encouragement and an autograph.

I just wanted to ask her *how?*

How do I take a broken life and allow God to use it for His glory? Is it possible that a girl rejected by her earthly father could actually be chosen and set apart for a divine calling? Could God really have a purpose for my life just as He had for hers?

I waited in line for my turn. Then, as I opened my mouth to speak, my throat tightened, my eyes filled with tears, and all I could squeak out was an emotional "How?" I wanted her to take me home with her and teach me. I wanted her to pack me in her suitcase and whisk me away from my meaningless life and into the life of one making a difference. I wanted her to share some quick and easy answer, three easy steps to the life you dream of, all for the low price of attending the seminar. But this speaker wasn't a magician, a slick salesman, or a woman looking for a new houseguest. She was a woman who had experienced deep hurts and bitter disappointments and who had chosen to surrender her life—with all its failure and pain—to God. Now she was being used by Him in a truly wonderful way.

She did not give me the quick and easy answer I was looking for. She didn't give me any profound wisdom or direction. We only had time for her to simply tell me how she got started, and then I found myself making my way back to my seat. But I wasn't heading back empty and without hope. What this speaker lacked in words, she more than made up for in example. I had seen Jesus in her. I had seen living proof of God's redemption. I thought to myself, *If God could do that with her, I think there's hope for me after all.* And something new and big and God-directed was born in me and confirmed in my heart in an undeniable way that day.

GOD WILL FILL IN THE GAPS

Though I still didn't know how God could possibly use me, I knew He could find a way. Though I didn't know when God could use me, I knew the timing was in His hands. Though I didn't even think I had much to offer, I knew God would fill in my many gaps. I simply knew God was calling me, inviting me, wooing me to something with His fingerprints all over it. And that was enough.

My life certainly didn't change overnight. I experienced a waiting period, a time of growth, development, and perseverance as God prepared me. Lessons on patience, trust, surrender, and learning to take hold all preceded my stepping out. But even in this seemingly unimportant time of pruning and trials, God was preparing me for the next step. This "getting ready period" was not a waste of time. It was an important part of fulfilling my calling. Though I couldn't see much fruit, God was getting my branches ready and healthy enough to hold all He knew was coming.

So I left the conference that day excited, only to be hit with a shocking dose of reality back home. There were still dishes to be washed, clothes to be folded, bottoms to be wiped, and everyday life to be dealt with. To be completely honest, I didn't like my mundane life. And yet what we call mundane is, in some very important ways, significant in God's school of preparation.

DREAMS AND DESPAIR

I can remember as a young girl looking out my bedroom window, dreaming of the man I'd one day marry and the children I'd one day hear call me Mommy. I counted the years on my small hand and delighted as each one ticked away. With each passing birthday, my anticipation grew. Like most other girls, I had other goals and dreams, but the fairy tale of my heart was being a wife and mother. I could hardly wait!

Then all of a sudden I was an adult woman, and God had indeed blessed me with both a loving husband and wonderful children...and I was miserable.

How could this be? What kind of terrible joke was this, that the very thing I dreamed would bring me ultimate happiness had actually ushered me into a deep despair? How ungrateful I felt. I had asked, begged, pleaded for God to give me these gifts, and now I was desperately looking for the return policy.

Was I missing something genetically? As I looked around at church and the mall and the grocery store, I saw other women who seemed delighted to be the June Cleaver of my generation. They'd walk by me, giggling and cooing at their baby as if they were in a romantic movie. They mentioned offhandedly that their husbands were whisking them off to New York that weekend. These women were, of course, all skinny, and their well-ordered shopping lists gave evidence that their homes were no doubt tidier than mine.

What was wrong with me? I felt like a failure as a woman. And most disturbing was the fact that I didn't like being a mother. I was a gold-star member of the Mommy Guilt Club almost from the moment my child exited the womb. Can you imagine feeling this way and then considering that God was calling you into ministry?

Who do you think you are? Do you really think God could use a woman like you to help others? Satan's whispers were relentless. Sadly, to be honest, I agreed with him. At the conference, I had felt such assurance of God's calling, but back in the midst of everyday life, I began to doubt.

My only recourse was prayer. I got down on my knees and cried out to the Lord for His assurance. And as He always does, God met me there at the point of my need. He assured me that He doesn't call the qualified, but He qualifies those He calls.

SURRENDERING INADEQUACY

My friend, I don't know where you are as you read these words. I don't know the circumstances of your life. I don't know the dream God has given you. Perhaps you don't either...yet. But I do know you have this book in your hands for a reason. God has a plan for you. A dream perhaps you can't even imagine, an assignment you can't figure out and wouldn't even dare to consider as being for you. I pray that as I have honestly shared the misgivings I had, you will find great hope that God really can use any woman who surrenders her inadequacies and circumstances to Him. I've seen Him do it time and time again in the lives of women who were willing to walk in faith. But most powerfully I've seen it in my own life.

Though it started small and happened slowly, I'm now able to live the dream God has given me. But also, and more importantly, I'm now a very happily married mother of five kids. I wake up most days excited about my life and can't wait to unwrap the blessings of serving, loving, and enjoying those whom God has entrusted to me.

Now don't get me wrong, I still have days when I feel like a failure, but they are fewer and far between. My circumstances haven't really changed since those early mommy days (except I have a lot more kids!), but my perspective certainly has.

Perspective is the key. If I'd never had the husband and the kids that I have, I'm convinced I would be incredibly self-centered and seriously lacking in character. God uses different things in different lives to shape and mold them, and my family was God's perfect tool for building my life. God used many everyday life experiences to shape and mold me for ministry. I learned so much by being faithful in little, everyday responsibilities, and eventually God was able to entrust larger responsibilities to me. Any woman who wishes to be used by God must be willing to honor God no matter what.

Any woman who
wishes to be used by God
must be willing to honor
God no matter what.

HONORING GOD

During those early years, God was asking me, "Lysa, as you start to feel overwhelmed with doing the laundry and caring for the kids and cooking meals and handling life, will you honor Me? Will you do it with a grateful heart? Will you see the blessings hidden in the long to-do lists? Will you surrender your plans of convenience and ease and accept My plans for your growth and maturity?"

When I aligned my perspectives with God's and decided to honor Him in all things, big and small, I was finally ready to step out in ministry. My circumstances were not perfect, but I knew whose face to seek when I fell flat on my own. So I declared in my heart I was a woman in ministry, dedicated to serving God, and I started to watch for His invitation to join Him.

Trust me—those first steps were the furthest thing from limelight ministry. They were everyday choices to honor God right where I was: spending time in God's Word even when the items on my to-do list seemed more urgent. Getting filled with Him first so I could love and give and serve out of an overflow rather than relying on my own strength.

Honoring my husband even when he'd said something that hurt my feelings. Choosing to keep a good attitude even when the grocery store clerk overcharged me and took longer than necessary to remedy the problem. Having patience with my children and handling a problem calmly when I really wanted to yell and send them to their room. Graciously serving other people without calling attention to my service. Honoring Him in these ways was a vital part of getting my heart ready to serve Him in larger ways.

God wants us to honor Him. He wants us to put personal conveniences aside, lay our own ideas down, and get past our stubborn will to have and do things our way and in our time. God wants our obedience, not just lip service. It's one thing to say we'll honor Him but another thing entirely to actually do it. Don't wait for the perfect day to start honoring God. Make that choice today. Don't think you're not doing what God called you to do just because things don't seem as glamorous as you thought they would be. If you are a woman who honors God right where you are, you are in ministry. Keep being obedient, keep looking for the next open door of opportunity, and above all else hold closely to our Lord.

BIBLE STUDY

Read Job 1:6; Luke 22:31; 1 Peter 5:8.

These verses show us how active Satan is in our world. His very name means "one who separates." His chief purpose is to separate us from God however he can. He wants us to chase after other things—even good things—so we miss God's best. He wants to keep us busy. He wants to fill our heads full of lies so that we can't hear God's truth. Too many times I have allowed his tricks to steer me down the wrong path. What about you? What tactics is he using to try to defeat you right now?

Read Ephesians 6:11; James 4:7; John 10:10.

Satan uses the same old bag of tricks, but we have God—who is infinitely creative—on our side. We can turn to Him as our support, wisdom, and way out under temptation (1 Corinthians 10:13). God gives us the strength to stand and the armor to protect ourselves from our enemy. Satan comes to steal our joy, to kill our spirit, and to destroy our hope. He masquerades as the angel of light, deceiving us with his false beauty (2 Corinthians 11:14). We must be aware of how he works so we can guard our minds, hearts, and steps as we set out on our amazing journey. Make no mistake, this is one trip Satan does not want you to take, and he will pull out every trick in his bag to try to stop you. Just remember the scriptural paradigm: Resist the devil and he will flee from you (James 4:7). Draw close to God and He will draw close to you (James 4:8).

List some practical ways to resist Satan.

List some practical ways to draw close to God.

....

Read Hebrews 10:35-36.

As we set out on our journey together, I want you to really ponder these verses. Copy them down in your notebook. This book is written to enable you to journey with confidence wherever God is leading in your life. Your journey will not look the same as mine—it is as unique as you are. But the same basic truths described in these verses apply to us all. Circle these words after you have copied down the verses: *confidence, perseverance*, and *promised*. My prayer is that you will find the confidence you need to persevere until you have received whatever God has promised you. Press on, my friend, and prepare to be amazed at what God has to show you through this study!

TWO

A LINE IN THE SAND

To honor God completely, you need enough faith to leave with Him. Leave? Leave and go where, you ask? Leave the way you've always done life and start doing things differently with God. Leave the attitude, leave the stubborn pride, leave the right to be right, leave the control, and biggest of all, leave the unbelief.

Now wait a minute, you say. I thought God was about to ask me to step up and do big things for Him, but you're saying the first step is leaving stuff behind?

Absolutely.

A couple of years ago, I drove an old minivan. It got me where I wanted to go but lacked many of the comforts and conveniences a newer model would have given me. For one thing, the rearview mirror had fallen off the windshield. I went to get a repair kit, thinking I would repair it on my own and save a little money. But as I read the instructions to use the super-duper repair glue, fear seized my heart, and visions of disaster started dancing through my mind. The instructions were very bold with the warning that you must not let the glue get on your skin or you could literally get stuck to whatever you were gluing.

I am not a woman of great coordination, and most embarrassing things often happen to me. So I became convinced that I would be the one out of a million who would actually have to drive herself to the emergency room because her thumb was permanently stuck to the windshield! Instead, I tossed the kit and drove around with the rearview mirror in my cup holder and used it only when absolutely necessary.

Fortunately, I learned to use other means of navigating the road, such as using my side mirrors or asking other passengers in the car to check the traffic. What I soon learned was that using the rearview mirror wasn't nearly as necessary as I once thought it was. To be honest, I used it for the wrong reasons anyhow. I used it to put my makeup on while driving—dangerous and unnecessary. I used it to fuss at my kids while driving—dangerous and unnecessary. I used it to speed into the other lane when the driver in front of me was going too slow in my rushed opinion—dangerous and unnecessary. You see, looking behind you and ahead of you at the same time is impossible. Can you imagine how dangerous the roads would be if everyone drove around looking in their rearview mirrors only?

It's much safer to stay focused on the road ahead and use the rearview mirror when absolutely necessary.

DON'T LOOK BACK

This might be a silly example, but it makes a strong spiritual point. We can't go ahead with God to new and exciting places if we're spending too much time looking back. We must leave our past behind, draw a line in the sand, and determine to proceed forward with God. As a matter of fact, every time God calls His servants to go to new heights with Him, they have to go through a leaving process first.

In Genesis 7, we find Noah and his family being called by God to leave and go into the ark. Because of their obedience, their lives were spared, as was the entire race of mankind. In the book of Ruth, we find the widow Ruth making the tough decision to remain loyal to her mother-in-law, leave Moab, and travel to Bethlehem. Because of her obedience, she eventually finds a new husband, and through their lineage, Jesus is born. In 1 Samuel 16, we find Samuel being sent to anoint one of Jesse's sons to be the new king. David, the youngest and least likely candidate, was the one chosen. Almost immediately after being anointed king, he had to leave the fields and flocks to go to the palace. Another interesting thing to note is that he didn't go to the palace to sit on the throne right away. He had to first serve the existing king as a harp player. Because of his obedience in leaving, we get to read about one whom God called a man after His own heart.

Jeremiah 1 tells the amazing story of Jeremiah being called. "The word of the LORD came to me, saying, 'Before I formed you in the womb I knew you, before you were born I set you apart; I appointed you as a prophet to the nations'." To which Jeremiah replied, "I do not know how to speak; I am only a child" (Jeremiah 1:4-6).

Now listen to the Lord's response to Jeremiah, "Do not say, 'I am only a child.' You must go to everyone I send you to and say whatever I command you. Do not be afraid of them, for I am with you and will rescue you" (Jeremiah 1:7-8). Did you see the word "go"? Yes, indeed, Jeremiah left his old way of relying on his own ability and accepted a new way of thinking. Because he was obedient to trust God, God promised to give him every word and power to accomplish the mission before him. "Then the LORD reached out his hand and touched my mouth and said to me, 'Now I have put my words in your mouth. See, today I appoint you over nations and kingdoms to uproot and tear down, to destroy and overthrow, to build and to plant'" (Jeremiah 1:9-10).

In the New Testament, when Jesus called His disciples, the first thing they had to do was leave wherever they were and whatever they were doing to follow Him. "As Jesus was walking beside the Sea of Galilee, he saw two brothers, Simon called Peter and his brother Andrew. They were casting a net into the lake, for they were fishermen. Come follow me, Jesus said, and I will make you fishers of men. At once they left their nets and followed him" (Matthew 4:18-20). Because of their obedience, we have a record of the life-changing actions and truths of Jesus.

Even when marriage is mentioned in both Genesis and Matthew, the mandate to leave is first. "A man will leave his father and mother and the two shall become one flesh" (Genesis 2:24; Matthew 19:5).

So is it any surprise that you will be called to leave as well? You may or may not have to change physical locations, but you will have to change your mind-set and your spiritual perspectives. Time and time again the formula for starting something new begins with leaving the old. Leaving is usually an act of obedience and not a desire of the heart. It is hard. It causes you to step outside of your comfort zone and enter a life that requires faith.

A POWERFUL FIRST STEP

I was teaching this principle at a weekend retreat once when a lady came up to me afterward and thanked me for the invitation to draw a line in the sand and leave her past behind. I had issued them a challenge: "Just because you came to this retreat one way doesn't mean you have to leave the same. If you came as a discouraged woman, leave encouraged. If you came defeated, leave victorious. If you came as a mom who yells at her kids, leave challenged to make better choices. If you came as a wife who doesn't honor your husband like you should, leave renewed with new perspectives. Wherever you fall short, let God fill in your gaps this weekend and empower you to leave changed. Experiencing life change is not a matter of chance, it's a matter of choice, choosing God's ways instead of your own."

With tears in her eyes, this dear woman hugged me and thanked me for giving her hope that things could be different—and permission to make it happen. A few months later, I received an e-mail from her telling me that she literally went home and drew a line on the ground. She lived in New Hampshire, so instead of drawing a line in the sand, the minute she drove in her driveway, she grabbed a hockey stick and drew a line in the snow. She stood behind her line and paused. She didn't want to make this declaration alone, so she beeped her car horn until her husband and all her children came out to greet her. She instructed them to come and stand behind the line with her.

Choking back tears, she told them she knew she had not been the woman of God she wanted to be or the wife and mom they deserved. But over the weekend, God had shown her some amazing truths, and she was making the choice to change. With that, her entire family held hands and stepped over the line together. Leaving is truly a powerful first step!

Time and time again

the formula for starting

something new begins

with leaving the old.

Was her life now going to be hunky-dory? No! Her circumstances were going to be just the same when she walked back through her threshold, but she was different. She was changing. She was determined to honor God and begin living a life that required faith. She would have to depend on God like never before.

YOUR NEW NAME

What might you need to leave behind? How will you change as a result of leaving? What might the cost be? What will be your reward? Later in this section we'll be taking a walk with Abraham, who went through all five phases to fulfill the calling on his life. We'll pay special attention to the leaving phase. Abraham was obedient to leave, and in the middle of Abraham's journey something significant happens. I want to point this out while you are asking these tough "leaving" questions.

> When Abram was ninety-nine years old, the LORD appeared to him and said, "I am God Almighty, walk before me and be blameless. I will confirm my covenant between me and you and will greatly increase your numbers." Abram fell facedown, and God said to him, "As for me, this is my covenant with you: you will be the father of many nations. No longer will you be called Abram; your name will be Abraham, for I have made you a father of many nations. I will make you very fruitful; I will make nations of you, and kings will come from you" (Genesis 17:1-6).

Now to paint the backdrop of what had been going on in Abraham's life, let's remember, he'd been disobedient to God. Thirteen years earlier he'd had a baby with his wife's maidservant. He was trying to make the dream God had planted in his heart come true through his own schemes and plans—through his own strength. Abraham had lost sight of God's ability to fulfill His promise. So God reestablished the promise, recast the vision, and breathed fresh life back into Abraham's dream. God told Abraham it was already done. Look at these words: "I have made you a father of many nations." Not I will make you a father of many nations, but I have already done it. In other words, God tells Abraham that He has everything under control.

And did you catch the previous sentence? God gives Abraham a new name. He was called Abram before this re-established-covenant encounter, but every time afterward, he is referred to by his new name. Abraham means "father of many."

God renamed Abraham, and He has renamed you as well. When you go through the leaving phase, you are asked to leave much behind. But you don't walk from this place empty-handed. You are going equipped with a new name. I used to be Lysa—a broken, insecure, and unable woman. But when I chose to leave that behind and walk with God, I became Lysa—a holy, chosen, equipped-by-God woman with a dream! I am not looking back! Equipped with your map and now focused ahead, you are closer than you think to the faith you've always wanted.

BIBLE STUDY

Read Hebrews 11.

We will refer to this chapter throughout this book, but I want you to take a moment now to read through it in its entirety. This chapter is known as "faith's hall of fame." As we begin this journey of faith together, the accounts in this chapter will inspire and encourage you. Record the names in Hebrews 11 in your notebook. What do you already know about them? Were they perfect people, or were they fraught with human frailties? Did they make all the right choices, or did their bad decisions become part of their learning process? Did God choose them because they were perfect saints, or were they ordinary people who trusted Him? Allow this chapter to minister to you as you reflect on the very imperfect people God has used in the past to do great things. He can use you too!

Read Isaiah 43:16-19; Philippians 3:12-14.

Walking in faith includes leaving the past behind. In the first chapter, we mentioned Satan's schemes to defeat us and separate us from God. One of his main tactics is to use our past mistakes to cripple us. He is so crafty at holding our past over our head, thus making us feel useless, ineffective, and unworthy. But God wants to do a new thing within you. He wants you to forge ahead, pressing on toward the promised land He has set before you, forgetting the failures of the past. While we all need to remember the Egypts God has delivered us from, we need to change our focus, throw away that old rearview mirror, and prayerfully seek His direction as we set out on our walk with Him.

After reading the verses in Isaiah, list some of your streams in the desert.

What does Philippians 3:12-14 say we're straining toward?

....

Read Psalm 147:4; Isaiah 62:2-3; Revelation 3:11-12.

Abraham, as we will see, eventually does have a son named Isaac. The name Isaac means "he laughs" because Abraham and Sarah both laughed when the Lord told them that they were going to have a son in their old age (Genesis 17:17; 18:12). Names do mean a lot to the Lord. He changed Abraham and Sarah's names. He told Abraham Isaac's name before he was even conceived. He also designated the name above all names for His only Son, Jesus. When we join God's family, He writes our names in the Book of Life. As He designates us as His beloved children, may we lay claim to our new names, which He has engraved in the palms of His hands (Isaiah 49:16). Do you know the meaning of your name? Do a little research today to find out what it means. Write the meaning of your name in your notebook and see if you can find a verse that correlates with the meaning of your name. Write down the verse as well and spend time thinking about how it applies to your life and God's plan for you.

THREE

GOD HAS A PLAN

As I've pursued my dream, I've experienced the leaving phase and all the other phases of faith several times. But each time, God brings me to a stronger faith than I had before. That's God's plan, you know. His ultimate goal is to grow us to be more and more like His Son, who had incredible faith. I must always keep this in mind because, for some reason, God doesn't seem to want to do things my way or in a time frame that I would choose. So to leave some things behind, we need to learn that God has a plan and to trust His plan.

In so doing, we'll find that we must leave our old identity behind. We just learned in chapter two that God has given us a new name, but sometimes we try to put our new name on our old identity. I had to learn to leave my wrong perceptions of myself and my bitterness from my past. Strangely, I'd held onto these like a security blanket. I was used to operating in a private realm, keeping everyone at a safe distance. I always thought to be in ministry meant painting the façade that I was perfect. Only then would I be a qualified servant of God. I quickly learned that people aren't impressed with fake perfection—they're turned off and intimidated by it!

God wanted me to be honest and real. That was to be my identity. He wanted to shine His grace, mercy, love, and redemption through my faults, failures, and frailties. He wanted to make me strong with His strength. He wanted to be glorified in any and all good that would come from my ministry efforts.

As I've mentioned, my dream—the ministry God gave me—started very small, right within the walls of my home. Eventually, God led me to a lady who felt passionate about writing a newsletter to encourage women. I agreed to help her write and promote the small newsletter. The newsletter subscriptions grew, and other opportunities for ministry resulted. Our local Christian radio station invited us to come on the air to give short devotional thoughts. From there we started to receive invitations to speak at small groups.

So, with shaking knees, a quivering voice, and some of the saddest-looking outlines you've ever seen, I booked my first few small speaking engagements. Somehow, the ladies were touched and the ministry continued to grow.

A BRIGHT IDEA

Eventually, I got the bright idea to write a book. I typed out my outlines in chapter form, thought of some catchy chapter titles, slapped a cover sheet on the ragtag collection, and called it a book proposal. Another friend of mine, Sharon Jaynes, and I naïvely headed to the annual Christian Booksellers Association International Convention, fully expecting to find a publisher eager to publish our proposed books. After all, the hardest part of getting a book published was writing it, right? Well, I quickly learned that couldn't be further from the truth. The wave of rejection letters that littered my desk in the months that followed the conference dashed my great hopes and big dreams.

Had I heard God wrong? I really felt He'd told me I would write books that help women. So I'd tried to force the dream to come true with my own formula, and it failed miserably. In my own reasoning, I had planned the trip to the convention thinking if I needed to find a publisher, I'd better go where the publishers were. But my efforts produced nothing but disappointment.

God did have a plan for me. But His plan started much smaller than mine. He opened doors for me to write smaller articles for more newsletters and some magazines. But there were rewards for doing ministry God's way. I'll never forget the first time I saw my name as the author of a published article. God might as well have opened the doors to the library and told me to count the books if

I could, for that's the number of books that would eventually come from Proverbs 31 Ministries. Not that I'd write them all but that women throughout the world would catch a vision for writing their messages and that I could have a part in giving them the courage to do so.

I believed that God would one day give me the chance to write a book, and I committed myself to wait on Him. I would no longer go chasing after publishers; I would wait until God brought one to me. I took my book proposals, placed them in a file, closed the drawer, and thanked God in advance for what would one day come to pass. I believed. I chose to embrace the leaving phase and trust God.

REALITY HITS

Three years later, I wrote an article for a financial publication. To be completely honest, I thought it was one of the worst articles I'd ever written. But the article made its way into a publisher's hands who read it, loved it, and offered me a book contract. Only God could do such a thing! I think God wanted to make sure I knew that a book contract had a lot less to do with me and a lot more to do with Him working through me—in His timing.

I was doing the happy dance everywhere I went. God did it! God really did it! I don't think my feet hit the ground for days. I was going to be a published author. I was thrilled beyond belief until a stark reality hit me: Getting a book contract is one thing, but actually writing the book—all 50,000 words of it—is another thing entirely. Was I nuts? Why did I want this, could someone please remind me? Did I know 50,000 words? Did I even know 1,000 words that I could somehow tangle together 50 different ways?

Though I was scared and unsure, I started gathering quotes and stories. I assumed a most authoritative writing voice and mechanically typed out my first 10,000 words. I sat back in sheer delight, realizing I would make my editor's first deadline. I was to send this first section of the book off to her for approval before continuing on. Like a proud mama of a newborn baby, I nervously let someone else hold my little darling. I couldn't wait to hear her glowing report of how beautiful and full of promise my words were. Instead, I got back two pages of corrections and the direction to begin again.

I got down on my floor beside my computer, buried my face into the carpet, and wept out loud. Oh, how this rejection hurt! I had embraced the leaving phase and was excited to be moving on. This was a call to leave again. It shattered my perception of what God was doing. It reminded me once again that I must leave something behind in order to be able to move ahead.

MY PLANS AND GOD'S PLAN

I realized I had two choices. I could cling to my dream and smother it to death, or I could release it and let my own attempts to do God's work fall to the ground. I chose the latter, even through my tears. With as much faith as I could muster, I placed my book in God's hands, and only then did I understand. God was calling me to simply lay my desire to write a book on the altar.

God did require a sacrifice, but it was not the entire book project. He let me use a substitute sacrifice. My substitute sacrifice was my first 10,000 words. The reward was a book where I found my place as my reader's friend rather than an official-sounding expert.

God's plan was perfect, and when I left my plans behind, God let me participate in His. Looking back, I wouldn't have wanted it any other way. I still remember holding that first published book in my hands. Seeing my name on the cover, leafing through the pages, and seeing God's fingerprints all over this project brought tears to my eyes. Once again, I was reminded that the book was not really about getting a book published. That was just an aside, a fringe benefit. The real treasure was walking with God through the project. Being reminded firsthand that God does indeed have a plan. Not just a good plan. Not even a really good plan. God has the perfect plan.

My new voice changed other aspects of my ministry as well. I tossed the crafty, sad outlines from the talks I'd been giving and traded them in for sharing the real me, the imperfect, desperate-for-God me. God honored my obedience and continued to unfold a plan that I could have never imagined.

God has

the perfect plan.

Proverbs 31 Ministries has now grown into an international women's ministry with a team of dedicated women who have caught God's vision.

EVERYDAY PEOPLE

I stand humbly amazed. My teammates stand humbly amazed. We are all average, everyday women. God certainly doesn't need us to do this ministry, but He allows us to be a part of it. God has a ministry assignment for you, and He wants you to join Him. Soon, you'll stand back in amazement as well.

At each of my speaking engagements, I set up a book table. Each title is a reminder to me. It may look like a little bundle of pages and words, wrapped in a cover, but to me it is so much more. The little seed of a dream to write books that would help others has sprouted and bloomed. These books take the messages God has given me and the other women on my team into places we could never go. They are His words on loan to us from Him. He uses these words to inspire, encourage, teach, and help other people. They are living proof that walking with God truly does take you to amazing places!

Are you ready to venture to your own unique and exciting places? Commit to leave your agenda behind, take God's hand, and hold on tight…the journey has just begun.

BIBLE STUDY

Read Nehemiah 9:7-8; Acts 3:25; Galatians 3:6-9.

As we've already seen in Hebrews 11, God doesn't seek out perfect people to do His work. I mistakenly believed at first that I needed to be perfect to serve God effectively. I think many people believe the lie that they must achieve perfection in order to begin a life of faith. But I learned that God uses our imperfections and our willingness to share our mistakes to reach the hearts of the lost. As I speak to women all over the country, I share my mistakes, my clumsiness, and my most embarrassing moments. While I am sharing, I watch. I watch their laughter give way to relief. These women seem to be saying to themselves, If God can use her, surely He can use me! Are you waiting until you have arrived at perfection to step out in service to God? Are you afraid to show the real you for fear it will hinder your ministry? Don't be afraid to start where you are and be who you are. Blessed are the transparent, for they shall be used by God in a mighty way! How might God use you, weaknesses and all, to minister to other people?

Read John 10:9; Revelation 3:7-8.

When I stepped out in my own strength according to my own timing, God didn't seem to be opening any doors. I battled frustrations as I questioned my calling. I wanted everything to work out, and I wanted it to happen according to my timetable. I showed God my agenda and expected Him to oblige. What I missed was that He is the door. This was not about me checking off my to-do list of accomplishments, but about me drawing closer to Him. As that happened, He would open a door that no one could shut. The time in which I thought He was not moving was actually the time He was moving in my heart. As I kept His Word and proclaimed His name, He was preparing me to walk through the door. I would not trade that time for anything as I serve in ministry now. He used that time to equip me to fulfill my calling and to prepare me to reach women who needed to hear my story.

What do the sheep find when they walk through Jesus' door?

How does this encourage you?

....

Read Joshua 24:14-15; Psalm 68:6; 113:9.

In this chapter, I said that my ministry began right within the walls of my home. Never has this been clearer to me than as I reflect on God's plan for my life. He knew to give me exactly the parents, sisters, husband, and children He has given me to specifically prepare me for my calling. I know without a shadow of a doubt that I wouldn't be the person I am without these people as part of my foundation. They contributed to my character growth and played starring roles in my family dramas. I thank God for their influence in my life through the years, for better and for worse. God has placed you exactly where you are according to His purposes. Thank Him for that today. Write a commitment to not dwell on how some of these people have let you down. Thank God for using the people in your family to help shape and mold you for your calling.

FOUR

LOVING GOD MORE
THAN MY DREAM

How alike we are to the children of Israel. The Old Testament chronicles the history of the Hebrew people and the lessons they had to learn the hard way. They had to learn over and over and over again to leave some things behind.

Walking with God will indeed take you to amazing places—but it won't always be where you thought you wanted to go, and the road won't always be easy. To help prepare you for the things you'll learn, see, and experience on this journey, I want to explore rich biblical truths beginning with the stories of Abraham and continuing through the deliverance of the children of Israel.

As we start with Abraham and one of his first conversations with God, we shouldn't be surprised that God calls him to leave. Genesis 12:1-2 says, "The Lord said to Abram, 'Leave your country, your people and your father's household and go to the land I will show you. I will make you a great nation and I will bless you; I will make your name great, and you will be a blessing.'" Verse 4 goes on to say, "So Abram left, as the Lord told him."

Amazingly, Abraham had to walk away from all that was comfortable—his family, his friends, and his wealthy lifestyle—in order to gain the blessings of the Lord. And I bet Abraham's understanding of becoming a great nation and being blessed was much smaller than God's amazing vision.

Walking with God
will indeed take you to amazing
places — but it won't always
be where you thought
you wanted to go, and the
road won't always be easy.

The same is true for our lives as well. Our thoughts about how God wants to use us are much too small. That is why we hesitate to leave our old ways behind. If we could taste the delights that await us in the promised land, we'd leave everything behind without hesitation…and yet God doesn't work that way. We must choose to leave first. We must see by faith the rewards ahead and then move toward them. What might God be calling you to leave? Check your answer with these other questions:

Does it line up with Scripture?

Would it cause me to become more like Christ in my thoughts and actions?

Do I have a peace in my heart about this when I pray?

As you answer, I'd suggest you spend some time in prayer asking God to show you His answers, and then remember to look for confirmations from Him throughout your day and record them. These confirmations will prove invaluable as you move into the next phase that comes shortly after leaving— the phase I call famine…and the topic of the next four chapters.

A FAMINE IN THE LAND

As we end our chapters on the leaving phase, I want to briefly alert you to the phases ahead so you see how they naturally unfold, one after the other, as God brings dreams to pass. Each new phase arises out of the previous phase and is an ongoing part of our life of faith. We will never arrive at a final stopping place in this life. We are always pilgrims here, looking forward to our final rest in heaven. But until then, we are called to participate with God in the fulfillment of a life dream…His plan for us.

So as the leaving phase closes, another one begins: the famine phase.

Genesis 12:10 says, "Now there was a famine in the land, and Abram went down to Egypt to live there a while because the famine was severe." How heartbroken Abram must have been to leave all that was comfortable and move to the land where God promised to fulfill his dreams, only to have to pack up and move away because of a severe famine.

During such a disappointing passage, your roots grow deeper, not just wider.

Don't second-guess what God is doing. Rather, look for ways to dig deeper into His Word, His character, and His faithfulness in this time. Growing deep roots isn't easy. Skimming the shallow dirt of the surface and growing outward is much easier, but roots that grow outward do not anchor the tree and sustain its growth through the years. Isaiah 61:3 says, "They will be called oaks of righteousness, a planting of the LORD for the display of his splendor."

During the time of famine we will have to dig deep, drawing our sustenance from God's Word. Not one of our biblical heroes escaped the famine phase before being used by God in a mighty way. Noah left to get on the ark and then had to endure the flood. Ruth left the banquets of Moab to glean leftover wheat from someone else's field. David left the gentle sheep to face the fierce Goliath. The disciples left with Jesus only to discover He was not going to be an earthly king but rather a crucified Savior. Abraham experienced a physical famine but also a dream famine as well.

God had promised to make Abraham the father of a great nation, yet Abraham's wife, Sarah, had been unable to conceive. How heartbroken Abraham and Sarah must have been to have God plant in their hearts this amazing dream of a family, only to watch the years tick by with no children to call their own.

So Abraham went to God and shared his distress. Have you gone to God and poured your heart out to Him? Remember, this journey will be a lot less about the places He eventually takes you and much more about the relationship He establishes with you along the way. He wants us to communicate with Him every day through every thought, every step, every victory, every defeat, every question, and every assurance.

In Genesis 15:5-6 God repaints the vision for Abraham, assuring him that it will come to pass, and gives him a visual illustration of how big God's dreams for us are. God took Abraham outside and said, "Look up at the heavens and count the stars—if indeed you can count them...so shall your offspring be."

Wow! What a picture. What a destiny. What a big promise. And verse 6 includes a sentence that made my heart jump. Abraham had been walking in obedience since God called him, but he never proclaimed that he actually believed God's dream for him. But this is where he is credited, not for doing something, but for establishing deep in his heart that God was to be trusted because Abraham knew that He would be faithful. "Abram believed the LORD, and he credited it to him as righteousness."

BELIEVING AND SEEING

After the leaving and the famine time comes the phase where we learn to believe God. We must watch for His beautiful confirmations and divine appointments, for they will be there if we take heed to look for them. We must never allow ourselves to be so distracted by the famine that we miss this wonderful new phase of really believing and letting that belief settle in even the deep recesses of our heart. This believing time is vital, for it will carry us through other tough times to come. It will remind us, assure us, comfort us, and motivate us that God is to be trusted through every circumstance—even the coming death phase.

THE DEATH OF THE DREAM

And then Abraham experienced the death phase shortly after God finally blessed him with his long-awaited son, Isaac. Probably when Isaac was about to become a teenager, God called Abraham to give him up. The dream was just about to be fully realized, and now death loomed on the horizon. Genesis 22:2 says, "Then God said, 'Take your son, your only son, Isaac, whom you love, and go to the region of Moriah. Sacrifice him there as a burnt offering on one of the mountains I will tell you about.'"

I fully believe that God had Abraham walk through this shocking test of obedience to see which came first—his dream or his God. We are tempted to give a quick answer and move past this uncomfortable question without giving it the thought it deserves. This is serious business to God. We quickly take possession of our hopes and dreams, and we don't want to ever give them back. Like a self-centered two-year-old, we scream, "Mine. Mine. Mine!" God can never let that be the cry of our hearts. Our heart must beat in tandem with His. The only way for that to happen is for us to constantly take our dream to Him with open hands and willingly declare, "Yours. Yours. Yours!" Abraham's dream to be the father of a great nation was God's dream first. God is the author of your dream as well. But He's not just the author of the dream, He's the perfecter as well (Hebrews 12:2). Our job is not to figure it all out, manipulate it into being, make the contacts, guard it fiercely, and stake an unwavering claim on it. God started it. God is faithful and more than able. God will finish it.

> Early the next morning Abraham got up and saddled his donkey. He took with him two of his servants and his son Isaac (Genesis 22:3).

Abraham did not hesitate. He believed God even to the point of death. He got up early and made God's command the priority of the day. I'm sure though his feet walked obediently, his heart ached for reassurance. Somewhere along the journey to the mountain, I believe God gave him assurance that He had it under control and that Abraham could trust Him completely. As Abraham left to take Isaac up to the altar, he says something very surprising to the servants being left behind, "We will worship and then we will come back to you" (Genesis 22:5).

How did Abraham know that both he and Isaac would return? Was it just wishful thinking? Was he just trying to protect the servants from the terrifying truth? Or did he trust that if God allowed the dream to die, He could certainly resurrect it as well? God provided a ram as the sacrifice for Abraham, and He provides it for each one of us as well.

> So Abraham called that place "The Lord Will Provide." And to this day it is said, "On the mountain of the Lord it will be provided." The angel of the Lord called to Abraham from heaven a second time and said, "I swear by myself, declares the Lord, that because you have done this and not withheld your son, your only son, I will surely bless you and make your descendants as numerous as the stars in the sky and as the sand on the seashore. Your descendants will

take possession of the cities of their enemies, and through your off-spring all nations on earth will be blessed, because you have obeyed me" (Genesis 22:14-18).

Only God can give such a dream, and only God can bring it to pass.

RESURRECTION

The final phase, which we will more fully explore in chapters 17–20, is the glorious resurrection. It is the fulfillment of that which God has promised and brought about Himself. Our greatest satisfaction will come when we stand in awe at what God accomplishes as we simply walk in faith.

How appropriate for Abraham's dream of a great nation and for our dreams as well. "And to this day it is said, 'On the mountain of the LORD it will be provided'" (Genesis 22:14).

BIBLE STUDY

Read Acts 7:1-8.

This is a New Testament account of the story of Abraham. This sermon, preached by Stephen just before he was stoned, is the longest recorded in Acts. Why do you think Stephen takes the time to recount Israel's history to his audience? What is his objective in reminding the people of these stories of their past?

As the Christian church is growing, Stephen reminds the Jews of their covenant relationship with God. By reminding them of the faith of their forefathers, he is also bringing to mind the patriarchs' response to God's call on their lives. What was their response?

Now read Genesis 12:4-9.

What was Abram's response to God?

Write down the verse that best states Abram's response to God. Is this your response to God as well?

....

If you are ready, write a prayer to God claiming this verse as your response to Him. Be sure to record the date that you prayed this prayer. Be prepared for what God will do in your life if you pray this prayer!

....

Read Proverbs 18:24; John 15:13-15; James 2:23.

God longs to hear our prayers. He wants to pull us up into His lap and hear about our day, our grief, our victories. Something happens through this process of pouring out our hearts to Him. As we commune with Him and depend on Him, we grow closer to Him. He truly becomes our Friend. He wants to be the first one we turn to when our hearts are broken, the one we go to seeking wisdom for a problem, and the one to give us a big thumbs-up when we are victorious. He is our Comforter and our Counselor, available 24 hours a day, just a prayer away. We can derive much confidence from implementing this truth into our prayer lives. Because he had a relationship with God that was based on faith, Abraham was called God's friend. We have the same opportunity today. What a Friend we have in Jesus, indeed.

Read Jeremiah 31:31-33.

I heard a Bible teacher once say that this verse was God's phone number! God has issued a new covenant with us through salvation. It is an everlasting, unchanging covenant initiated by God because of His great love for us. All that He asks for is obedience on our part. We do not have to be brave or smart or witty. We don't even need to know exactly where we are going—just whom we are following. Will you step out as Abraham did—with a new name and a new heart, one that desires to follow God every step of the way, leaving the familiar, the comfortable in search of God's best for you? Write down what you feel God is calling you to leave and ask Him to help you take steps away from these things.

PHASE TWO

Famine

FIVE

THE ADVENTURE OUR
SOULS WERE MADE FOR

We have experienced the leaving phase, and we've stepped out with God. Unfortunately, we aren't immediately ushered to the land of great promise and dreams fulfilled. This new place is dusty, unfamiliar, and unexpected. This is where the dry, barren, uncomfortable famine begins. In this new place of sacrifice and surrender, God will take you outside your comfort zone, and you'll learn to depend on Him like never before.

It was a hot day inside and outside at the orphan village in Liberia. The soaring temperatures were inescapable, but at least outside there was a breeze. The boys playing soccer in the field didn't seem to mind the heat because the constant excitement of the game kept them plenty distracted. The 12 boys inside, practicing their choir music, found their eyes wandering often over to the soccer field, where the promise of fun and the cheers of their friends tugged at them. Was membership in the boys' choir worth sacrificing their free time playing soccer?

They were feeling the pain of surrendering to their calling, sacrificing their time, and stepping out of their comfort zone. The famine of fun was hitting them hard. But the 12 boys determined the choir was worth the sacrifice, and they stayed true to the task at hand. Other boys had come and gone from the choir, deciding to satisfy their immediate desires for fun instead of staying true to this calling. And a calling it was.

Liberia had been ravaged by a civil war that left more than 25,000 orphans to be cared for. One of the men called to this daunting task was Pastor Kofi. To raise money and support for the hundreds of orphans in his care, Pastor Kofi had his oldest son form an a cappella boys' choir. This choir was to travel throughout the country of Liberia and perform in churches to solicit support. Little did Pastor Kofi or the boys who signed up to be in the choir know that their vision was way too small. God had a plan that these boys could never have imagined.

A STEP OF FAITH

A woman from the American embassy attended one of the choir's Liberian concerts. Her heart was stirred, and she determined to help the boys get the necessary paperwork completed to be able to come to America. Through this woman's relentless determination and God's divine intervention, the boys were headed to the United States for a concert tour.

Once there, God continued to work miracles. He brought a businessman forward to manage the choir and book concerts. Soon, they were scheduled to sing at more than 130 churches throughout the southeast. Through the concerts, they were able to raise awareness and prayer support for their home country and enough money to feed and care for the many children back in the orphanages for that entire year.

The boys in the choir had made great sacrifices, giving up their favorite time of the day playing soccer to practice their singing. The only promise they had was that they would have a chance to tour around their home country of Liberia to encourage the people in churches. But oh, how God blessed their sacrifice! Little did they know that their step of faith to honor God would result in their biggest dreams coming true.

DREAMS COME TRUE

Amazing things happened to each of the boys in that choir. One boy was named Seebo. When I first saw Seebo sing, I was struck that he didn't seem to be singing to the crowd of people in front of him. No, his head was tilted and his eyes focused on the only "Daddy" Seebo had ever known—his heavenly Father. The big voice trumpeting from his small frame poured out songs of joy and hope and peace and love. Though his life circumstances had been void of the things that bring joy, hope, peace, and love to most children, these qualities were evident in his life because God reigned so richly in his heart.

Seebo's joy wasn't a temporary happiness that comes on sunny days and then quickly fades. His hope wasn't based on a bright future. His hope was rooted in Jesus and Jesus alone. His heart was filled with peace and love even though he didn't have a warm bed in a nice home with parents who tucked him in with a prayer and a kiss each night. He had no home or parents to call his own, but he knew God was his Father and he had a home in heaven. He also knew that God answers the prayers of His children, so he prayed that God would make a way for him to find a mommy and daddy.

Meanwhile, David and Debbie were living a great life. David had just been promoted to CEO of a major Fortune 500 company. Debbie was the women's ministry director in one of the fastest-growing churches in her city. They'd just sent their second son off to college, and the time had come for them to do those things they'd waited for. They had plans to travel more and finish decorating their house, and Debbie was going to go back to school for a counseling degree. They were both gifted speakers and teachers and considered using these gifts in some kind of ministry together.

All of that came to a screeching halt when God brought Seebo and his friend into David and Debbie's life through the concert tour. Instantly, David and Debbie fell in love with these two boys and prayerfully decided to adopt them. After these boys settled in, David and Debbie kept hearing them talking about their brothers, sisters, and a special friend still in the orphanage. Soon, this empty-nest couple became the proud parents of eight children—two biological and six adopted from Liberia.

FAITH IN THE FAMINE

Little Seebo had been a forgotten child in a third-world, war-torn country. But he was a boy who prayed, stayed strong in his faith, and was obedient to walk through every open door before him, and so the orphan became the son of one of the most influential and powerful businessmen in America. Do we serve a big God with big plans or what? Rest assured, my friend, the same extraordinary God is looking for faithful people through whom He can reveal His extraordinary purposes and ways.

Seebo's story issues a challenge to us all. The more we really believe the truths God calls us to believe, the more we will take chances with God. We can press through the pains of the famine and find comfort in knowing that God has a good plan even in our discomfort. Yet most of us sit in the dust of famine and cry out for comfort and security. We may even turn back to the mud puddles we left behind. All the while, ahead of us are the pure rushing waters our souls were designed to dive into. A sweet place of complete trust in God, great faith, and dreams come true is out there. And inside of us something calls us to dive in and experience the riches of the deep. Something in us wants to believe that God could have great things in store for us too.

Now, think back for a minute to the seemingly ordinary day when Seebo decided to give up his soccer to come inside and join the choir. Do you think he had any idea that this decision of obedience and sacrifice would one day lead to his biggest dreams coming true? Could he have possibly known that he would profoundly affect many other children's futures as well? Sadly, I think about the multitude of Christians who have decided they'd rather be comfortable and play games than get on with the adventure our souls were made for—living a life that requires faith.

A LIFE THAT REQUIRES FAITH

A life that requires very little faith is not a life that God will use. When we are willing to embark on a life that requires faith, we are more aware of God and His ability to provide for us in every detail of our lives. We won't wait until

The more we really believe the truths God calls us to believe, the more we will take chances with God.

everything in our lives is in order and then decide, *Okay, now I have time to work on living by faith.* We will never have everything in order, and faith can't be dispensed like a can of soda from a machine. Faith is learned through life. Through the messy and unpredictable everyday events that often stumble us, we become aware of our desperate need for God. I have determined that once I leave the mud puddles of the past, I'll not look back regardless of how hard the famine gets. I'll focus on what is ahead and find joy in knowing God always comes through.

Let's play a simple game. Without looking, can you name the people whose faces appear on the one-dollar bill, the five-dollar bill, and the ten-dollar bill? I recently posed this question to more than a thousand people in a church service. I then told them to raise their hand if they could say without a shadow of a doubt all three answers. The crowd looked around to see only three people out of a thousand raise their hands. Odd, isn't it? These bills pass through our hands on a daily basis, and yet we live our lives so unaware. Did you know the answers?

Washington, Lincoln, and Hamilton, in that order.

The point isn't that we should pay more attention to money. The point is that we must get to the place where we pay more attention to God at work in our daily lives. If we live our lives unaware of God in the small things, we're probably living unaware of His presence in the big things as well. How vitally important it is for us to surrender our hearts to God and ask Him daily to reveal His plans and perspectives to us so we don't miss His activity and His glorious plans for our future.

Look for God's activity around you each day. Your outlook will change, your faith will take on a fresh excitement, and you'll start walking toward the amazing places God is so excited to lead you to.

BIBLE STUDY

Read Psalm 15; 24:3-6.

Are you ready to climb God's hill so that you can get closer to Him? These two psalms reveal some of the character qualities God looks for in His people. Though these qualities are not possible in our fleshly nature, with God we can aspire to be righteous because He is at work within us. In your notebook, note particular areas you would like to work on throughout this study. Perhaps you have a friend or someone in your group that you could ask to hold you accountable. Above all, remember that this list is here to inspire you, not to overwhelm you or condemn you.

Read 1 Samuel 16:7.

God looks at your heart for Him most of all. How quick we are to condemn ourselves and think we can never measure up! God sees you trying. He knows when you are doing the best you can. He saw those young men in Africa make the choices they did, and He honored and blessed their choices. Of course, we can all work on our character and our actions as we constantly seek to become more like Christ. But we must also give Him time to work on us from the inside out, molding and shaping our hearts according to His design. What are some heart issues you need to ask for God's help in working on? Do you harbor unforgiveness toward someone? Is a secret sin haunting you? Are you bitter toward someone who does not meet your expectations? Pour out your heart to the Lord in your notebook. Ask Him to reveal the truth to you, ask Him to cleanse your heart, and pray for wisdom and courage to do what He tells you to do.

....

Read 2 Chronicles 1:11; Psalm 119:72; Jeremiah 15:16; Romans 10:1.

What is your heart's delight? Is it God's wisdom and understanding? Do you delight in His Word?

....

Matthew 6:21 says, "Where your treasure is, there will your heart be also." My pastor often reminds us that it is easy to tell where someone's heart lies—just take a look at their checkbook and their calendar. Where does your money go? Where do you spend your time? God longs to be your heart's delight. Psalm 37:4 says, "Delight yourself in the LORD, and he will give you the desires of your heart." Determine to delight yourself in Him, and trust Him to work out the rest.

SIX

GOD'S EXTRAORDINARY
INVITATION

Perhaps you read the previous chapter and thought, *Well, that's an inter-esting story, but what does it have to do with me?*

Well, let me tell you the rest of the story.

Two of the teenage boys in that choir, Jackson and Mark, had been orphaned as babies when their parents and most of their siblings were killed by rebel forces. Those babies, along with so many others, were brought to the orphanage and were taught how to pray, how to have faith in the face of extreme adversity, and, despite times of starvation and deadly attacks by the rebels, how to keep God's joy dancing in their hearts.

Night after night these boys knelt beside their makeshift beds and poured out prayers of thanksgiving and hope that one day they'd hear six simple yet life-changing words, "You are my child—welcome home." Though they couldn't always see God's hand at work, they trusted His heart and rejoiced in the sim-plest of blessings each day.

God had a perfect design for their prayers to be answered and worked mir-acle after miracle to bring these boys to America.

But little did I realize that Art and I were to be part of the answer to those boys' prayers. Our life was busy and full, and we were enjoying being the parents of three little girls. So you can imagine my surprise the night I went to the boys' choir concert at our church, only to have our family's life changed forever.

MOVED AND TERRIFIED

I remember as I sat in the concert that night that from out of nowhere, God whispered to my heart that two of those boys singing in the front of the church were mine. *Right*, I thought. *Sure.*

I felt like sticking my fingers in my ears and singing, *La, la, la, la, la...I'm not listening to You, Lord!* But my song didn't deter the Lord, and the assurance seemed to grow more certain. I decided to try a new tactic with Him. *Lord, I just came here tonight to bring my girls to a simple little cultural event. I'm not looking for a major life change. My life is already very full with speaking and writing and homeschooling three girls. We don't do BOYS in our house. We "think pink," and my husband is okay with that. Besides, all my friends would think I was crazy, and my husband would never think this is a good idea.*

God wasn't discouraged by my response. As a matter of fact, His stirring in my heart grew more and more intense as the evening went on. After the concert, I asked one of their directors which of the boys still needed homes (just so that I could pray for them). He told me that eight of the twelve boys still needed to find families to adopt them. He encouraged me to walk into the reception area where the boys were greeting people. If God intended for some of these boys to be ours, he was sure I would know it.

I rather reluctantly walked into the reception area, and in a matter of seconds, two boys, Jackson and Mark, walked up to me, wrapped their arms around me, and called me Mom. I was moved and terrified at the same time.

How could I call Art and drop this bomb on him? I wouldn't even consider bringing home a new pet without talking extensively with him, so how was I to explain that two boys from halfway across the world are calling me Mom?

We were the last family to leave the concert. My girls and I hugged the boys goodbye and started making our way home. I flipped open my cell phone and with trembling hands called Art.

How? Why?

For several weeks, we cried out to God, desperate for His guidance and wisdom. We talked to our friends and our parents, and most of them did think we were more than a little crazy. We pondered every aspect and wrestled with this decision deep in our spirits. Art's questions centered more on the how aspects. How could we financially increase the size of our family? How would we find the time in our already crammed schedule? How would we raise boys? How could we protect our girls? How would we find room in our home? The list went on and on with a host of other How questions.

My deepest questions centered more on the why. Why us? I'm not even sure I do this motherhood thing right with just three kids, much less five! I want to be a great mom, but sometimes I just get tired, frustrated, angry, and out of sorts. God, shouldn't You call someone who looks a little more like the Old Woman in the Shoe and who can handle loads of kids with a smile?

Then there's the whole perfection thing. I like my house to be neat, tidy, and quiet. This has been doable with three girls—but boys are loud and messy, especially teenage boys. And finally, I'm busy. Lord, You've blessed me with a ministry that's grown beyond my wildest imagination. I travel and speak, and I don't feel You calling me to give that up. But it's not humanly possible to add two more children and continue with my calling, is it? Why me, Lord? Why me?

HEAVEN SENT

I called my dear friend Sheila one day and asked her this question. I poured out my heart. I unloaded all my doubts and questions. She patiently listened without much response. "Why me, Sheila? Why me?" Then quietly and prayerfully she answered. "Because God knew you'd say yes, Lysa."

I was stunned. It was the highest compliment I'd ever received. My heart was filled with joy as suddenly memories filled my mind of the years of spiritual training God had taken me through to get me to the place where I could be called a woman who says yes to God.

There were other confirmations for me and for Art. One came when we were on a plane traveling together to speak at a marriage conference. We were having one of our "Are we crazy?" discussions when a woman from the row behind us approached our seat and leaned in to speak with us. She told us that God had been prompting her for more than an hour to say something to us, but she was nervous about intruding into our conversation. We smiled and reassured her that we'd like to hear what she had to say. She went on to tell us that she and her husband had three daughters when God called them to adopt some foreign children, and God wanted us to know that everything would be all right. As she turned to leave, she handed me her business card, which had the words printed across the top: Heaven Sent.

GOD'S FINALE

When we returned home from that trip, we asked the boys' director if we could schedule one of their final concerts at our home church. Many of my friends thought we were crazy, so I thought they might be more understanding if they heard what I heard that first night as these precious boys sang of the joy of the Lord. I also thought the visit might help give our boys an easier transition into the church body. But God had a grander design for the evening in mind.

The night was magical—one of the last concerts of their tour. They'd sung in more than 130 churches and raised enough money to feed all their friends back home in the orphanage in Liberia for a year. Their mission had been a great success, but six of the boys still needed homes. They needed a miracle. And a miracle is exactly what God had designed for that night. Those friends who thought we were so crazy are now proud parents of Liberian boys!

People lined up at the end of the program to get to know the boys, and we had more willing families than boys to adopt. All of the rest of those boys found parents that night, and at the writing of this book, more than 22 kids (siblings and friends of the boys) from the Liberian orphanage have now been adopted by families in our church.

David and Debbie Alexander, mentioned in the previous chapter, really had their doubts when we first told them of our decision to adopt. They thought what we were doing was commendable, but taking teenage boys into a family of only young girls? Yes, they thought we were crazy. But Debbie came to that concert that night and then she understood. Recently Debbie wrote me to thank me for being crazy, for it led to their six new blessings!

JUST SAY YES

Now think back to me sitting in that church pew, just going about my ordinary life when God's extraordinary invitation burst forth. I could have so easily walked out of that church and ignored God's stirring. I've done that more times than I'd like to admit. But look at everything we would have missed out on had I done that.

My involvement in God's perfect design began with one simple answer: Yes. Yes, God, I will embrace what You have for me. Though it's hard and doesn't even seem to make sense, I will embrace it as Your perfect design because Your ways are higher than my ways!

What a picture for our orphaned souls. That's what we all were until many centuries ago the cries of a newborn baby proclaimed that our King, our Savior, our Lord of lords, our Prince of Peace, Jesus Christ was born. Then He lived and loved and submitted to death on a cross. Three days later, death was defeated as Jesus rose from the dead and became the way for our longing hearts to hear those six simple yet life-changing words: "You are my child—welcome home." That's what God says to all who trust in Him and accept Jesus Christ as Lord of their life.

Let me encourage you that your spiritual journey doesn't end the minute you become a Christian—that's where it really begins! Being a follower of Christ is a continual process of learning, growing, stretching, and trusting. Each day we can look and listen for God's invitation to join Him in His wondrous work. It was never part of my plan to have more children, but praise God, it was part of His plan.

Being a follower
of Christ is a continual
process of learning,
growing, stretching,
and trusting.

LOOK FOR THE JOY

Has it been easy? No. I left my comfort zone and entered into a famine place where I am forced to depend on God like never before. Are there some days I feel like tearing my hair out and wish I had less laundry, fewer messes, lower grocery bills, and more "me" time? Yes. But this life is not about me. It's about joining hands with Jesus to fulfill whatever tasks He sets before me and to share His love with all He brings my way. Don't miss this point—though the famine phase is hard, it does not have to be void of joy. Look for the joy. It is there. Answered prayers, treasures of wisdom, and the peace of God's provision are waiting for you in this phase. Depending on God brings such joy as I would never know any other way.

For example, our three daughters have grown more spiritually this past year than I could have ever imagined. They aren't just reading about loving others, they are living it. They've adjusted wonderfully. And my ministry? Adopting these boys has taken me away from the ministry quite a bit, but God has grown the ministry more this year than ever before. Had I not adopted the boys, I could have worked hours on end trying to make things happen, but I could never have accomplished what has come from God's hand.

I'm convinced breakthroughs come during this famine phase, not when we're striving to make them happen. Breakthroughs happen when we get about the business of honoring God moment by moment, step-by-step, day by day by what we do and, more importantly, with the thoughts we think while we do. People who don't say yes to the Lord can still live a good life. But only those who fully embrace God can experience the wonder and awe of a "yes" heart that lives the great life He intends.

What is God calling you to do His way today? You may never be called to adopt children from a foreign land, but God is calling you, wooing you, pursuing you, inviting you to something richer with Him. May your ordinary be invaded with His extraordinary invitation to press through the famine phase and to live life His way!

BIBLE STUDY

Read Psalm 37:5; Proverbs 16:3.

Is God calling you to something big—really big? Is it bigger than you could ever accomplish on your own? Write down what is stirring in your heart.

It's time to commit whatever God is laying on your heart to Him. Lay your burdens, anxieties, fears, and misgivings on Him, and let Him take care of the details. He is your Father, and He wants to help you work it out. Write a prayer, laying down your burdens and asking for the Father's help.

Read Matthew 6:25-27; 1 Peter 5:7.

When you're embarking on an adventure with God, it's easy to get bombarded by all the "what ifs" of the task at hand. I know Art and I dealt with our share of these when we were considering our adoption. We had our own fears, our well-meaning friends and family expressed their doubts, and Satan added his insistent whisperings. Instead of looking at the impossibilities of the adoption, we ultimately decided to step out in faith according to what we knew God was telling us to do. When doubt began to take root, we depended on God to work out the unknowns. We returned to the throne room many times to cast our cares on Him. We knew we served a big God who could handle all that we had to cast upon Him. He took it all and—as I shared—worked out every detail. He put to rest every fear. Record one way God has already started putting your fears to rest through some confirmation from Him.

....

Read Jeremiah 6:16; Mark 10:21-22.

When God calls, not everyone says yes. These two passages give us glimpses of those who decided not to take a great adventure with God. What do you think stopped them?

How many of us have divine appointments with the God of the universe but ignore them because we are paralyzed by our fear of the unknown? What is stopping you or has stopped you in the past?

God holds the future in His hands. Spend time in prayer asking God what your next step is (not the whole plan). You may want to write down your prayer in your notebook. Proverbs 23:18 says, "There is surely a future hope for you, and your hope will not be cut off."

SEVEN

GOD IS WITH YOU

When Art and I were struggling about whether or not to adopt Mark and Jackson, we continued to look for confirmations from God. Many confirmations came, and we decided to proceed with the adoptions without doubt. We trusted that God was with us and that He would work everything out. But one thing kept nagging at me: How in the world will I fit two more lives into my already busy schedule? Do I give up being in ministry? Do I give up homeschooling? Do I give up writing?

I was smack-dab in the middle of a famine, and though I knew the purpose was to learn to depend on God like never before, it was hard. The more I prayed about and pondered trying to make everything fit, the more I kept saying, "There's no way...there's just no way." I wasn't feeling led to give up anything in my busy life, which made no sense. Something had to give. So I continued to pray and watch for God's answer. I would stop trying to figure it all out and simply wait for God.

JESUS IS THE WAY

A few weeks later I flew to California to teach at a women's retreat. I prayed off and on the entire four-hour plane ride and two-hour drive to the retreat center. I kept looking for some kind of assurance from God that He was hearing my prayers and that He knew my struggle. When I arrived at the retreat center without that assurance, I was disappointed. I would be ministering to the ladies. The time had come for me to give, not to receive…or so I thought.

I walked to the registration desk to check in, and the woman behind the counter handed me a name badge. Every woman was being given a name badge with her name on it along with a name for God from the Bible. When I glanced down at my tag, I was shocked. The name of God I'd been given was The Way. For days, I'd been telling God there was no way, and now He was reminding me that there is always a way with Him.

In John 14:5, Thomas asks, "Lord we don't know where you are going, so how can we know the way?" What a great question. Like me, you may have asked this many times, especially during the famine phase. You've stepped out of your comfort zone and you feel uncertain, so now what? In the next verse Jesus tells us plainly, "I am the way and the truth and the life. No one comes to the Father except through me."

Thomas had just asked Jesus the way to heaven, but in an even deeper spiritual sense, he was asking the way to assurance. Jesus' answer was good enough for Thomas, and it's good enough for us as well. Jesus is the way, our certain path in life, our way out of the famine. He is the truth, God's promises made real. And He is the life—the only way to live with purpose now and the only way to receive life eternal.

MOVING MOUNTAINS

We must expand our vision. In our own strength, achieving our dreams may be impossible. But with God, there is a way! We must begin thinking in a new way—His way. I can live with my limited vision, convinced that there is no way and overcome with uncertainty in my time of famine, or I can take God's hand and confidently proclaim Him to be my way. I wish I could impress you with my great organizational skills that allow my life to flow seamlessly, but I can't. I plan and I delegate, but I rely daily on God to fill in my many gaps. I am

Jesus is the way,

our certain path

in life, our way

out of the famine.

amazed that God so freely gives His help when I ask for it. We all need help to get through our times of famine, so ask Him to help you.

God constantly reminds me of details I've forgotten. He sends people who are available to help me. He goes before me and arranges carpools and schedules in a way that shocks me. When I sit down to plan out my weeks with my husband, I'm always amazed that each week works. But I really shouldn't be because God is truly the way.

God wants you to succeed in His plans. Do you really believe that? Have you changed your thinking enough to trust that to be true? You can't go on this grand adventure with God and keep your old way of thinking. Remember, we've left that behind in the last section. Like the wine, you must have a new wineskin—a new pattern of thinking for this new way of living. Remember, the purpose of this famine phase is for you to learn to depend on God like never before.

Art and I aren't the only ones who had adjustments to make. Our boys have had to make them as well. In order to step into this new life God offered them, they had to leave all that was familiar back in Liberia. And when they left, they did not step immediately into their promised land. They progressed through each of the phases of faith when they joined our family. In their famine phase, they realized that life in America is not nearly as laid-back and relaxed as life in Africa, especially at school. They have a lot of catching up to do.

Jackson has always been an eager learner, so the transition hasn't been as difficult for him. Mark, however, would just as soon forget about school. Sometimes education looks to him like a huge overwhelming mountain that will only be moved by the miraculous hand of God. He even prays for God to work a miracle and drop the knowledge he needs into his brain. Though he is a bright kid, reading, writing, and arithmetic are very challenging at times.

I'm Mark's primary teacher, and I must admit that I too have prayed for God to move this mountain of knowledge right into Mark's brain! The Bible tells us in Matthew 17:20, "I tell you the truth, if you have faith as small as a mustard seed, you can say to this mountain, 'Move from here to there' and it will move. Nothing will be impossible for you." Some people read this verse and get frustrated because even though they have faith, the mountains don't seem to be moving. Such was the case with Mark. Though he was believing and trying, the mountain didn't seem to be moving.

So Mark decided to try going around the mountain. The next time I gave him a math test, he scored a whopping 100 percent! But his answer to the last problem included a note to the teacher from the answer key. How my heart broke as I realized he'd cheated.

Though we forgave him and made him retake the math test, his punishment needed to be a visual reminder that God can move the educational mountain. Art had Mark move a huge pile of rocks a short distance from one spot to another spot. The rocks were heavy and could only be moved one at a time. He worked for a long while and felt frustrated that he'd hardly made any progress. But several hours later, he stood back amazed. The mountain had been moved. Though God could have instantaneously moved it, He chose another way. He gave Mark the strength to move it one rock at a time.

Yes, faith still moves mountains. But sometimes the greater act of faith is not praying for the mountain to move instantly but rather hanging in there while God helps you to move it bit by bit.

During this famine phase, many people are tempted to doubt and sometimes even give up. Maybe we heard God wrong. Maybe God isn't with us. The doubts bombard us and steal our passion to press on. When this happens, we are looking at the entire mountain and losing sight of the part God wants to help us move today. Don't try to make your whole dream come true at once. Just fulfill the small part of the mission He's asking you to do today. Just carry that one rock. Ask God, *What is my assignment for today?* Do that part and be satisfied that God is pleased. Be encouraged and continue to press on!

BIBLE STUDY

Read 2 Samuel 22:29-46; Philippians 4:13.

God's way is perfect. We may not understand His plan, but we know we can trust it to be better for us than anything we could devise for ourselves. God sees the big picture—beyond the famine time and all the way to the promised land. Our limited vision is finite and unreliable. The more we realize this, the more we know that we are better off depending on God. Second Samuel 22 shows us what we can do with God's help. Read through this list a few times. What do you need God to help you accomplish right now? Write down your answer and ask God to show how you can experience the same type of victorious Christian living that David is describing. Second Samuel 22:31 says, "As for God, His way is perfect; the word of the LORD is flawless." God showed me that He is the Way. Let Him show you that too through His Word.

Read Judges 21:25; Isaiah 53:6.

We can easily forget that Jesus is the way, choosing to go our own way instead. Though these are both Old Testament passages, they definitely still hold true today. God is loving and patient with us, His rebellious children who stubbornly try to do things our way. Isaiah tells us "each of us has turned to his own way." Without exception, every one of us is included in that verse. We allow our pride, our independence, and our sin nature to get us off the path of God's way and onto a path that leads us to less than God's best. We take our eyes off

God and do what is best in our own eyes. In this time of famine, Satan comes to tempt us to go his way. He makes following him look enticing and easier than God's way—a shortcut. Just remember that God's way may not include shortcuts, but it does lead to success by God's design, which will never disappoint (Romans 5:3-5a). Meditate on these verses and record your thoughts in your notebook.

....

Read Proverbs 16:3; 2 Corinthians 6:4-10.

Godly success and worldly success rarely look the same. In God's economy everything is upside down from the way the world sees things. That's because we live in a fallen world run by the prince of this world, Satan. Satan wants us to believe that second best just doesn't cut it, but God says, "The last will be first, and the first will be last" (Matthew 20:16). As we hope to realize godly success, may we strive to understand exactly what godly success even looks like. Using the concordance of your Bible, look up the word *success* or *succeed* and find out what God has to say about success. Remember to keep seeking God in all that you do, and success will follow. Record your verses in your notebook.

EIGHT

REFUSING TO GET BOGGED DOWN IN BITTERNESS

I must caution you not to get bogged down in bitterness during this famine phase. This is a season of learning to depend on God. As a result, things will be stripped from you that hinder the relationship He wants to have with you. You may experience a shake-up in your finances, your friendships, your position of leadership, your expectations, or one of a thousand other things that we put our trust in. God wants our complete trust. So whenever He strips something away, He does it for our good and not to harm us.

Resist getting bitter with people or circumstances. Take great comfort in knowing this is but a season, it will soon pass, and one day you will actually thank God for taking you through this. This time of loss will lead to a time of great celebration one day.

As we look at the story of Joseph, take courage from one who has gone before you. Put yourself in his shoes. Watch him make the constant decision to honor God during his famine phases, and watch how God restores his life back a hundredfold time and again.

Also, take heed of his brothers in this story and watch how their poor decision to let bitterness consume them hurts them. What will be the story of your famine phase?

JOSEPH'S LEAVING PHASE

To set the stage, we must remember Abraham from our chapters on leaving. God promised Abraham that he would be the father of a great nation. The only problem was that Abraham and his wife, Sarah, experienced years of infertility. Had Abraham heard God wrong?

No, God just had a much different timetable than Abraham and Sarah had. When the couple was quite old, they were blessed with a son named Isaac. Isaac grew up, married, and had two sons, one of whom was Jacob. Then Jacob grew up, married, and had 12 sons by four different women. His favorite wife bore him his favorite son, and then she died giving birth to a second son. The favored son was Joseph, and his brothers grew to despise him.

Genesis 37:4 says, "When his brothers saw that their father loved him more than any of them, they hated him [Joseph] and could not speak a kind word to him." In this same chapter, verse 11 goes on to state the obvious: "His brothers were jealous of him." The brothers held such bitterness and animosity against Joseph that their hearts became cold and their judgment clouded. One day as they were tending the sheep on a hillside, they saw Joseph coming in the distance and plotted to kill him. The oldest brother stepped in and convinced the others not to kill Joseph but rather to throw him into an empty pit and hold him captive.

Before long some merchants passed by on their way to Egypt, giving the brothers their perfect answer. By selling Joseph, they acquired some money and got rid of their hated brother all in one transaction. They took Joseph's beautiful coat, which had been a gift from their father, shredded it, dipped it in animal's blood, and returned home to break the news to their father that Joseph had been killed by a wild animal.

Meanwhile, Joseph is making a journey of more than 30 days through the desert on foot, chained, and probably treated worse than an animal. After all, he was now merchandise to be sold once he reached Egypt. I can't help but think about how Joseph must have felt during those long hot days and harsh lonely nights. But the Scriptures make clear that God was with Joseph just as He is with all of His wronged and brokenhearted children.

GOD WAS WITH HIM

Joseph finally reaches Egypt and is sold into slavery. His life there sees many ups and downs, trials, tragedies, and triumphs, but God is with him through it all. Whether he was held in captivity by slave traders, serving as a slave, or in prison, the Bible constantly reminds us that the Lord was with Joseph. Genesis 39:2-4 says, "The LORD was with Joseph and he prospered, and he lived in the house of his Egyptian master. When his master saw that the LORD was with him and that the LORD gave him success in everything he did, Joseph found favor in his eyes and became his attendant. Potiphar put him in charge of his household, and he entrusted to his care everything he owned."

Oh, my friend, think of what a bitter person Joseph could have been. He could have claimed his right to charge that he'd been mistreated and abused. He could have let bitterness wrap his heart in a web of anger, anxiety, and revenge, but he didn't. He chose not to. He made the conscious choice to honor God with his actions and his attitudes, and God honored him. Notice also that God didn't immediately pluck him from the situation but rather honored him in the situation. How many times do we ask God to take away an unpleasant circumstance, and He doesn't? Seek to honor Him and then remember to look for the ways He's honoring you, not by removing you but by sending blessings to you in that place.

FROM PRISONER TO PRINCE

And we must not overlook the fact that the people around Joseph observed him honoring the Lord. People are watching you. Even when you think they aren't looking, they are. They want to see if your claims about God's faithfulness hold true even when life gets hard. Joseph's master saw God in Joseph and was drawn to God's Spirit in Joseph. We must remember that our bitterness turns people away. Being filled with God's sweet fragrance of acceptance will attract and bless and, most importantly, draw people to God. Joseph honored God time and time again, and God blessed and honored him in return.

Still, life didn't go as we would hope for Joseph. Potiphar's wife tried to trap him in sin and had him thrown in prison. "But while Joseph was there in prison, the LORD was with him; he showed him kindness and granted him favor in the eyes of the prison warden" (Genesis 39:20-21).

Eventually, Joseph interpreted a dream for Pharaoh. God was warning Pharaoh to prepare for seven years of plenty followed by seven years of famine. Pharaoh was so impressed by God's Spirit in Joseph that he placed Joseph in charge of the entire land of Egypt, second only to Pharaoh himself. Joseph, once a forgotten slave boy, now wielded the power of a king. Ring any bells? God did this for Joseph. He did it for the Liberian boys. And God has done it for you too. You were once a spiritual orphan with no hope, but now you are adopted as a child of the Most High King!

ORDINARY DECISIONS CAN HAVE EXTRAORDINARY EFFECTS

Pharaoh wisely heeded Joseph's predictions, and during the seven years of plenty, Egypt diligently saved up grain to be used when famine hit. Sure enough, seven years later, a terrible famine struck the land, and the grain saved the lives of the people.

Jacob and his family were also experiencing extreme famine, and they heard that Egypt had grain. So Jacob sent some of the brothers to Egypt to get some grain to feed their families. The story once again takes many twists and turns, but eventually Joseph recognizes the brothers, has mercy on them, and gives them food, and Jacob's entire family moves to Egypt to live.

All 12 sons of Jacob grow up, marry, raise their families in Egypt, and become the 12 tribes of the nation of Israel. Many years and several generations later, a Pharaoh arose who did not remember Joseph and his great service to Egypt. He was concerned that the very large nation of Israel was a potential threat and could disrupt his powerful Egyptian empire.

Exodus 1:11 says, "So they [the Egyptians] put slave masters over them [the Israelites] to oppress them with forced labor." Verses 12-13 go on to say, "But the more they were oppressed, the more they multiplied and spread; so the

You were once a spiritual orphan with no hope, but now you are adopted as a child of the Most High King!

Egyptians came to dread the Israelites and worked them ruthlessly." So goes the story of how the entire nation of Israel wound up as slaves in Egypt.

Think back with me to that day many years before when a group of bitter brothers were tending sheep on a very ordinary day and made one tragic decision. They caused harm not only to their family but eventually to the entire nation of Israel. Had they never sold Joseph to be a slave, the nation of Israel would have never wound up as slaves being treated so cruelly in Egypt.

Sadly, those brothers were living their lives very unaware of the tragic consequences that can come from one act of disobedience. The brothers' bitter hearts caused trouble for many on that ordinary day (see Hebrews 12:15). And the effects of their bad decision haunted generations who came after them. As we make ordinary decisions on ordinary days, do we, I wonder, have any idea of the impact and influence those decisions have on the people around us and the generations to come?

ALL THINGS ARE POSSIBLE

Thank God the Liberian boys were aware that with God all things are possible. They didn't get stuck in the bitterness that surely came knocking at the doors of their hearts. After all, their mothers, their fathers, and many of their biological siblings were massacred by evil rebels. Put yourself in their shoes.

You're at home one night with all of your family. Suddenly the front door crashes in, and everyone you love is slaughtered right in front of you. Your home is burned and your money is taken away. Miraculously, you survive, but what future do you have now? You have no money, no one to care for you, nothing. You are taken to an orphanage and left there. You are now a forgotten child in a third-world country.

But God was with those boys. God was with Joseph. And God is most certainly with you too. He has not forgotten you. He knows your circumstances. He knows bitterness has certainly come knocking on your door as well. Don't answer that knock. Don't listen to the voice of bitterness. Don't even crack the door to peek outside. Ask God to slay this unwanted visitor and carry him away. And then you choose daily to never resurrect him.

The decisions you are making today matter. Thank God Joseph was aware that with God all things are possible as he saved the nation of Israel despite being betrayed and hurt by them. What might God have in store for you after the famine? What treasures are you discovering? Have you learned how to depend on God like never before? More importantly, do you have a sure answer settled in your heart that yes, with God, all things are possible?

BIBLE STUDY

Read Acts 7:9-15.

This passage is a continuation of Stephen's sermon, particularly dealing with the story of Joseph in this section. Notice verse 9 points out that "God was with him." Many times in the Bible, people are described as having God with them. Read Genesis 21:20; 26:3; 39:2; 1 Samuel 18:14; Luke 1:66; and Acts 11:21 for just a few of these references. In these passages, God is clearly with those who follow Him. I picture Him walking right beside us as the perfect traveling companion. He walks with us and talks with us and calls us His own, as the old hymn says. How blessed we are to have God as our companion in life. In your notebook, write out one of these verses and record your name in the place of the person's name in the verse. Gain the confidence and strength you need just by knowing that God is with you, just as He was with Joseph and other heroes of the faith.

Read Genesis 41:16.

Joseph refuses to take any credit for his success in this verse. He is standing in the presence of the Pharaoh—the most powerful man in the world at that time—who does not worship Joseph's God, yet Joseph is not afraid to give God the glory before Pharaoh. His willingness to glorify God resulted in many blessings for him personally and politically. Read Genesis 41:38-45, and in your notebook, list the blessings God provided for Joseph.

Joseph could have given up, felt betrayed, and turned his back on God when he ended up in Egypt as a slave. Instead he used the opportunity to grow his character and increase his faith all the more. Because of his positive perspective on the situation, he was allowed to see God work out a desperate situation for good. We can have the same perspective according to Romans 8:28 (NKJV): "And we know that all things work together for good to those who love God, to those who are the called according to His purpose."

....

Read Genesis 41:50-52.

After Joseph is blessed with his new position as second in command to the Pharaoh, he marries and has two sons named Manasseh and Ephraim. These two sons' names are both significant to Joseph's life, as the verse says. Write down what the verse says each son's name meant.

By the time Joseph married and assumed his new position of leadership, he had spent 13 years in slavery. Was slavery part of God's plan for him? Proverbs 20:24 says, "A man's steps are directed by the LORD. How then can anyone understand his own way?" Joseph knew that God had a plan for his life, and he accepted God's sovereignty regardless of what happened. He knew that God had directed his steps into that pit his brothers had dug for him just as He had directed his steps into a place of power. God had shown Himself faithful from the pit to Potiphar to prison to power. Joseph's sons, in turn, became a living testimony to his conviction that God was with him every step of the way. In your notebook, briefly retrace God's faithfulness through some of the experiences in your life.

PHASE THREE

Believing

NINE

A MOST
UNLIKELY PATH

Art's family loves to go camping, and I don't mean in a cushy campground with hot showers and power hookups. Oh no, they like a true wilderness, Survivor style of camping experience. One where you set up a tent village complete with a makeshift outhouse—a hole in the ground with plastic tarps covering three sides. You can imagine their horror when Art brought Princess, the nickname I have affectionately earned, to participate in the family tradition, pulling an air-conditioned pop-up camper to the remote riverside campsite. They were speechless when their peace and quiet was invaded by the roaring sound of the generator. Then the last straw was when I stepped out of the camper the first morning, having fixed my hair and makeup.

Now in my defense, I met the challenge head-on, and by the end of the week my hair dryer and makeup were things of the past. I even tried bathing in the muddy river like everyone else. I actually enjoyed communing with nature and bonding with my family as we left the modern world behind.

On one of the last days of our adventure, all the kids decided to go swimming in the river. I wasn't concerned in the least as we'd all grown quite comfortable around the water. While they were splashing and laughing their afternoon away, I sat on the bank, delighting in my kids having such a good time with their cousins. Suddenly, something strange caught the corner of my eye. Something was floating on top of the water a short distance from the kids. It appeared to be a stick. There were lots of sticks and other natural debris in and on the water, so I brushed it aside. A few seconds later a question flashed through my mind…was it floating or swimming? Sticks don't swim on top of the water—snakes do!

I gasped as one of my worst fears was making its way toward my children. I knew I couldn't panic, so I calmly got all the kids' attention. I told them sternly that it was very important for them to listen to my voice and do exactly as I directed. They needed to get out of the water quickly—but this wouldn't be possible going the normal route toward me. The embankment I was on was too steep, and only one child could slowly climb up at a time. They had to swim across the narrow river to the sandy beach on the other side. Then all the kids could get out of the water quickly, and the men could get the boat between the children and the snake.

I didn't want them to know about the snake and have them panic, so I just said it was very important to do as I was instructing, and they would have a surprise on the other side. The thought of a surprise was all the motivation they needed as they calmly but quickly did exactly as they were told. When the men got to the stick-like creature, they confirmed it was indeed a poisonous snake. Yes, the kids certainly got a big surprise as they realized why it had been so important to make it out of the water, just as I had told them to.

TOO REAL TO DENY

Life is a lot like that snake experience. God knows the best routes for us. He sees dangers and temptations that we don't see along the way. Sometimes we get frustrated with God when He takes us through places we hadn't planned on going. His route sometimes appears to be out of the way, inconvenient, tiresome, and confusing. But we must recognize His voice, listen carefully, and do exactly as He instructs. My kids did this because they knew me, trusted me, and had been conditioned to obey me.

We must trust God in the same way. When you leave the famine phase, you enter into this wonderful new place of believing God like never before. You've always wanted to believe Him and His promises, and now that you've left your comfort zone and pressed through the pains of the famine, He's become too real to deny.

The longer we walk with God, the more easily we hear His voice and trust His instructions. Throughout Scripture God calls His people "sheep" and refers to Himself as the Good Shepherd. Phillip Keller makes this note in his classic book, *A Shepherd Looks at Psalm 23:*

> In the Christian's life there is no substitute for the keen awareness that my Shepherd is nearby. There is nothing like Christ's presence to dispel the fear, the panic, the terror of the unknown. We live a most uncertain life. Any hour can bring disaster, danger and distress from unknown quarters…Then in the midst of our misfortunes there suddenly comes the awareness that He, the Christ, the Good Shepherd is there. It makes all the difference. His presence in the picture throws a different light on the whole scene. Suddenly things are not half so black nor nearly terrifying. The outlook changes and there is hope…It is the knowledge that my Master, my Friend, my Owner has things under control even when they may appear calamitous. This gives me great consolation, repose and rest.[1]

GOD WILL HELP YOU WANT TO OBEY

Every day the Good Shepherd asks, Do you trust Me? Do you believe Me? Will you follow My commands even when they don't make sense to you? We sheep must give a resounding yes, laying all our own questions aside. God has probably taken you on some unlikely paths before, and you can almost be guaranteed that more lie ahead, so why not make peace with this now? Why not just confirm right out loud that you do trust God and are willing to travel the unlikely paths because you know they are His best?

I challenge you to do this even if you don't feel like it. Feelings follow correct behaviors, not the other way around. Make right choices to honor God, and your feelings will eventually catch up. And though at first following God this way may appear to make your life harder, it actually does the exact opposite. It makes your attitude more in line with His, thus enabling you to weather whatever comes your way.

Though I've tripped and stumbled many times along this most unlikely path with God, He has allowed me to understand what Philippians 2:12-13 means when it instructs, "Continue to work out your salvation with fear and trembling, for it is God who works in you to will and to act according to his good purpose." In other words, it's okay to be scared that you might mess up. It's okay to be honest enough to admit you don't always want to obey. This is human nature. Ask God to help you make wise decisions. Ask Him to help you to want to obey. God will work in you to help line your will up with His if only you'll ask.

Have you ever dared to ask this? Have you ever dared to say to God, Lord, whatever Your will for my life is, that is what I want? Believing God is not for the weak at heart. It's only for those who want to discover the rich blessings of walking close enough to God to hear the constant drumming of His heartbeat.

GOD'S HEARTBEAT

I've heard this heartbeat many times. I heard it very clearly on a day that my world could have come crashing in around me. But there it was, thump-thump, thump-thump, thump-thump. So real. So close. Too close to deny that He was right there with me. So, what could have been a day of devastation was but a bump in the road. I heard His instructions, I did exactly as He told me to do despite my feelings, and He delivered me safely to the other side.

Several months prior to our camping trip, Art told me he wanted to invest our entire life savings in the stock market. A couple of stocks showed great promise, and he wanted to get in on what was sure to be very profitable. I'm not very investment savvy, but I didn't like the sound of putting all our eggs in one basket, so to speak. I voiced my concern but let him do what he thought best.

Then came the day. The day the market crashed. Art came home, and I went

Feelings follow correct behaviors, not the other way around. Make right choices to honor God, and your feelings will eventually catch up.

to the front door to greet him with some trivial details from the day. The look on his face made me stop speaking. I watched as he slumped down in front me, wrapped his arms around my legs and sobbed, "I've lost it all. Our entire life savings is gone."

Thump-thump, thump-thump, thump-thump. I knew the Lord was close. I knew He would provide. I knew He was allowing this to happen for a reason. He could restore our investment as quickly as He allowed it to go away. Thump-thump, thump-thump, thump-thump. I knew all this, but my flesh screamed out to say, I told you so! You fool! How could you have done this? But how could I dishonor God when everything I know about Him reminds me of His constant provision? Did I really think our life savings came from our hard work, or did I know and believe that everything we have comes straight from Him? Thump-thump, thump-thump, thump-thump.

I knelt down in front of Art and cupped his face in my hands. "I loved you yesterday when we had everything. I love you today when we have nothing. I love you, Art, not for what you have but for who you are." This became a marriage-defining moment for us. It was not a path I would have ever freely chosen, but it was the best path. I chose to believe God in this moment. I chose, by the Holy Spirit's power, to honor what I knew to be true about God even though my feelings lagged behind. Now, on the other side of this experience, I can say that what it did for our marriage was priceless. I would have freely given every penny we lost to have what we gained.

God knew best. He always does. Thump-thump, thump-thump, thump-thump.

I had a complete and very unexpected peace. I could have wallowed in what I'd lost and stayed in the hard place of the famine. But something in my soul reached out for God's perspective and grabbed hold of the certainty of His presence, and suddenly I was ushered from famine to believing. The minute I trusted God this way, my famine was over, and I began a new phase of believing God like never before.

You see, in the believing phase your circumstances might not be that much different from what they were in the famine phase. However, the difference is in how you look at them. You have changed. Your outlook has changed. Your belief in God has changed, for you now know this for sure: People may change, and things may change, but God never does. God does not change, and neither do His promises.

BIBLE STUDY

First read Job 37:1-5; Psalm 29:3-9; and then read 1 Kings 19:11-13; Isaiah 30:21.

In the first set of verses, God's voice is described as a mighty thunder, loud and commanding and awe-inspiring, just as you might expect. In the second set of verses, though, God's voice is quiet and still, barely more than a whisper. I must admit, sometimes I wish I could hear God's voice as loud as thunder so I would know for sure that I had heard Him correctly! But I am grateful that God is gentle with me—whispering His words of affirmation and encouragement. I have learned to listen for the sound of His voice just behind me saying, "This is the way, walk in it." As I take tentative steps forward, I grow more confident in my walk and realize He is with me always.

Read 1 Samuel 15:22; Psalm 95:7-8; Hebrews 3:7.

As we learn to listen for God's voice, the next step is to obey His voice. These verses show us that God speaks to us with the expectation that we will obey Him as a result. And yet how many of us ignore His voice, argue with His voice, or try to drown out His voice by allowing other noises to fill up our world? As we saw, God's voice is that gentle whisper that can be heard only when we intentionally listen for it. In Psalm 95:7, the original word for "hear" means to hear with the intention of obeying. We must take that next step of listening for His voice and then obeying what He has asked us to do. God's Word gives us many examples of how we will miss out on the many blessings He has in store for us if we do not obey His voice, just as the children of Israel missed out on their promised land.

Read Psalm 37:23-24; Proverbs 4:11-12; John 11:9.

Sometimes we hear God's voice, and we set out on the path according to His direction, only to stumble along the way. God's Word warns us that we will stumble from time to time, but He will keep us from falling. James 3:2 says, "We all stumble in many ways." Jesus taught us that we must walk according to God's will. When we are doing that, we have nothing to fear. It is better to walk in obedience than to live in fear of stumbling.

TEN

ROADBLOCKS
AND REASSURANCES

W*hat exactly are You up to, God?* I shook my head in disbelief as I drove slowly down the driveway. I was facing an impossible situation. God was asking me to extend grace to someone who was hurting me. He wanted me to love her when she was doing everything possible to destroy my comfort, my security, and my joy. I felt in no way like honoring God in this moment. I had a whole list of emotions coursing through my body, none of which were loving and kind. But I couldn't shake this overwhelming sense that God was waiting, watching, wooing me to act contrary to my feelings and simply walk in His truth. I was to love this woman who so desperately despised me.

BLOCKADE!

It all started over a dispute about the boundary lines of our property. We soon discovered that indeed we had made a mistake, and part of our driveway was on land that did not belong to us. We tried to buy the small parcel from her to no avail. We tried to reason it out and thought of every scenario possible to fix the problem without having to spend an exorbitant amount of money to dam up part of our pond and move the driveway over. But no solution was acceptable to her, and it became apparent that we'd have to do the least desirable option.

The timing was also a problem. We needed to wait until the dryer summer months when we could drain the pond. But even this was unacceptable, and soon we were greeted by various blockades in our driveway. Huge rocks, saw-horses and boards of wood, and No Trespassing signs blocked our way. Months went by, the blockades got worse, and the less-than-kind letters to us got more frequent. I felt threatened, frustrated, hurt, and bewildered.

Here I was, a woman in a Christian ministry who spends my life teaching women to love one another, and my neighbor couldn't stand the sight of me. I was brokenhearted and rattled, and I began to question myself. Worst of all, I couldn't fix the problem. I cried out to God and begged Him to remove the problem, soften hearts, change minds, or best of all, supernaturally move the driveway. But it was not to be. Week after week, I'd find myself driving down my long winding driveway, only to be halted by the latest blockade attempt.

GOD'S SOLUTION

Then came the day God moved. Not the driveway, and not even the other person's heart. God moved in me. It was the day I came home and found work-ers building a fence across the drive that would permanently block us from going to and from our home. I was infuriated. How could she do this? Why would she do this? I ran to call someone to help me, someone to rescue me. As I stormed into my home, God suddenly broke through my anger and anxiety and prompted me to take my fence-building adversary a cup of water.

It was a hot summer day, and building a fence is not an easy job. She was tired and thirsty. But the reason she was tired and thirsty was because of all the energy she was exerting to hurt me! Now I was supposed to go give her water to refresh and reenergize her efforts? God, this is not fair. This does not make sense! She probably won't even take the water I give her. So this is the place I was in as I slowly made my way down to the fence. As I got out of the car and started toward her, I had to will my feet to walk this obedience path. But then as my arm reached to give her the water, the heaviness lifted, and I so clearly felt God's impression on my heart: Today it will be physical water, but this is one of the things that will lead to her receiving the living water.

Her silent stare let me know today was not the day to try and give her the living water, but seeds were planted in her heart and mine. How these seeds will be nurtured is up to the Lord.

Tears filled my eyes as I silently walked back to my car and turned to go back up the driveway. God has the most amazing way to work in the unseen details of life and work out His plan despite our stubbornness. Here I was, kicking and screaming through this situation that I thought seemed so pointless, and all along God had a plan. A plan for her and a plan for me.

GROWING UP

How I wished I could have embraced God's plan sooner than I did. All I could think about was changing the circumstances that were causing me disruption and discomfort. Now I realize that for that season of my life, my assignment from God was to learn to love an enemy. What enemy do you need to love at this moment? Maybe it's a neighbor, a prodigal child, an angry spouse, or an unforgiving friend.

We don't like hard places. Our souls long for the perfection of the Garden of Eden that we were designed for, and yet the world we live in bounces us from one imperfection to the next. Soon we find ourselves empty and exhausted, trying to fix problems that interrupt and inflict pain and heartbreak. We even become frustrated with God. We know He could fix this problem. With one snap of His holy hand, He could heal the hurts, rearrange the circumstances, restore the broken places, and provide a way out. So why doesn't He?

The answer is that He loves us too much to leave us the way we are. Think about a baby inside his mother's womb. He is warm and well fed. He likes this place of security and safety, but a time comes when he must leave. He must go through the painful shock of being born. It is hard, but if he resists, growth will no longer be possible, and he will die.

Our spiritual life is very much the same. We must continue to grow and embrace God's plans for the life we've been given. We don't grow by changing the adverse circumstances. We grow by embracing God's plans for the circumstances and allowing Him to have His full way in us. Allow Him to work out kinks and imperfections in the core of your soul. Let Him help you find a perspective beyond your own. Only then can you find incredible peace in the storms of life.

The enemies to a great life are not tragedy, heartbreak, and hard times. The enemy to having a great life is to simply lead a good life. A life where you seek comfort and ease above growth. A life where you avoid the risk of taking chances with God. We live in a fallen world, so no one can avoid every pothole in the road of life. You will have hard times. You will get bumped and bruised, but you don't have to get bewildered. Say yes to God now. Say yes to whatever He brings your way. Seek Him wholeheartedly through it. Ponder what He is teaching you. Surrender what He is requiring from you. And know that He is working out His wonderful plans for you right now behind the scenes.

EMBRACE HIS PLAN

This hard place you are in is not a distraction. You are not being sidetracked. This is His way. "'For I know the plans I have for you,' declares the LORD, 'plans to prosper you and not to harm you, plans to give you hope and a future'" (Jeremiah 29:11). You've probably heard this verse quoted time and again, but put it in context with the verses that come after it, and you'll see the call to not only trust God but to have peace in knowing He will carry you through. Verses 12-14 go on to say this:

> "Then you will call upon me and…find me when you seek me with all your heart. I will be found by you," declares the LORD, "and will bring you back from captivity. I will gather you from all the nations and places where I have banished you," declares the LORD, "and will bring you back to the place from which I carried you into exile."

My favorite call to action here is to seek God "with all your heart." Not just the parts of your heart crying for ease. Not just the parts of your heart crying for restoration. But find that place in your heart eager for growth, and let it cry out as well. Embrace this perfect plan, and you will find God, see His plan from His perspective, and enjoy peace right in the middle of the storm. In the meantime, my favorite promise here from God is that He will carry us. He carried us into this hard place, this exile of sorts, and He will carry us back out.

This is a season of growth. This is a part of the plan. The road will not be hard all the way through. Continue to call on Him in great confidence, realizing that nothing, no hard place, can separate you from God's comforting presence and boundless mercy. This will soon pass, and on the other side wait rich perspectives, beautiful growth, and yes, stronger faith.

THE REST OF THE STORY

So, whatever happened with the driveway? We had to drain the pond and move the driveway. It broke our heart to see the pond get to such a sad state, and the process of moving the driveway was very expensive. However, God provided every penny we needed to move the driveway in the most surprising ways. Now you can't even see evidence of the great driveway escapade. The barren ground sprouted grass again, and the driveway sits securely on our land. I still pray for my neighbor, who has since moved, and I still hope one day we'll be friends. But the most beautiful restoration that took place was with the pond.

Our pond had taken years to fill, so we assumed it would take years to refill after being drained. But God had a different plan. Do you remember what He asked me to give my neighbor? One cup of water. Do you know what God gave me back? He brought a rainstorm right over our pond—the heaviest downpour I'd ever seen—and refilled that pond in one day! My friend, those weren't just raindrops that fell that day. To me, it was God lavishing His love all about me and reminding me that He is in absolute control. One cup of water led to the blessing of millions of gallons.

Hosea 10:12 says, "Sow for yourselves righteousness, reap the fruit of unfailing love, and break up your unplowed ground; for it is time to seek the Lord, until he comes and showers righteousness on you."

Now let me have you read that verse again with a few personal additions: "Sow for yourselves righteousness [right choices that honor God even when you don't feel like it], reap the fruit of unfailing love [love for the lovely and unlovely alike], and break up your unplowed ground [whether that be the blockades in your driveway or blockades in your heart]; for it is time to seek the Lord [embrace Him with all your heart], until he comes [and He most certainly will] and showers [more than you could ever hope for or imagine] righteousness on you."

This is the secret to living the life God has given you and loving it whether you are rejoicing in the sunny good times or feeling tossed and turned in a storm. You have His peace because you have His presence. Give your heart permission to grow in fertile soil by making right choices that honor God every step of the way. Take your eyes off the problem and focus on the good and loving God who has great plans for you. Watch for God to rain down more than you could have ever even thought to ask for. He will restore what has been taken from you in His perfect way. Then you will dance in that rain and drink up every last drop! "The LORD will open the heavens, the storehouse of his bounty, to send rain on your land in season and to bless all the work of your hands" (Deuteronomy 28:12). Are you starting to be amazed by the things that happen when we walk with God?

BIBLE STUDY

Read Proverbs 25:21-22; Mark 9:41; Hebrews 6:10.

When God asked me to bring my neighbor a cup of water, I was initially resistant to His gentle nudging in my heart. After all, she was persecuting me and putting me and my family through unnecessary turmoil. She did not deserve any acts of kindness from me. And then God broke through my selfishness and pointed out that if His judgment was based on what we deserved, I would surely never see heaven. I knew that I needed to stop telling God why my neighbor did not deserve my kindness and simply obey Him. Later, as I reflected on this situation, I thought of these verses, which specifically deal with bringing water in His name. I was encouraged once again by the relevancy of God's living and active Word (Hebrews 4:12) and by His promise that it would not return void (Isaiah 55:10-11). I can rest in that truth, knowing that God has and will use that simple cup of water in my neighbor's life and is now using this story in your life.

Read Matthew 25:40; Acts 10:4; Romans 12:13-21.

My assignment was to bring cold water to the person who was trying to block me from entering my home. Your assignment will probably be to bless someone who is just as unworthy in your eyes. Every day, God invites us to reach out in His name to the poor and needy. These people aren't just the financially poor. They are poor in spirit, poor in resources, poor in perspective. They don't just need money or handouts, they need encouragement, kindness, and hope. Many of them don't deserve these things and will probably not appreciate them at first. When I offered that water to my neighbor, she refused it. But God assured me that my willingness to offer it was enough for Him to accomplish His purposes in that time and place. No miracle occurred in that moment;

she went on building the fence, and I went home still unaware of exactly how God was going to resolve the situation. But one thing I knew: God was at work, and in that I could rest.

Who is God leading you to reach out to as you read these words? Is there someone in your life who is "the least of these"? Maybe you have an unlovely neighbor as I did. Maybe your "least of these" person is a family member or business associate—or maybe more than one. Pray for God to show you who these persons are and what you can do for them in His name—not because they deserve it but because you know that blessing them honors and pleases the Lord. Write down some names and your service in your notebook. Be sure to include the date, and remember to go back later to write what happened as a result. Trust God to multiply your efforts beyond what you can see with your limited vision.

....

Read John 4:4-42.

Though you have probably read this account of the woman at the well before, read it this time paying special attention to Jesus' references to the living water He had to offer her and to what she did after her encounter with Jesus. He so impacted her that she went back and told everyone she could find to tell (verse 28). Verse 39 tells us that "many of the Samaritans from that town believed in Him because of the woman's testimony." Who is God leading you to share your testimony with? Share His living water by telling about your encounters with Him and how He has changed your life.

ELEVEN

GOD WILL MAKE A WAY

After such an incredible ending to the last chapter, you might think that God would send the rain, teach me these great principles, and have the person and me reconcile so we could dance off into the sunset together while "And they lived happily ever after" scrolls across the screen. Well, it was not to be.

About a year after we moved the driveway, a sheriff showed up at our home to serve me papers to appear in court. We were being sued for rent on the time our driveway sat on her property. I almost fainted. Some people have snake phobias, others a fear of heights...not me. I have an overwhelming fear of being taken off to jail. So seeing the sheriff at my door shook me.

Suddenly, my absolute belief that God was in control started to waver. This wavering made me madder than having to go to court. I wanted to believe. I willed myself to stay strong in my belief. I read and reread many "believing" verses like Psalm 118:6-7: "The LORD is with me; I will not be afraid. What can man do to me? The LORD is with me; he is my helper. I will look in triumph on my enemies." Still, I didn't feel assured.

I cried out to the Lord. On my more spiritual days my prayers sounded like Psalm 25:1-2: "To you, O LORD, I lift up my soul; in you I trust, O my God...nor let my enemies triumph over me." I knew my "enemy" was not this person—it was Satan wanting me to miserably fail this test. Oh, how I wanted to pass this test, but I was so scared. On my more grumpy, wavering days, I prayed more like Psalm 5:6: "You destroy those who tell lies; bloodthirsty and deceitful men the LORD abhors." Terrible but true.

TREASURES TO DISCOVER

On and on I vacillated. I was afraid God wouldn't show up for me. What if we lost the court case? How would that make us look? Worse, how would that make God look? The truth all along was that God didn't need me to worry about how He would look or figure out a way to make things turn out okay. God doesn't need us to make excuses for Him when His children simply make the choice to believe whether they feel assured or not. Our feelings do not have to dictate our choices.

We can choose to believe and walk in that belief with our head held high and our confidence sure. Psalm 118:24 reminds us, "This is the day the LORD has made; let us rejoice and be glad in it." This day has treasures for us to discover. We will find treasures of truth and treasures of God's presence if we choose to look for them. If we walk through this day with our head downcast, we'll miss the treasures. We'll miss His presence. We'll miss His assurance. And for sure we'll miss out on rejoicing and being glad in this day.

THROUGH THE BLOOD

If the only things we focus on are the doom and gloom our present circumstances bring us, then we'll wallow in the mud. The mud will cloud our vision, skew our focus, and make us forget that the sun still shines above us. But if we make the choice to rejoice and keep looking up, when we hit the inevitable mud puddle, our shoes might be a little dirty, but it will not affect the way we see life.

The day of our court case I was much calmer than I expected. Though my hands were shaky, my heart was confident. I knew God had gone before us and would work everything out regardless of which way the judge ruled.

Our accuser presented her side of the case, and we presented ours. We were thankful that the judge dismissed the case. At the instant the judge said "dismissed," a beautiful picture popped into my head. One day Jesus will stand between us and our sin, and because of His blood shed on the cross we will hear, "Case dismissed!" What a glorious day that will be!

My heart was rejoicing in this truth as I turned to make my way out of the courtroom. Suddenly, something strange caught my attention and literally took my breath away. It was a trail of blood droplets that led from our courtroom all the way down two halls and out the front doors of the courthouse. (Apparently, some man had a nosebleed. Bless his heart, I feel bad he had to be the one to provide the blood so I could have this wonderful visual!) This man's blood made me think of the blood Jesus shed and of the fact that Jesus' blood leads us out and onward with full assurance. The blood could not be denied that day. It was real. I had to walk through it. Art had to walk through it, and yes, even our accuser had to walk through it. There was no way out except through the blood.

THE PAIN HAS A PURPOSE

That's when I understood why God allowed this land issue to happen. Romans 8:17 says, "Now if we are children, then we are heirs—heirs of God and co-heirs with Christ, if indeed we share in his sufferings in order that we may also share in his glory." It was a small way to identify and align our hearts with Jesus. And really in the big scheme of things, this was such a little way to suffer. Even if the court ruling had gone the other way, it would have still been such a small way to suffer.

A friend of mine later gave me added perspective. I was telling her about the day the sheriff came to the door and how horrible it was. On and on I went until she asked a simple question: "Lysa, do you know what happened in my life the last time a sheriff knocked on my door?" I didn't know what to say. Her response eliminated my pathetic pity-party: "He was coming to tell me my dad had committed suicide. Do you know how many people are out there today who had a visit from a sheriff? I can almost guarantee you that most of them would trade your visit with theirs in a heartbeat."

I was humbled. Yes, we will suffer in this life. Something may be causing you to suffer right now, but the pain has a purpose, and you aren't alone. Jesus is right there with you to comfort you in a way only He can, for He knows what real suffering is like.

We can't even begin to imagine the way Jesus suffered for us. Even our worst sufferings cannot compare to taking the sin of the world upon His body, being nailed to a cross, and dying for people who were beating, spitting on, mocking, and killing Him. Nor can we compare our suffering to God giving His only Son for all this to happen as He, His Father, had to turn and forsake His Son. Yet He did all this so that we can share in His glory. We only have to suffer in comparatively small ways, but we will share in His glory in the grandest of ways.

RENEWED DAY BY DAY

Yes indeed, we have no way out except through the blood. This blood-stained path is the way God has made. Through the blood of Jesus we can be saved, we can be healed, we can be taught, and we can be part of an eternal glory that we can't even imagine. Second Corinthians 4:16-17 assures us, "Therefore we do not lose heart. Though outwardly we are wasting away, yet inwardly we are being renewed day by day. For our light and momentary troubles are achieving for us an eternal glory that far outweighs them all."

All parts of that verse are true for me. The eternal glory part is true. The renewed part is true. The troubles part is true. And rest assured, the day-by-day part is so very true. This journey is very day by day for me. Good days, bad days, and all in between days are true for me as well. Some of the comments I receive sound as if people think I lead a very charmed life. Trust me, my life is so not charmed. My life is very much like yours.

I get aggravated with those I love the most. I get frustrated with other drivers on the road, especially the ones that beep at me because I drive like Granny Mae. I find myself stepping onto the dreaded scale only to beat myself for not being more self-disciplined. And I'm forever vowing to be more organized, but

I keep misplacing the lists my organized friends encourage me to make. No, life is not charmed in the TerKeurst camp any more than it is in your camp.

But I do experience God in spite of my circumstances and failures. I see Him. I hear Him. I know He's always close. This is not because I'm special or more spiritual. I experience Him because I choose to. I make choices every day to look for Him, listen for Him, and acknowledge Him. Even though the world tugs at me to serve many lesser gods, in the depths of my heart, I choose Him.

AN OPEN HEART

The decision must be made deep in our heart—not our physical heart but our inner self as a whole. Our thoughts, emotions, intellect, and spirit all combine to form this beautiful spiritual heart within us. The Bible has a lot to say about the heart. It's mentioned more than a thousand times in God's Word. Here are just a few of my favorite verses regarding the heart:

- Serve the LORD your God with all your heart (Deuteronomy 10:12).
- Return to the LORD with all your heart (1 Samuel 7:3).
- My heart trusts in him (Psalm 28:7).
- So teach us to number our days, that we may gain a heart of wisdom (Psalm 90:12 NKJV).
- Trust in the LORD with all your heart (Proverbs 3:5).
- May he strengthen you with power through his Spirit in your inner being so that Christ may dwell in your hearts (Ephesians 3:16-17).

To make the decision to experience God, you must have a heart that's open to Him. When we forget to be renewed day by day by looking and listening for God, we lose our eternal perspective, get entangled in the troubles of today, and close our heart to Him.

A closed heart simply and tragically forgets God.

Though I may fall short in many areas of my life, I will not close my heart to

To make the
decision to experience
God, you must
have a heart
that's open to Him.

God. I will rejoice in really believing Him. The purpose of this phase will then be fulfilled when I know He is too real to deny. In every circumstance I face, I know God makes a way, not because life is always hunky-dory but because I've chosen to experience Him too many times to live any other way. May it be so with you as well.

BIBLE STUDY

Read Isaiah 29:13; Matthew 15:8.

These two passages talk about following a religion based on rules and regulations without committing our hearts to Him. Honoring God with our lips by merely talking about Christianity is one thing. Honoring Him with our hearts by entering into a relationship with Him is another thing entirely.

Read 1 Samuel 3:20.

God promises that if we honor Him, He will honor us. We can honor the Lord in many ways. I have listed below some key ways to honor God. Read each verse for yourself and write down specific ways you can apply it to your life as you honor God.

- Psalm 50:23—We can honor Him with our thankfulness.
- Ephesians 5:21-33—We can honor Him as His bride by giving ourselves up for Him and respecting Him.
- Psalm 91:15—We can honor Him by calling on Him, making communication part of our daily relationship with Him.
- John 14:23-24—We can honor Him by obeying His teachings.

Proverbs 8:17 says, "I love those who love me, and those who seek me find me." Seek God with all of your heart, and don't be satisfied with merely paying lip service to having a relationship with Him.

Read Luke 11:28; John 13:17; James 1:22-25.

These passages highlight three key elements: hearing the Word of God, doing what it says, and receiving a blessing as a result. Isn't it interesting how this chain of events works? These passages describe hearing the Word by taking it in, allowing it to work within you, and then using what you have learned to benefit others and to further God's kingdom. Jesus came to serve us as a living example that we are to follow in our lives. As we serve those around us—our husband, children, parents, or even those we consider to be unlovely—Jesus has blessings in store for us. Just as we cannot merely follow a religion without a relationship, neither can we merely hear the Word without acting on it. Do not allow yourself to have eyes that do not see and ears that do not hear. Do not go through life with a closed heart. Take steps today to live out your faith in a way that impacts those around you. Write down one way that God is leading you to become a doer of the Word. Prayerfully commit before the Lord to take this step today.

Read Hebrews 13:20-21.

I shared in this chapter about the blood we had to walk through as we left the courthouse and the powerful visual reminder that was for me. This verse tells us that through Jesus' atoning blood, we are equipped with everything we need to do His will. Through Jesus, God has fully provided everything we need and made us ready to actively live out our faith according to His plans and His purposes for us. We don't need to worry about our abilities or our shortcomings when we know we already have all we need through Jesus. What inadequacies inhibit you from stepping out and acting on your faith? List them in your notebook, and as you draw a line through each one, thank God today for covering all of them through Jesus Christ, to whom be the glory for ever and ever. Amen.

TWELVE

LEARNING TO LEAD

G od is calling you to live out His dream for you, and part of the dream is to lead. As we seek to believe God like never before, we will set an example for others to follow. I never pictured myself as a leader until God revealed to me that like it or not, people were watching and modeling my life. If you are influencing people, you are a leader. You may not stand before crowds or be the next Kay Arthur, but in some way, God will use you to lead others through your influence in their life. Do you not only believe God but also believe in God's calling on your life?

Maybe your reaction to this revelation is like Moses' three-part response.

1. I'm not _____ enough!

"Who am I that I should go to Pharaoh, and that I should bring the children of Israel out of Egypt?" (Exodus 3:11). In so many words, we tell God, I'm not qualified. I'm not educated enough. I'm not old enough. I'm too old. I'm not wealthy enough. I'm not smart enough. I'm not brave enough. I'm not bold enough. I'm not organized enough. And on and on and on we go with excuses.

2. What if others reject me?

"But suppose they will not believe me or listen to my voice; suppose they say, 'The LORD has not appeared to you?'" (Exodus 4:1). Who are we more concerned about pleasing: other people or God? We are not responsible to control how others act and react. We are simply responsible to do what God tells us to do. Certainly, we should listen to wise, godly counsel. But laying our agendas and desires aside, we must first go to God in His Word and in prayer, spending time listening to Him.

3. What if I mess up?

"O my Lord, I am not eloquent, neither before or since You have spoken to Your servant; but I am slow of speech and slow of tongue" (Exodus 4:10 NKJV). As we've seen already, one thing was true about each of the heroes of the Bible—they each messed up. But they chose not to wallow in the mud of their mistakes. Instead, they kept a responsive heart toward God. We need to be like David, who is the only one God ever called a man after His own heart. When he messed up, he cried out, "Create in me a pure heart, O God, and renew a steadfast spirit within me. Do not cast me from your presence or take your holy spirit from me. Restore to me the joy of your salvation and grant me a willing spirit, to sustain me. Then I will teach transgressors your ways, and sinners will turn back to you" (Psalm 51:10-13).

God will reveal to us not only when we mess up but how to return to Him if we constantly seek a pure heart. Is it easy? No, it's extremely difficult to come face-to-face with our sin and admit our failures. That's why David had to ask for a "willing spirit." But did you catch the beautiful outcome? God will redeem our failures! God will take our mess-ups, what Satan meant for our defeat, and use the situation for His glory. People stuck in the same sin you're in will find their way back to God by hearing your story.

GOD USES INADEQUATE PEOPLE

God has already given you a place of influence, and you are the right person for the job. God calls inadequate people so He can work through them and He can receive the glory that is only His. When you experience God working through you despite your human shortcomings, your confidence in Him and His abilities will grow more than ever before. God rarely uses people who look perfect. He uses imperfect people.

You know the "perfect people" I'm talking about. We've all had people in our lives who think they are experts on every topic that comes up. Maybe we've even acted this way at times. The Bible calls this being "stiff-necked," which is a picture of being deceived and hardened. Second Chronicles 30:8 says, "Do not be stiff-necked, as your fathers were; submit to the LORD."

Think about this picture. A stiff-necked person has one of two problems. Either she refuses to turn her head or she refuses to bow her head. If we are too proud and think we know it all, we are stiff-necked because we refuse to bow our head and admit our inadequacies. If we are too insecure, we are stiff-necked because we refuse to look at the possibilities that God is placing around us. The cure for either is submission to God—which means yielding our thoughts, emotions, fears, and wills to Him.

THE CURE FOR A STIFF NECK

Moses overcame his stiff-necked attitude and inadequate feelings by walking in obedience with God. Step-by-step, he started obeying God and eventually became the leader God knew he could be. In Deuteronomy 10:12-16, Moses gives the children of Israel a description of what God expects from us.

> O Israel, what does the LORD your God ask of you but to fear the LORD your God, to walk in all His ways, to love him, to serve the LORD your God with all your heart and with all your soul, and to observe the LORD's commands and decrees that I am giving you today for your own good? To the LORD your God belongs the heavens, even the highest heavens, the earth and everything in it. Yet the LORD set his affection on your fore-fathers and loved them, and he chose you, their descendants, above all the nations, as it is today. Circumcise your hearts, therefore, and do not be stiff-necked any longer.

We all have stiff-necked tendencies. Before we can overcome them, we must have our hearts circumcised. The males of Egypt were required to be circumcised surgically. Moses learned the extreme importance of this when he almost lost his life due to not having his own son circumcised in a timely manner. God could not have Moses be the deliverer of His people until the requirement of circumcision had been fulfilled. And the same is true of our hearts being circumcised as well. The physical act of circumcision gives us a visual of this spiritual truth. The commentary in the *Life Application Study Bible* includes this note:

> But God wanted them to go beyond the surgery to understanding its meaning. They needed to submit to God on the inside, in their hearts, as well as outside, in their bodies. Then they could begin to imitate God's love and justice in their relationships with others. If our hearts are right, then our relationships with other people can be made right too. When your heart has been cleansed and you have been reconciled with God, you will begin to see a difference in the way you treat others.[1]

ACTIONS AND REACTIONS

So to be the leader God wants you to be, you have to not only believe in God's calling on your life but also believe that the people you are leading are valuable and worthy to be honored. Moses learned to be a good leader by walking in obedience to God. Moses developed into a great leader by being consistent enough with his habits of obedience that they became the natural reactions of his heart. The way to be a good leader is for your actions to be reflective of God reigning inside you. But to be a great leader is for your reactions to be reflective of God reigning inside you. Did you catch that? Your reactions are key.

We can easily choose to act obediently to the Lord and honor others in times of less stress. I can be the best mother in the world sitting quietly at the library reading parenting books while my kids are at home with a sitter. The real test is when I go home and something happens to turn the stress up a few notches. How will I react? That reaction is the real litmus test revealing the condition of my heart. My reactions let me know whether or not my belief in God and His ability to shape and mold me is real. Remember, the purpose of this believing phase is to get you to the place where your experience of God is too real to deny.

Nothing will make God so real to you as seeing Him change your character. Not change who you are—your personality, your strengths, and your abilities—but how you are—your character. I like what the *Life Application Study Bible* says in its commentary on Moses:

> In Moses we see an outstanding personality shaped by God. But we must not misunderstand what God did. He did not change who or what Moses was; he did not give Moses new abilities and strengths. Instead, he took Moses' characteristics and molded them until they were suited to his purposes. Does knowing this make a difference in your understanding of God's purpose in your life? He is trying to take what he created in the first place and use it for his intended purposes.[2]

MOSES AND THE PHASES OF FAITH

Moses struggled with both his actions and his reactions. God taught Moses to obey by letting him live with the consequences of his disobedience. His time in the desert after murdering an abusive Egyptian proved to be invaluable. He had to leave the comforts of the palace he'd grown up in (phase one) and endure a famine-like experience of becoming a lowly shepherd (phase two) to get to the place where he could learn to really believe (phase three). This is another example of God taking a bad situation and using it for good. Living in the desert, herding a flock, and learning to hear from God prepared Moses for the role he was destined to play. And it prepared him to move through the next two phases of death and resurrection.

Those are some of the many experiences God used to make Moses into the man that Hebrews 11:24-27 describes:

> By faith Moses, when he had grown up, refused to be known as the son of Pharaoh's daughter. He chose to be mistreated along with the people of God rather than to enjoy the pleasures of sin for a short

How will I react?
That reaction is the real
litmus test revealing the
condition of my heart.

time. He regarded disgrace for the sake of Christ as of greater value than the treasures of Egypt, because he was looking ahead to his reward. By faith he left Egypt, not fearing the king's anger; he persevered because he saw him who is invisible.

Oh, to have such things said about me when I'm gone!

BELIEVING OR GRUMBLING?

When I consider all the lessons Moses had to learn, the one experience that I learn the most from is the one that prevented Moses from entering the earthly promised land. This scene breaks my heart, but it's worth studying because of the rich spiritual truths it demonstrates. The children of Israel left Egypt 40 years earlier. Most of the original people had died, and only their children and grandchildren remained. Moses, Aaron, Joshua, and Caleb were among the remaining few. Sadly, the children of Israel were singing the same grumbling song: "Why did you bring the LORD's community into this desert, that we and our livestock should die here? Why did you bring us up out of Egypt to this terrible place? It has no grain or figs, grapevines or pomegranates. And there is no water to drink!" (Numbers 20:4-5).

Most of these Israelites had never personally tasted a fig, grape, or pomegranate. They only knew desert life. All they knew about what they were missing was what they learned from their disobedient and grumbling parents. These parents had many stories they could have shared to constantly remind their children of God's faithfulness. Instead, negative attitudes consumed their hearts. So, tragically, this is what they passed to their children. This is probably what grieved Moses the most as he threw himself facedown before the Lord and asked what to do.

MOSES' DISOBEDIENCE

The LORD said to Moses, "Take your staff, and you and your brother Aaron gather the assembly together. Speak to the rock before their eyes and it will pour out its water" (Numbers 20:7-8).

In Exodus 17, God had instructed Moses to strike a rock, and water came out. But this time Moses was to only speak to the rock. God was teaching the people to do what He says, though it makes no sense, and watch Him keep His promises. In Joshua 6, the walls of Jericho fall by the shouts of the people. Therefore, Numbers 20 records a pivotal moment that could have proved to the people that God can use voices—He can bring water from a rock or, as they would later see, tear down walls. But Moses, in his frustration and bad reaction to the people's grumbling, did not obey the Lord. Instead of speaking to the rock, he struck it twice.

The water came, but so did God's harsh punishment for Moses. "But the LORD said to Moses and Aaron, 'Because you did not trust in me enough to honor me as holy in the sight of the Israelites, you will not bring this community into the land I give them'" (Numbers 20:12).

We might expect this point of the story to be filled with great weeping and gnashing of teeth. But we have no record of any kind of negative reaction. No begging for mercy, no cry for a "do-over," no pleading for an exception, no long "that's not fair" speech...nothing. Moses' reaction appears to finally have been shaped and molded to reflect God's reign in him.

MOSES AND THE PROMISE

Moses never physically entered the promised land, but two additional points are worth noting. First, Moses desired God's presence more than he desired to enter the promised land. In Exodus 33:18-23, Moses' secret desire to see God comes to pass. Though he only got to see His back, he saw God nonetheless. Once he saw God, everything else paled in comparison. Maybe this is why being excluded from the promised land didn't appear to rattle him. He remained focused and continued leading the people. My flesh would have been tempted to leave those whiny Israelites to fend for themselves in the desert while I went off and pouted the rest of my dying days under a rock somewhere. But Moses didn't react in his flesh. He remained faithful and true. He unselfishly finished his mission. Hebrews 11 remembers him as one who "persevered because he saw him who is invisible."

Secondly, many years after Moses' death, he appears with Jesus on the Mount of Transfiguration, which just happens to be in the physical location of the promised land. "Just then there appeared before them Moses and Elijah, talking with Jesus" (Matthew 17:3). Did you catch that? Moses was standing in the promised land, talking with Jesus. When he desired to see God before, he could only see His back, but now he sees Him face-to-face. How precious of God to give us this beautiful reminder that He always comes through for us. He wants our dreams to come true more than we do. He has everything planned out, and even if things don't seem to work out on this side of glory, we can't even imagine how amazing eternity will be. "No eye has seen, no ear has heard, no mind has conceived what God has prepared for those who love him" (1 Corinthians 2:9).

My friend, I pray that along this journey of walking with God toward your dream, your greatest joy will be seeing and experiencing God, for that is the real joy of this entire adventure!

BIBLE STUDY

Read Exodus 2:1-10; Acts 7:20-22; Hebrews 11:23.

God, Moses' parents, and Pharaoh's daughter all saw that Moses was no ordinary child. Indeed, he was the chosen deliverer God raised up as the leader of all Israel. Though Pharaoh's daughter didn't know it at the time, she was participating in God's plan for one special child. Only God could arrange for Moses to live in the palace of the very man who was trying to kill him! Because of his upbringing in the palace, Moses had the finest education and resources of the day. He understood Egyptian culture from the inside, which gave him a perspective unlike any other Israelite of his time. The only thing Moses lacked from his Egyptian upbringing was a close walk with God. Moses' 40 years in the desert gave God ample time to remedy that situation.

As Moses served as a shepherd and lived as an outcast from his people, God worked in his heart. God used Moses' time in the desert to work on his character, making his preparation complete. In the desert, God revealed His plan for Moses. God's plan for each one of us includes a unique preparation for our particular assignment. What has God prepared you for? What is He preparing you for now? Is God speaking to you in a desert time? Is He preparing your heart for something big enough to take your breath away? God gave us Moses' example to assure us that He is working a plan for our lives even when we cannot see it. Moses became a man of influence because God prepared in advance for Him to be one. In your notebook, write down some of the truths you have learned from your desert times. How is God using those truths to prepare you?

Read Exodus 4:10-17; Ecclesiastes 4:10; Mark 6:7.

When Moses offered up excuse after excuse to God, God responded by providing him with Aaron, his brother, to speak for him. God recognized Moses' need for a partner who would encourage and support him in his calling. We also read that Jesus sent His disciples out "two by two." Clearly, God understands we need people in our lives to stand by us and cheer us on in our calling. Has God provided you with a friend, spouse, or relative who encourages you in your walk and prays for you? Thank God for that person today. If that is something you lack, you can ask God to provide such a person for you. Above all else, remember that God has already given you "a friend that sticks closer than a brother" (Proverbs 18:24). Spend some time today thanking God for being your Friend.

Read Exodus 4:19-20; Jeremiah 10:23.

Once Moses fully trusted God and overcame his fears, he returned to Egypt. God assured him that he would be safe in his travels, and Moses set out on his faith journey step-by-step. Sometimes our steps feel like baby steps, and we wonder if we are getting anywhere. All God asks is that we take steps of obedience and let Him take care of the rest. What step is God asking you to take? Don't worry about where the journey will take you. Trust God with the journey as you take each step. You take care of the possible and let Him take care of the impossible.

PHASE FOUR

Death

THIRTEEN

DEATH DOES NOT MEAN DEFEAT

The third phase of the walk of faith, the beautiful time of believing God like never before, is a wonderful time that we might hope will continue forever. But God has more to teach us, and we must be willing to enter into yet another season of growth. Surprisingly, the fourth phase is called Death. But don't let the name discourage you. Death brings about a new life that can't be found any other way. Indeed, death does not mean defeat.

I went to college to get an education, but that's not all I wanted. The degree I really wanted was not a bachelor's or even a master's but a Mrs. I had it all planned out, really. I would find Mr. Wonderful, we'd fall in love, date throughout college, become engaged my senior year, and get married the weekend after graduation. So, right from the first day on campus I scanned every crowd looking for him. I was subtle about it and played hard to get, but I mentally crossexamined every guy I met to discern if he could be the one.

I didn't discover him until my sophomore year. But the minute I first laid eyes on him, I was captured. He was tall, dark, handsome, and the star of the football team. He was on billboards throughout the town and posters all over campus. And he was supersmart. Majoring in physics, he maintained a 4.0 GPA. Though I had never graced the halls of the science building, I signed up for Physics 101. Then, I proceeded to fail my first test and suddenly was in desperate need of a tutor. What a beautiful plan to get to meet with him on a regular basis!

To protect the innocent, we'll call him Flicktoid, or Flick for short. Before long, our tutoring became less and less about physics and more about the chemistry budding between us. I dropped the class, but the relationship was in full bloom and continued long after physics was forgotten.

THE BIG SURPRISE

We dated all throughout the rest of our college career. I filled pages of scrapbooks that would one day be a treasure to show our children. I imagined the faces of mini-me's and mini-he's all gathering around our kitchen table, gazing in delight as I recounted our romance. Here's a petal from the first roses Daddy gave me. Oh, and here's a picture from a formal dance we went to in the mountains. And look, Daddy's football team won the national championship that year. What a star he was. There's Mommy cheering him on from the stands. I went to every game.

Flick graduated a year before me and went on to a graduate school that was four hours away. We continued dating, and as my graduation approached, my anticipation grew. We had talked about getting engaged, and I thought the big question could come anytime. Each time we saw each other, I imagined this could be the big day. But graduation came and went, and still no ring.

When I was deciding on where to move after graduation, he encouraged me to get a job close to his school. I was able to move only a few hours from him, and I was sure this was a good sign. Though I was lonely in this new town, I was encouraged by the fact that my birthday was only a few weeks away. I decided this must be what he was waiting on and swept away any doubts as to the future.

Flick arrived late for our date on my birthday, complaining about the drive being too far for just a dinner date. As the evening wore on, other clues should have warned me that things weren't going as I'd hoped. But my Pollyanna attitude just kept me wishing for the best. At the end of dinner, Flick pushed back his chair, took my hand, and looked me straight in the eyes. Oh, finally, the big moment!

It was big all right. Flick announced he'd met someone else. I had hardly picked my jaw up off the floor when he continued, "And I really need to be getting back. Do you have a few bucks I can borrow for gas?" I was in such shock that I not only paid for my own birthday dinner but also for his gas to get back to the new Flickette!

THE PIT

The story sounds funny now, but at the time it seemed worse than death. I was so alone. I had uprooted my whole life and planned my future around him. Now he was gone, and so were all my grand dreams to get married. I was angry, hurt, depressed, and devastated. The rejection from this man I trusted stung deeply. It sent me into a dark pit of depression. I couldn't eat, couldn't sleep, and couldn't fathom how I'd ever get over this hurt.

I crawled into bed, pulled the covers over my head, and didn't care if I ever saw the light of day again. Though my responsibilities eventually made me get out of bed, I just went through the motions of living. Inside my heart, I was under that blanket of darkness.

One Saturday morning, my roommate bounded into my room, holding up a newspaper ad for a large church near our apartment. Though she was not a churchgoer herself, she encouraged me to go and meet some people my age. She quipped, "That church is so big, you might even find your husband!"

So I went to that big church the next day. Though I found no husband right away, I did find some great friends who helped me get over Flick. More importantly, I shifted my opinions about what really mattered in a husband. Almost a year later, one of my guy friends from my Bible study group introduced me to the most handsome man I'd ever met…handsome on the outside, and even more importantly, handsome on the inside as well. We became friends, but I secretly hoped for more.

NOTHING BUT THE BEST

About this time—you guessed it—Flick started calling again. Things hadn't worked out with Flickette, and he claimed to now see the error in his ways. He wanted me back. He wanted us to be together again, forever. Even though I didn't know if the new young man I had taken an interest in would ever ask me out, I knew I was at a major crossroads. Flick was everything I thought I wanted. A year earlier, I would have given anything to have him back—but not now. I had a new vision for what love was supposed to be. My new interest treated me nicely, encouraged me in my relationship with the Lord, and bought my dinner when a group of us went out—and we weren't even dating!

I called Flick and told him it was over for good. Nothing he could do or say would change that. Though there were no assurances that anything would ever work out with the young man from church, I was assured that God didn't want me to settle for anything less than His best.

A few weeks later, the young man from church finally asked me out. His name was Art TerKeurst…and eight months later, we were married. Now, I must say, our marriage has not always been easy. I now know that all those years of so desperately wanting someone to love me were not cries for a husband but rather for a Savior. My soul yearned for a relationship with the Lord though my heart had been fooled into thinking all my wrongs would be fixed with a husband. But Art has weathered my emotional and spiritual storms in a way that Flick never would have.

GOD'S WAY MIGHT NOT BE THE SHORTEST WAY

God knew what I needed so much better than I did. Thank God for not answering the prayers for Flick and me to get married. Flick breaking my heart was one of the best things that ever happened to me. It was a death of sorts but not a defeat. It was a victory in disguise.

So much about my life has been like that. The very things that feel like death are really a birth of something so much better. Later in this section we'll learn a lot about the children of Israel and their journey to the promised land. But first I want to recap their initial day of deliverance. It wasn't the day they left Egypt; it was the day God radically delivered them from the pursuit of their captors.

The children of Israel were led by God, not on the shortest route but rather the ordained route. Exodus 13:21 says, "By day the LORD went ahead of them in a pillar of cloud to guide them on their way and by night in a pillar of fire to give them light, so they could travel by day or night." God was with them and reassured them of His presence in visible ways. But they reached a point in their exodus from Egypt when, though they knew God was there, they felt defeated. Just when they thought they'd escaped the Egyptians, Pharaoh's army appeared on the horizon, barreling toward them. "They were terrified and cried out to the LORD...'It would have been better to serve the Egyptians than to die in the desert!'" (Exodus 14:10-12).

HIS WAY IS PERFECT

Oh, how I can relate to their anguish and utter dismay. I too was in a strange place when Flick broke up with me. I couldn't understand why God had brought me to this place only to allow my heart to get broken. But if I'd never moved to be closer to Flick, I would have never met Art. It wasn't the shortest route or even the safest in my opinion, but it was God's best, and I'm so thankful I stuck with Him. Left to my own opinions and plans, who knows where I'd be today.

Just as God didn't abandon me, He didn't abandon the Israelites either. "Moses answered the people, 'Do not be afraid. Stand firm and you will see the deliverance the LORD will bring you today. The Egyptians you see today you will never see again. The LORD will fight for you; you only need to be still'" (Exodus 14:13-14).

The minute they stopped fretting, the Lord started fighting. He told the Israelites to move on through the sea. Moses raised his hand over the sea, and the water parted, allowing the Israelites a way of escape. With a wall of water to their right and left, the Israelites crossed over on dry land. When Pharaoh followed them, the Lord caused the sea to crash back on top of them, and the Egyptian army perished that day.

The sea in front of them must have looked so big, so dangerous, so immovable. The army behind them was deadly, horrifying, and so seemingly unstoppable.

But the Lord was bigger than the immovable and stronger than the unstoppable. Israel had no way to escape, but God cut a new path and made a way. Not only did He make a way but He defeated the Egyptians, so as God had promised, Israel never saw those Egyptians again. His strength was perfect. His timing was perfect. His plan was perfect.

DEATH IS DEFEATED

And so it is with our lives as well. Death seems frightening, but it is not to be feared. As you walk through death times in your journey of faith, rest assured that God has already defeated death. "Since the children have flesh and blood, he too shared in their humanity so that by his death he might destroy him who holds the power of death—that is, the devil—and free those who all their lives were held in slavery by their fear of death" (Hebrews 2:14-15).

God not only has defeated death but is providing victory through it. This is not your defeat; this is your valley in the shadow of the mountain your soul longs to climb—a mountain of greater faith and closer intimacy with God than you ever thought possible.

> I have set the LORD always before me. Because he is at my right hand, I will not be shaken. Therefore my heart is glad and my tongue rejoices; my body also will rest secure, because you will not abandon me to the grave, nor will you let your Holy One see decay. You have made known to me the path of life; you will fill me with joy in your presence, with eternal pleasures at your right hand (Psalm 16:8-11).

When you die, your body will go to the grave, but you can rest assured that with God your soul will never taste defeat.

God not only
has defeated death
but is providing
victory through it.

BIBLE STUDY

Read Jeremiah 23:23-24.

God is not a distant God, seated on a throne far away. He is a living, active God—aware of every thought, every need, every heartbreak, every death in our lives. We need only to call out to Him, and He will invade our dark secret places full of shame and tears and shine His light in our hearts. Little by little we can know His love and let His hope replace our sorrow so we can look ahead with our trust firmly rooted in Him. In your notebook, write a short prayer asking God to be real to you.

Read Psalm 139:1-10.

Some days I do this thing called life really well. That's when I feel like verse 8: "If I go up to the heavens, you are there." On those days, I am communing with God, and His praise is on my lips. Then there are those days when I really stink at life. I feel cut off from God as though my prayers hit the ceiling and bounce back down into my lap. David finishes verse 8 with this: "If I make my bed in the depths, you are there." God is with us on our "praising Jesus" days and in our "want to curl up in bed with the covers over our head" days. He is still there on our bad days, singing over us (Zephaniah 3:17), wiping our tears (Isaiah 25:8), and taking care of our future (Jeremiah 29:11).

When I lost my college love, I thought my life was over. I "made my bed in the depths" for a while as I grieved this loss. I could not see that what I thought was an ending was only the beginning. God was working out His plans for me—I just had to trust Him. Do you need to trust God with something?

...

Maybe God seems very far away right now. Don't believe that lie. He is a very involved Father, as the Scriptures show us. Write out these verses and note how God is personally ministering to you through each: Isaiah 25:8; Jeremiah 29:11; Zephaniah 3:17.

...

Read Habakkuk 1:5; Acts 13:26-41.

Think back on your life for a moment. Try to recall a time when you can definitely see God at work in your life even though at the time you wondered if He had forgotten you. Death did not mean defeat then, and it doesn't now. Write about this time and pray about sharing your story. If you are not going through this book with a group, pray about sharing your story with a friend.

You might want to pray Ephesians 3:20-21 when you are finished with this portion of the Bible study. Spend some time really praising God for how He has brought about victories in your life. Praise Him that the power that resurrected Jesus is at work in our lives today! Write some of your praises in your notebook.

FOURTEEN

PRESSING
THROUGH THE PAIN

Every person Mary touched was changed for good. In big ways and small ways, Mary was a woman of grace, love, and sweet influence. Being invited to one of Mary's parties was always the highlight of any holiday. Her goal was to let her gift of hospitality shine for God's glory, and shine it did. Though she always wowed attendees, her goal wasn't to impress people but rather to love them. Whether at a simple family gathering or a grand gala with many, she always made each person feel special and important.

So you can imagine how loved Mary's husband always felt. They had been married since Mary was 20 years and two weeks old, and they were madly in love even after 40 years of marriage. Ken and Mary moved down the street from me several years ago and always inspired me with their love, devotion, and life full of fun. Their sunny yellow house was as happy on the inside as it always looked on the outside.

When Mary found out she had cancer, she handled the news with the same cheerful poise and positive attitude that she'd handled all of life. She and Ken battled the disease together and were two of the bravest fighters I've ever witnessed. He was always at her side. She was always smiling.

Everyone thought Mary would beat the cancer and come out skipping on the other side, but it was not to be. They traveled to Houston to participate in a very aggressive treatment program and kept up with family and friends through website postings.

I couldn't read these postings in Mary's last days without sobbing. When she finally went to be with the Lord, I felt as if the whole world paused for a minute of sadness as this ray of sunshine left this place. And there was Ken, alone. The hand he'd held for most of his life was now still. The smile he'd found such joy in seeing was now gone. The voice he'd delighted in hearing was now silent. How do you press through such pain?

ENJOY LIFE

A few weeks after the celebration of Mary's life, I ran into Ken when my kids and I were out eating lunch. He was alone. I asked how he was doing, and though he smiled, his response broke my heart.

"The silence is killing me," he admitted.

Without pausing, I insisted he come to our house for dinner. I gave the disclaimer that I'm not the best cook, I couldn't guarantee what the house might look like, and we are quite a lively bunch but I could guarantee there would be no silence. He accepted.

When Ken arrived, life was very hectic at my house. The boys were picking on their sisters, the puppy wet the carpet again, the phone was ringing, my youngest was jumping on the couch, and I was trying to manage the two pots and a casserole dish that contained our dinner. I apologized for not remembering to offer him something to drink right away. When he graciously said, "No problem," he added, "Enjoy this, Lysa. Enjoy every moment. It goes by so fast."

Throughout the evening, Ken continued with this same gentle reminder. Though he said it in different ways and at different times, the message was always the same. Savor every moment of this precious time. Life is here. Precious, loud, hectic, messy, beautiful, rich, irreplaceable life is here. And the time to enjoy life like this is short.

LOOK FOR HIS ANSWERS

We had a delightful evening with Ken. We'd invited him to dinner as a gift, but we were the ones who received the real treasure. As he was leaving and Art was walking him to his car, he stopped halfway down the sidewalk. He walked over to a gardenia bush planted in front of our house—a bush I've breezed by without enjoying for 11 years. He bent down to a flower on one of the lower branches and buried his face in it while breathing in deeply.

The sight made my breath catch in my throat. I knew Ken had been crying out to the Lord to fill in the gaps Mary left—her gentleness, her sweet smell, her beauty, and her way of brightening up any place she went. Ken prayed expectantly. He expected God to answer and therefore was able to recognize the answer when it came. A flower handcrafted by the hand of God was designed, I'm convinced, just for Ken.

That's the secret of pressing through the pain. Really, it's the secret of pressing through all of life. Learning to depend on God, asking for His provision, and then remembering to look for His ready answers. God did more that night than remind Ken of His faithfulness. He reminded me of what is really important and how to press through the pain with perspective.

As a woman, perspective sometimes gets lost in the sea of emotions that course through my heart. A woman's heart is a deep, wild, and wondrous place full of secret desires. I desire for my life to count for something. I desire for my kids to grow and become good people. I desire for my marriage to always be full of love and devotion. I desire to live a life of no regrets. But my greatest secret desire must always be for more of God in my life. This is the only desire that's certain to never disappoint and can never be taken from me. My husband, my kids, and my life as I know it could be stripped away in an instant. But God will be there through it all. I just have to make the choice to make my relationship with Him of utmost importance.

Knowing this for sure, I can press through any and every pain, disappointment, and even death. God is near. He's drawing me close, teaching me lessons I can't learn any other way, revealing more of His character, allowing me to experience Him in even more amazing ways. Yes, death is hard and extremely painful. Whether it's a loved one, a lifestyle, or a dream, death hurts. I know—I've passed through this phase many times in many different ways. But rather than only looking at what the death phase takes, I've learned to see the good it gives.

GOD'S PRESENCE IN LITTLE THINGS

Sometimes when we go through the death phase of our faith walk, we get so consumed with trying to find the big resurrection that we forget to see God reveal Himself in smaller ways throughout our day.

I asked a friend who is going through a very hard death phase to write down every little thing the Lord had done the previous day to remind her of His love. She was amazed how much more clearly she could see God's hand as she retraced her steps and stopped to ponder this. She'd gotten lost traveling home from visiting family and cried out to God how unfair it was that she was lost. But her circuitous route took her by her favorite restaurant, where she was able to enjoy the very thing she wanted for lunch and still make it home on time. On the same trip, at one point her cruise control stopped working. She slowed down to adjust the knobs to try and fix it. Only then did she realize the speed limit had decreased and a police officer was behind her. Had her cruise control not malfunctioned at that moment, she probably would have kept going the same speed and gotten a ticket.

My friend sensed God's presence in her favorite lunch and no speeding ticket. Ken saw His handiwork in a beautiful flower. How has God revealed His presence to you today? If your desire is for more of Him, you can rest assured that He is working to show you something wonderful right now.

BIBLE STUDY

Read Exodus 15:1-21.

As the children of Israel crossed the Red Sea and emerged on the other side, they stopped and sang praises to the Lord. As we see God at work in our lives, do we stop and praise Him? Do we pause in the midst of our busy lives to deeply inhale the beauty of His creation? Do we choose to focus on the special moments He has given to us and treasure them as a praise song in our hearts to Him? Record your thoughts in your notebook.

Read Psalm 22:3-5; 99:1-3.

These verses tell us that God—who is holy and majestic beyond our comprehension—inhabits our praises. If we want to experience a closer walk with Him, we need only to praise Him. His presence will overwhelm us when we choose to get off the normal path and notice the blessings He sends our way each day. May we learn to send up prayers of thanks and praise as we go through our days.

We can pray prayers of thanksgiving for what He does for us: Thank You, Father, for the sound of laughter. Thank You, Father, for the beautiful weather. Thank You, Father, for knowing what is best for me. Thank You, Father, for Your plan for my life. Record some things you are thankful for.

We can also praise Him simply for who He is. *I praise You, Father, for Your sovereignty. I praise You, Lord, for being Lord of all. You, O Lord, are my King, my Rock, my Redeemer. I praise You and You alone.* This song can be always on our lips as we commune with Him in the midst of our days. Record some praises for who God is to you personally.

Do the same thing I asked my friend to do: Think back to yesterday and write down every little way God assured you that He was with you.

....

Read 2 Corinthians 10:5.

Underline the phrase "take captive every thought." God is a God of details. He is orderly. He is in control. He is intentional about everything He does. And so He desires us to be intentional too. Just as we should take captive every thought, so we should take captive every moment to praise Him. Are you letting these moments pass you by? What is distracting you from praising God more often, and how can you make praising Him more often a priority?

I walked down my sidewalk for 11 years, never diverging from my routine to stop and take captive a moment to rejoice in a gift God had waiting for me if I only looked. Ken's lesson to me that night was to take captive every moment to notice the blessings in my life, both big and small, and to give God the praise when I do.

Write down a praise to the Lord in your notebook. Specifically praise Him for a way He provided for you recently. Your provision may have come in an unexpected way but was no less an answer to your prayers. Ken prayed for more time with his beloved Mary. Instead he is learning to see God's provision in other ways on earth until the day he will join Mary to praise Him in heaven. God will meet all of our needs just as He has met Ken's. Take captive every moment to focus on His gifts to you, regardless of your circumstances. Write your praise for His provision for you in your notebook.

FIFTEEN

GOD ISN'T
SURPRISED BY DEATH

Have you ever noticed that nature doesn't resist God? Think of the little seed that is planted. It's pushed down into a place that's dark and messy. Then it must go through a death of sorts. The seed must cease to exist as a seed as its shell starts to disintegrate and crack open before life can spring from it. When it follows God's design, life springs from the seed, pushes through the dirt, and finds life in the light. Who would have thought that a glorious plant could come from a tiny seed in a dark place?

What would have happened had the seed resisted God and retained its original shape? It would have avoided the trauma of change, but think of all it would have missed out on. It would never have known God's best. How we are so like that little seed at times!

THE SEED OF A VISION

I have acted like that seed and resisted God when the task placed before me seemed too big, too time-consuming, too risky, too costly. I acted like that seed when God gave me the vision for my personal ministry assignment. How, God? I felt so small, so unable, so afraid of trying and failing. As my ministry began, I was willing to take on the small tasks God gave me. I did so for many years, reaching many women with a message of encouragement. But I knew God wanted me to take a new step. *How, God?*

Then the thought struck me that maybe I could speak at an arena event along with other speakers.

The other, more famous speakers could draw the crowd, I could fulfill my own assignment, and we'd all sing Kum-ba-yah and go home happy. So I started praying for an arena event. Don't you just love it when people try to make suggestions to God? (Ugh…note to self: this is not a good idea.)

I was thrilled when I finally received the invitation. I was invited to speak at an arena event with an expected attendance of five thousand people. I was so excited the day I boarded the plane to fly to the event. At last my prayers were answered, and life was good…at least until the next morning at 7:50 AM.

THE SURPRISE

I was to be the opening 8:00 AM keynote speaker. The day's schedule was packed from early morning to evening, with sessions running every hour to be presented by a host of different speakers. At 7:50 AM I began to get a little nervous as the crowd had not yet arrived. I busied myself at my book table—not that the table was busy, but shifting and straightening these books gave me someplace to release my nervous energy. I smiled at the other speakers doing the same thing. We all just shifted and straightened and smiled.

Then two people walked in, and suddenly a new step was added to our awkward dance. It became a four-step movement of shift, straighten, smile, and welcome. These two overly welcomed women were a bit shocked to have such ample choice of seating. They'd brought along Barbie umbrellas so they could signal their friends arriving a little later of their exact location in the large arena.

At 8:00 AM it was time to acknowledge the big elephant in the room. Two people were in the arena, and about 4,998 people were missing! The attendees tucked their umbrellas underneath their seats and busied themselves with a nervous dance of their own. Theirs was a two-step of sorts: chat and look. They'd chat a while and then look around the arena. I think we all kept thinking that these silly little nervous dances would somehow woo people to come and fill the place and we'd proceed on with the conference as planned. But it was not to be.

GOD WAS NOT SURPRISED

The time continued to pass with not much improvement. At 10:30 our crowd reached its peak of 12 ladies. Determined to make the best of an odd situation, one of the other speakers and I took charge. We asked the ladies to help us move folding chairs into the lobby, where they could sit in a circle while we delivered our messages. Soon it didn't matter how many people were there as we knew without a doubt that God was with us. We laughed, we cried, we ordered pizza, and we fulfilled God's purpose for that day. Our plans still didn't go perfectly as we were interrupted by the loud gospel band playing to an empty auditorium, so we decided to move our chairs out to the parking lot. Then came a sudden infestation of flies (I counted 17 on me at one time), a remote-controlled airplane flying over us that sounded like a dying cow, and of course rain. Hey, at least we made use of those Barbie umbrellas!

But God. I love this two-word phrase because life can literally be falling apart around us, but God is good, and no mess we find ourselves in can change that fact! Remember the little seed. Oh, how I wanted to resist God that day. I wanted to pack up my things and fly home. Many of the speakers did, but I knew God was telling me to stay in the hard place. Fulfill the mission in a God-honoring way. Love on these ladies who did come. Be okay with letting your dream die for today because life will eventually spring from it.

God is good. He is way more interested in developing our characters to match our calling than in manipulating our circumstances to make us happy. God could have filled that arena that day. He could have changed all kinds of circumstances. But God's economy is different from our own. I told those 12 ladies that I believed that God had paused for us in this place to get all of our attention for different reasons, and He would use the circumstances of the day for great things.

Did I immediately see huge blessings from my cooperation with God? No. When the event coordinators came to pick my assistant and me up the next day to take us to the airport, conversation with them was awkward. I was still feeling a little shell-shocked by what had happened, and yet God was calling me to forgive their lack of planning, encourage them, and love them. So I did.

Did God immediately bless me for cooperating? Again, no. About an hour from the airport their car broke down, and my assistant and I wound up having to hitchhike to the airport! Once we were finally on the plane headed home, I didn't know whether to laugh or cry. To be honest I didn't know what to feel. The seed was cracking in the deep, dark place, and it hurt.

BEING BROKEN IS
NOT BEING SIDELINED

Was this the death of my dream? Why would God plant a vision in my heart and then let it turn out like this? At times like this, I have to live my life based on the truth of who God says He is and not my feelings. My feelings were hurt, my heart was broken, and I couldn't process this event in a way that made me feel better. So I had to rely on the truth that God is good, He has every detail in His perfect control, and this will turn out okay; in the meantime, I can't rely on my emotional thinking. I must seek God's perspective. Even in my broken state, I had to press on seeking Him.

If you were to ask most people if they desired a life of extraordinary faith, they would probably say yes. So why aren't more people living out this desire? Because they confuse brokenness with being sidelined by God. Brokenness is what must happen before God can put the pieces back together in the way He can shine through the best.

The very first recorded sermon that Jesus gave to the crowds in the Bible is the Sermon on the Mount. We find it in Matthew 5, right after He tells His disciples in chapter 4, "Come, follow me." So this was an important speech for Jesus. Though He'd been teaching and preaching throughout the land, this sermon must have held special importance and is the first time we get to hear Him word for word. Of all the topics He could have chosen to speak on, He spoke about brokenness.

Think about that. He had invited the disciples to leave everything and follow Him. He attracted quite a crowd. He was the talk of the town, the main attraction, the one everyone wanted to see. Can't you feel the excitement of the disciples? Can't you see their puffed-up chests and their confident stride? So Jesus pulls them close and rallies them with a real boost of self-confidence right?

No, He teaches them the importance of brokenness.

> Blessed are the poor in spirit…
> Blessed are those who mourn…
> Blessed are the meek…
> Blessed are those who hunger and thirst for righteousness…
> Blessed are the merciful…
> Blessed are the pure in heart…
> Blessed are the peacemakers…
> Blessed are those who are persecuted because of righteousness…
> (Matthew 5:3-10).

In all my years of reading these Scriptures, I read them as individual statements and missed an incredible insight. What if Jesus didn't mean for us to read them separately but rather as fluid stages of brokenness like this:

> Blessed are the poor in spirit…
>   the broken people.
> Blessed are those who mourn…
>   broken to the point of great weeping.
> Blessed are the meek…
>   weeping to the point of being humbled past worldly things.
> Blessed are those who hunger and thirst for righteousness…
>   humbled and desiring to be filled with God alone.
> Blessed are the merciful…
>   filled with God and able to overflow mercy to others.
> Blessed are the pure in heart…
>   freely extending mercy and living with a "yes" heart for God.

Blessed are the peacemakers…
    saying yes to God and bringing His peace everywhere they go.
Blessed are those who are persecuted because of righteousness…
    so certain in His peace that even when they face hardships,
    they trust and confidently walk with God no matter what.[1]

Beautiful, isn't it? Then Jesus goes on to say in verses 13-16, "You are the salt of the earth…the light of the world…let your light shine before men, that they may see your good deeds and praise your Father in heaven."

O Lord, thank You for shedding this new light on the beauty and value of brokenness. May I forever look at the broken places and experiences in my life in a new way. Thank You for loving me enough to save me from my ideas and desires. Only Your perfect way through brokenness can reveal the best road to travel. I know death doesn't surprise You, Lord, and brokenness doesn't mean an end. Praise You for new beginnings even when we can't see them yet. Thank You for the privilege of being broken enough to shine Your light through my life.

BIBLE STUDY

Read Hosea 13:14; 1 Corinthians 15:55-57.

Jesus defeated death once and for all on the cross. God had a plan for our salvation so that none would perish (2 Peter 3:9). God, in His sovereignty, offered up His only Son so that we could be redeemed. Death did not surprise God then, and it does not now. Even when Jesus was on the cross, He was in control of death. In Luke 23:46, He says, "Father, into your hands I commit my spirit." John 19:30 says, "When he had received the drink, Jesus said, 'It is finished.' With that, he bowed his head and gave up his spirit." He chose the moment of His death. He was not really killed by those who crucified Him, nor was He surprised by His body's weakness. He chose to commit His spirit into God's hands. John 10:17-18 shows us that God is in control of all things—even death. Record your thoughts in your notebook.

Read 1 Thessalonians 5:1-11.

God is not surprised by death. In His mercy, He has provided us with a way not to be surprised by things of this world either. Verse 4 of this passage tells us, "But you, brothers, are not in darkness so that this day should surprise you like a thief." The passage goes on to tell us that we are "sons [and daughters] of the light" (verse 5). God has given us His light in our lives, and that light shines brightest when we are in His Word. He has given His Word to prepare us, to equip us, and to fit us for battle as described in verse 8. He loved us enough to reveal Himself to us so that we would not be surprised by the things of this world either. Commit in your heart to become better acquainted with the God of the universe through His Word. Look at Psalm 119 and list some of the things God's Word does for us.

....

Read Luke 19:10.

Jesus' mission was to build His kingdom by offering salvation to all who believe. The compelling truth about Jesus' dream was that He was willing to die for it. In fact, His death was the pivotal component of His dream. In order to achieve His desired outcome, He had to lay down His life. The Scriptures show us that He was human and felt the same emotions about dying that we would feel. Luke 22:42 tells us that Jesus decided to accept God's will—even to the point of death. Death was always part of God's plan to achieve His dream. Even though He may require death, you can trust His perfect plan for fulfilling His dream for you. God loves you and is always there. This truth is woven throughout Scripture. Take some time to reflect on these promises, and then go through the Bible and find promises that really speak to you. Write them down and refer to these verses during this time. If you are doing this study with a group, share some of your verses as an encouragement to each other.

SIXTEEN

GOD'S PORTION, POSITION, AND PROMISE

I've had quite a week with my sweet five-year-old, Brooke. Let me just give you a few of the highlights:

Miss Thing, as we affectionately call her, got in trouble at home for making a smart remark and had to be spanked. The next day, as I was getting ready in the bathroom, I spied her in the tub, giggling. When I asked her what was so funny, she replied, "Well, I promised myself I wouldn't tell you this, but I just can't help it. Before you spanked me yesterday, I put on five pair of underwear and the thickest pants I could find. I didn't even feel the spanking!" *What? My sweet Brooke...is she really that conniving?*

I had hardly recuperated from the spanking fiasco when my nine-year-old informed me that she caught Miss Thing shaving her legs with her daddy's razor. When I confronted Brooke about this, she smiled and said, "Mom, my legs are too hairy. I 'razored' them and didn't cut myself one time, so what's the big deal?" The big deal? "The big deal," I replied back, "is that you are five years old, and you will not be 'razoring' your legs. Not today, not tomorrow, not for years to come!" *My sweet Brooke...is she really that sneaky?*

Then came the real doozie! My babysitter had taken my girls to a jewelry store to pick up a charm bracelet we were giving as a gift. They weren't in the shop long before visions of her own charm bracelet started dancing through

Miss Thing's mind. With her birthday just weeks away and Christmas only around the corner, it never occurred to her to simply ask for her own bracelet and wait for it to be given to her. She wanted a charm bracelet now. The sitter told her no, and we thought that was the end of that.

That is, until the next day, when her sister reached into the pocket of the pants Brooke had been wearing at the jewelry store and found eight silver charms inside! I marched her back up to the store, returned the charms, and made her give a most humble apology.

THE COLD HARD FACT

Where have I gone wrong as a mother? I mean, she's such a precious child—or at least she was a few days ago. But I had to face a cold hard fact. The easy answer would be to point the finger at myself and try a little harder to be a better parent. And I always have room for improvement, but that's not the whole answer. As much as I would like to think of Brooke as the sweet little angel she appears to be, I can't let her big blue eyes and wavy blond hair fool me. She is a sinner. She is infected with the same sin nature the rest of God's children are infected with—myself included. Without God, she would be left to her own bad decisions and faulty thinking. But with God, she has hope for a different kind of life.

When I study God's children, I feel much better about my own. Even He, the perfect Parent, had some pretty conniving, sneaky, apt-to-sin kids! I must admit, in the past I have been quite harsh in my thinking about the children of Israel at times. I can't help but read their story and think, *You crazy fools! How could you see what you saw and experience what you experienced and still doubt and grumble against God!* The sad truth is that the same is true in my own life. I've had my own parting of the Red Sea, I've delighted in His provision time and again, and still I go my own way at times.

Just like the children of Israel and my sweet daughter Brooke, I am a sinner.

As long as we live on earth, we will sin. But sin doesn't have to rule us and ruin our lives. If we can remember a few lessons from the children of Israel, we'll be much better equipped to avoid the pitfalls of sin. Understanding God's portion, position, and promise will be key as we progress from the death phase to the sweet promised land of resurrection.

GOD'S PORTION

Not long after the children of Israel saw the parting of the Red Sea and witnessed the dead bodies of their enemies washing up on shore, they forgot God's amazing ability to provide. In Exodus 15:21 we find songs of praise to the Lord: "Sing to the LORD, for he is highly exalted. The horse and its rider he has hurled into the sea." But just three verses later, the praises have faded from their lips, and in their place we find a very different tune. "So, the people grumbled..." (Exodus 15:24). And they continued grumbling though God promised to take care of them and provide for them.

Psalm 78:22-25 says,

> For they did not believe in God or trust in his deliverance. Yet he gave a command to the skies above and opened the doors of the heavens; he rained down manna for the people to eat, he gave them the grain of heaven. Men ate the bread of angels; he sent them all the food they could eat.

Though they didn't deserve His provision, God still had mercy on them and provided. The way He provided required them to pursue a relationship with Him on a daily basis, receiving their portion every day. God continued to reveal Himself to His people through the manner in which He provided. He still does this with us as well.

The Big Lie

I think one of the biggest tools Satan uses to keep people from growing in their faith and following after the dreams God has placed in their hearts is the lie that we have to do everything right before God will pay attention to us. We have to pray long and lofty prayers. We have to set aside chunks of time in the wee hours of dawn to do in-depth Bible study. We have to have a seminary-level knowledge of the Bible and be able to do expository preaching on any and every subject that might come up in our conversations with others. Once we reach this pinnacle in our faith, then God sits up, takes note of our devotion, and pays attention to us.

No! That's not the way it works!

Yes, God wants us to pray, read our Bible, and tell others about Him. But He wants us to do those things as a natural response of a heart that delights in our relationship with Him. God loves each of us and wants to spend time with us, not because it's on our to-do list but because we desire to stay in contact with Him throughout our day. He wants to be there for us. He wants to fill in the gaps where each of us falls short.

Our Weakness

When Paul pleaded with God to remove his "thorn," God refused and said, "My grace is sufficient for you, for my power is made perfect in your weakness." Paul goes on to say, "Therefore I will boast all the more gladly about my weaknesses, so that Christ's power may rest on me. That is why, for Christ's sake, I delight in weaknesses, in insults, in hardships, in persecutions, in difficulties. For when I am weak, then I am strong" (2 Corinthians 12:9-10).

Along the same line, God provided for the children of Israel in a way that made them admit their weakness and God's ability to provide. "Then the Lord said to Moses, 'I will rain down bread from heaven for you. The people are to go out each day and gather enough for that day. In this way I will test them and see whether they will follow my instructions. On the sixth day they are to prepare what they bring in, and that is to be twice as much as they gather on the other days'" (Exodus 16:4-5).

Every day the Israelites had to actively receive their portion. I have learned to do the same. Wherever I'm feeling weak, unable, or inadequate, I ask God to be my portion and fill in my gaps. Whether I run short on patience with my kids, love for my husband, forgiveness for someone who hurt me, or one of a myriad of other ways I sometimes miss the mark, I wake up in the morning and start my day by asking God for my portion of what I need.

We find these "portion" prayers throughout the Bible. Psalm 73:26: "My flesh and my heart may fail, but God is the strength of my heart and my portion forever." Lamentations 3:22-24: "Because of the LORD's great love we are not consumed, for his compassions never fail. They are new every morning; great is your faithfulness. I say to myself, 'The Lord is my portion; therefore I will wait for him.'" Even Jesus, when teaching us the Lord's Prayer, prayed for His portion: "Give us today our daily bread" (Matthew 6:11). If He had to pray for His portion, why would we think that we wouldn't have to?

Wherever you are falling short, ask God to be your portion and fill in your gaps. Then watch for His hand at work and thank Him for the many ways He'll reveal Himself to you each day!

GOD'S POSITION

God not only wants us to rely on Him for our daily portion, but He also demands we keep first place in our lives reserved for Him. It's easy to get so consumed with our promised land that we forget the promise Maker. We lose sight of the fact that God planted this dream in our heart and He will surely carry it through to fruition.

> You shall have no foreign god among you; you shall not bow down to an alien god. I am the LORD your God, who brought you up out of Egypt. Open wide your mouth and I will fill it. But my people would not listen to me; Israel would not submit to me. So I gave them over to their stubborn hearts to follow their own devices. If my people would but listen to me, if Israel would follow my ways, how quickly I would subdue their enemies and turn my hand against their foes! (Psalm 81:9-14).

> But their idols are silver and gold, made by the hands of men. They have mouths but cannot speak, eyes, but cannot see; they have ears but cannot hear; noses, but cannot smell; they have hands, but

God not only wants us to rely on Him for our daily portion, but He also demands we keep first place in our lives reserved for Him.

cannot feel; feet, but they cannot walk; nor can they utter a sound with their throats. Those who make them [idols] will be like them, and so will all who trust in them (Psalm 115:4-8).

Ask yourself this question: *What do I want more than anything else?* If your answer is anything other than more of God in my life, then you are worshiping an idol of some sort. Ask God to reveal to you the idols of your life, and turn back to Him.

He feeds on ashes, a deluded heart misleads him; he cannot save himself, or say, "Is not this thing in my right hand a lie?" Remember these things, O Jacob, for you are my servant, O Israel. I have made you, you are my servant; O Israel, I will not forget you. I have swept away your offenses like a cloud, your sins like the morning mist. Return to me, for I have redeemed you (Isaiah 44:20-22).

GOD'S PROMISE

Honestly, sometimes I get tired of the constant battles in my life. I hardly get one issue resolved when another seems to pop up. Not that I go looking for trouble, but somehow it always seems to find me. I've learned to view troubles in my life as "growth opportunities." They give me a chance to recognize God shaping and molding me to fit the calling He's given to me. God is interested in my character, not my comfort.

Last year, my girls and I went to a silversmith's workshop. When we walked into the shop, I was impressed by this man's artistic ability. His pieces were magnificently beautiful. They were so pure and smooth that I could see my reflection perfectly. Only when we went into the workroom did I understand what it took to get the silver to look as it had in the showroom. The pounding, turning, heating, and pounding some more gave me a new respect for all that silver must endure to be showroom quality. For that silversmith to put his name on a piece, it had to submit to treatment we might say is harsh and cruel. But I dare say the silver in the showroom would say it was worth it.

Max Lucado describes the process this way:

> Heating, pounding. Heating, pounding. Deadlines, traffic. Arguments, disrespect. Loud sirens, silent phones. Heating, pounding. Heating, pounding. Did you know that the smith in silversmith comes from the old English word smite? Silversmiths are professional smiters. So is God...God guards those who turn to him. The pounding you feel does not suggest his distance, but proves his nearness. Trust his sovereignty.[1]

God allows the heating and pounding, the abrasive rubs and polishing in my life for a reason. They are purifying and smoothing me so I will reflect Him. "The LORD will perfect that which concerns me" (Psalm 138:8 NKJV). "My Father is always at his work" (John 5:17). In the same way, God spent time molding and refining the children of Israel as well.

The Desert and the Promise

His promise was to deliver them to the promised land. God kept His promise as He keeps all His promises. But they didn't get there as quickly as they would have liked. Their disobedience and need to deepen their relationship with God kept them in the desert for 40 years. Maybe you feel like you're wandering in a desert of your own. Maybe you are wondering, while you're wandering, where God is and what He's up to. Maybe you feel frustrated with God and feel as though your desert experience is just a waste of time.

Rest assured, God is working in you just as the silversmith works with his silver. But He's also working around and about you. Just as an actor must spend time learning his lines and getting familiar with his part, you've got to learn your part as well. God is building the stage, perfecting the sets, and gathering the audience. Don't rush through what God intends for you to learn today. Stay close to Him, be open to His teachings, be faithful in the rehearsals—opening night is on its way.

God was around and about the children of Israel while they were wandering in the desert as well. But their frustration and grumbling prompted Moses' warning in Deuteronomy 6:10-12:

> When the LORD brings you into the land he swore to your fathers, to Abraham, Isaac, and Jacob, to give you—a land with large, flourishing cities you did not build, houses filled with all kinds of good things you did not provide, wells you did not dig, and vineyards and olive groves you did not plant—then when you eat and are satisfied, be careful you do not forget the LORD, who brought you up out of Egypt, out of the land of slavery.

What would be more important for the children of Israel to do, build cities or build a solid relationship with God? Fill houses or fill their hearts with more of God? Dig wells or dig into God's truths and let them change their attitudes? Plant vineyards and olive groves or let their own roots grow deep and steadfast as people of God?

Their death phase in the desert was actually a gift. It provided time to spend with God and to grow in their relationship with Him. In the meantime, God was setting the stage. He was preparing their promised land while teaching His children to learn to simply love and trust Him. "Trust in the LORD with all your heart and lean not on your own understanding; in all your ways acknowledge him, and he will make your paths straight" (Proverbs 3:5-6).

O child of God, let Him be your daily portion. Esteem only Him in your life and keep the Lord's position as number one in your life. And watch as He always has and always will keep His glorious promises! The death phase is coming to a close, and your resurrection is near...

BIBLE STUDY

The portion: Read John 1:12-13; 1 John 5:4-5; Revelation 2:17.

When we read in the Old Testament about God sending manna from heaven for the Israelites, we might think that's just a nice old story that doesn't really apply to us today. These New Testament verses help us to see that God is still providing manna to His children. This manna doesn't visibly fall from the sky, but it's no less available to us as Christ's followers. As these verses tell us, we are overcomers when we become children of God.

The Israelites were God's chosen children, but we are also His children through Jesus' sacrifice and God's mercy. As part of God's family, He gives us hidden manna, which refers to the sufficiency of Christ for the believers' needs. May we all become more intentional about allowing Christ to be our portion of manna for each day. Write a prayer asking for God's provision in a particular area of your life.

The position: Read Habakkuk 2:18-20.

What exactly are idols? In Old Testament times they were graven images carved from wood or stone as described in these verses. But today idols can take many different forms. An idol is anything that becomes a barrier to your relationship with Christ. Anything. Even those precious children He has blessed you with. Even very worthwhile pursuits like volunteering or homeschooling can become idols if they take priority over God in your heart.

Now read Judges 6:25-32. This passage describes Gideon's first directive from God after he was called to deliver the people. Why did God require this of him?

I think God wanted an outward sign of Gideon's inner devotion to the Lord. This was accomplished by physically tearing down his father's altar and replacing it with an altar for God. God wants us to do the same. We may not need to smash the TV with a baseball bat, but we may need to drastically reduce the amount of time we spend in front of it. We may not need to give up our dreams, but we must *surrender* the dream. We should place the dream squarely behind God on our priority list.

In Matthew 6:33, Jesus reminds us to "seek first his kingdom and his righteousness, and all these things will be given to you as well." Spend some time in prayer, asking God to reveal the idols in your life to you. Record one of them and write down how you can restore proper perspective in your life.

The promise: Read Exodus 15:13.

When we are in a desert time, we might think God is absent and begin to doubt His promise to us. We wonder, *Did He really call me to this?* and *Did I really hear that from Him?*

Losing our focus is easy when the desert seems so vast and endless. In this time we must focus on God's covenant of unfailing love. The Hebrew word for this love is *hesed*, which means loyal, steadfast, unfailing love. His love is there for us—working out His plans for us, protecting us, and guarding us as we make our way through the desert. Take a moment to thank God for His *hesed* for you today. Record your thanks in your notebook.

PHASE FIVE

Resurrection

SEVENTEEN

GOD'S DREAM,
GOD'S WAY

Resurrection—the final stage in our walk of faith—happens only after death has had her fleeting reign of victory. In other words, the only way to rejoice in the resurrection is to have sorrowed through death first.

Strange, isn't it? To the soul who has a lesser trust in God, the death phase could almost seem cruel and unnecessary. But the closer we walk with the Lord, the more we start rejoicing in it. For we've come to recognize this as the sign that the new life we desperately desire and can't get any other way is just around the corner.

And the death makes us people who can accept the accolades of resurrection without pride. Remembering the death phase keeps us humble and keenly aware that the resurrection has nothing to do with us. Our talents, our creativity, our manipulating, our arranging, our being in the right place at the right time—none of it brought about the good that is dawning.

God's dream planted in us is brought about by His hand alone. Only now can we let credit go to where credit is due. Not by our own efforts but by God's grace did this happen, and that we now know full well.

God's dream for us must come to life God's way.

A RESURRECTION STORY

My dream of writing a book had to die before it could finally come to life. My efforts to solve the problem with my neighbor had to fail for me to see

God's hand providing His beautiful provision. My thoughts of what my family would look like had to die so that a dream I didn't even know I had could bring the joy of my adopted sons. My suggestion to God for an arena event had to flop miserably before God's plan could be revealed. Yes, even that escapade has a resurrection story.

After I returned home from that most humbling of experiences, I have to admit, I felt weary, insecure, and vulnerable. And that was a good thing, for that very week I went to the concert where I first met my Liberian boys. God humbled me and taught me a lot through the failed conference, but He also helped me to be especially sensitive. He could easily speak to me the night of that concert because I had just been broken.

I was broken and humbled enough to no longer desire worldly things. I wanted to be filled with God alone, living with a "yes" heart for Him, bringing mercy and peace to others in a way I could not have otherwise. But there was even more to the end of this story than that.

My assistant, who had been with me at the arena event, was burdened for the couple who had arranged the conference. They were now in debt in a big way. They owed thousands of dollars to the arena, the musicians, the speakers, and other businesses involved with the conference. Repaying the debt would take a miracle. I figured I would never see the balance of my speaker fee or a reimbursement of my plane fare, and I made peace with that fact and moved on.

But my assistant couldn't let it go. She prayed for this couple. She tried to figure out a way to help them. She sought out a donor to help dig them out of their financial hole. Finally, she prevailed and was reeling with joy as she told me how she was going to be able to help. There was only one catch. I had to forgive the part of the debt owed to me, and then the rest would be paid. She looked at me with a questioned expression and said, "That will be all right with you, won't it?"

I considered this. Every other speaker was going to get paid, but not me. No one else, not even the irresponsible planners of this event, would suffer financially from this event, but I would. I suddenly felt as if I were eight years old and being punished for something my sister did. I put on the biggest pout I could and looked right up in the direction I assumed God's face might be and said…nothing.

Though my flesh wanted to scream, "Not fair! Not fair! Not fair!" God's Spirit inside me made me pause for just a minute. Remembering God's faithfulness time and time again, I silently prayed. *God, this isn't fair, but I don't need to tell You that. So I'm choosing to honor You here for no other reason than that I love You.*

"Yes," I replied. "Of course I will forgive my part of their debt." I willed my mouth to say it. I wanted to honor God even when my flesh screamed for me to do otherwise. And trust me, my feelings took a while to catch up, but eventually they did.

Though I'd made a different choice many times before, this time I chose wisely. It felt good. It felt freeing. It felt enabling. Somehow, this time, I'd battled the evil desires within me and won. Romans 12:1 says, "Therefore, I urge you, brothers, in view of God's mercy, to offer your bodies as living sacrifices, holy and pleasing to God—this is your spiritual act of worship."

YOUR PROMISED LAND IS CLOSE

In other words, in light of all the mercy God had extended to me, which is quite considerable, this sacrifice was small. This was an opportunity to offer my desires as a sacrifice. One that was holy, or "set apart." This was a sacrifice that couldn't be understood by worldly wisdom but that truly pleased God. In doing this, I worshiped God, and in that He would delight.

Psalm 37:4 says, "Delight yourself in the LORD and he will give you the desires of your heart." The very day I released the debt, a most amazing thing happened. I received an invitation to speak at a real arena event. And not just one. I am now under contract to do five events for these new sponsors.

The resurrection may seem to have happened immediately, but it did not. God had other things that needed to happen first. Opportunities for me to be obedient before I even hoped for a resurrection of the very thing my heart desired. Worth noting here is the fact that the resurrection didn't happen until the debt was released.

Are you in a waiting period right now? Though your resurrection may not happen as quickly as you would like, it is coming. Your promised land is close. In the meantime, look for opportunities to honor the Lord today. Look for an opportunity to release a debt, forgive someone who has hurt you, or choose to bless the one cursing you. Resist the urge to feel angry, disillusioned, or jealous of those who seem to have the very thing you keep waiting on. Determine to bless the one you are angry with, encourage the one who discourages you, and cheer for someone you are feeling jealous toward. Doing these things will break the downward spiral you will otherwise be pulled into.

STRENGTH IN GOD'S PROMISES

Doing these things would be impossible on your own, but God's promises will give you the strength. Romans 12:14,21 says, "Bless those who persecute you; bless and do not curse...Do not be overcome with evil but overcome evil with good." Your good choices will cause Satan to flee...flee from you and flee from your situation. Isn't that what you desire?

Second Peter 3:9 says, "The Lord is not slow in keeping his promise, as some understand slowness. He is patient with you, not wanting anyone to perish, but everyone to come to repentance." This verse is actually referring to Jesus' return, but look at the reason for the delay: His patience. He is waiting for His people to get ready. In the same way, He is being patient with you in this waiting period as well. Like any good parent, God is desiring to make good things happen for you, but He won't do it until you are ready to receive them.

THANK GOD FOR SAYING NO

As I write this, I'm sitting in a Barnes and Noble bookstore. A child is screaming from the back of the store, "I want it! I want it now! I want it, want it, want it!" My friend with me just looked up and smiled as we were having the exact same thoughts. If that mom gives in and lets the child have whatever he wants right now, he'll stop screaming, but he'll never appreciate what he's been given. If, however, this mom perseveres, the child stands to learn some very valuable lessons:

"No" doesn't mean the world comes to an end. It simply means not now, not yet, not necessary, or not in your best interest. If you wait for what your heart desires, you treasure it more when you finally do get it. Kicking and screaming and having a bad attitude while you wait is no fun for you or for those around you. Getting the thing you want might be the worst thing for you.

Often, we are very much like that screaming child. I thank God for the nos and the not yets in my life. Though they may not be what I want, they are exactly what I need. God is getting me ready to receive the promised land.

I must learn to be content in His provision today. Think back to the story of the manna in our last section. God was faithful to provide the children of Israel just enough of His portion for each day. But like that screaming child, one day they demanded more. Dissatisfaction came as they focused on what they didn't have instead of what they did have:

> The rabble with them began to crave other food, and again the Israel-
> ites started wailing and said, "If only we had meat to eat! We remem-
> ber the fish we ate in Egypt at no cost—also the cucumbers, melons,
> leeks, onions and garlic. But now we have lost our appetite; we never
> see anything but this manna!" (Numbers 11:4-6).

Does that sound like a child in need of some serious discipline or what? Notice the word "rabble." These were the mixed crowd of Egyptians and others who followed along with Israel out of Egypt. God could take the people out of Egypt, but He had to discipline the Egypt out of them. And discipline them, He did. "Now the LORD will give you meat, and you will eat it. You will not eat it for just one day, or two days, or five, ten or twenty days, but for a whole month— until it comes out of your nostrils and you loathe it—because you have rejected the LORD, who is among you, and have wailed before him" (Numbers 11:18-20).

The people didn't ask God to fill their real need—their ache within. They came up with their own solution and demanded it now. They got what they asked for, and as we later learn in Numbers 11:33-34, it became the death of them. So close to the resurrection, they let evil consume their hearts in their waiting time and missed the promised land entirely.

God's dream must be experienced God's way. If you settle for anything else, you'll never be satisfied. "Yet the LORD longs to be gracious to you; he rises to show you compassion. For the LORD is a God of justice. Blessed are all who wait for him!" (Isaiah 30:18).

BIBLE STUDY

Read Psalm 27:13-14; 33:20; 40:1; 130:5-8.

As we read these verses, we see that David struggled with waiting as much as we all do. It's not easy to wait on God when we want to move forward. We think we know how things should turn out, and we want to see resolution. These verses show us ten things we can do while we are waiting. A friend of mine calls this "actively waiting."

1. Do not lose confidence in God's goodness.
2. Be strong.
3. Do not lose hope.
4. Let God be your shield and your help.
5. Be patient.
6. Continue to cry out to God.
7. Cling to His Word.
8. Watch for His answers.
9. Trust in His unfailing love.
10. Rejoice in His redemption.

Continue to practice these ten things as you wait for the resurrection that will surely follow death.

What are you waiting for? How will this help you?

Read Matthew 6:9-13.

Most of us are familiar with this passage, having recited it or sung it countless times. But have we read it from the Bible and really applied it to our own prayer life recently? When we are in a time of waiting, we can communicate with the Lord and cry out to Him as the psalmist said. Jesus taught us how to pray in this passage. Verse 12 stood out to me: "Forgive us our debts as we also have forgiven our debtors." I thought of my assistant asking me to cancel my debt, and I remembered Christ went to the cross to cancel mine.

Write out a personal prayer using the Lord's Prayer as a guide. Using the key points from the verses you have read, begin with these phrases:

> Lord, I praise You for…
> Help me to do Your will by…
> Lord, I need…
> Please forgive me for…
> And help me to forgive…
> I am struggling with…
> Please help me to stand firm, for You alone are Lord,
> and I give You all the glory. Amen.

Read Psalm 16:2; 73:25; Philippians 3:8.

Though we will never arrive at a point of spiritual perfection, we must remember that these three verses are our goal. As we journey with God, we should desire nothing more than to fellowship with Him. Anything that you desire more than that is an idol. Knock it down just as Gideon tore down the altar. Is there still something in your life that is more desirable than God? If you can, write about it in your notebook and then ask God to help you tear down that barrier to Him in your life.

EIGHTEEN

A PROMISE MADE
IS A PROMISE KEPT

About six months before I met my two sons from Africa, I wrote this in my journal:

Sometimes I get overwhelmed with all the ministry opportunities that surround me every day. Children are starving in distant lands, a single mom is struggling financially down the street, a crisis pregnancy center in town needs volunteers, and friends from church could use a home-cooked meal brought to their home. I see homeless shelters and battered women's homes and people in dire situations who walk the streets of my city every day.

We live in a fallen world, where people's circumstances belie what God meant for His people to be and become. Yet here I sit in a warm home with a pantry stocked full of food and three little people who are looking at the way I live and patterning their lives after mine. This thought pounds in my head: I am only one person, I have three small children, limited resources, and an already full schedule. What can I do? I can't right all the wrongs of this world. I can't possibly help all the helpless. So I turn my head and do nothing.

Oh sure, I serve through Proverbs 31 Ministries and in my local church body, but what about the helpless? What about those who truly have nothing and nobody to turn to? Who will be Jesus to them today? Who will live out the biblical response to those in need?

James 2:14-17 says, "What good is it, my brothers, if a man claims to have faith but has no deeds? Can such faith save him? Suppose a brother or sister is without clothes and daily food. If one of you says to him, 'Go, I wish you well; keep warm and well fed,' but does nothing about his physical needs, what good is it? In the same way, faith by itself, if it is not accompanied by action, is dead."

I am determined to stop turning my head. I vow that even though I cannot reach them all, I can reach one. God, show me which one.

A DAILY ASSIGNMENT

Not long after writing this, I heard of a little boy named Sergei living in an orphanage in Belarus. Through another family who adopted a son from this same orphanage, I was able to obtain photographs of the living conditions these boys face every day.

My heart broke. I wanted to do whatever I could do to help him, and I started praying for God's direction. Each day I asked God for an assignment to help Sergei. Some days I was to pray for him. Other days I would call and send e-mails, inquiring of the possibilities to let him travel to spend time in our home. Though I had limitations, God blessed my obedience and gave me assignments I could do.

I received one of my most precious assignments in the middle of the night. I woke up with tears streaming down my face. At first, I was confused and asked the Lord why I was crying. God gently touched my heart by answering, *You are taking Sergei's tears today. That is what you are doing in My Name to change the world today. One orphan will go to bed tonight without one single tear.*

God was certainly stirring something in my heart. These were more than just prayers for an orphan child; they were the beginning of new adventures with God. Something was awakening in my spirit. My heart was becoming more aware of how to beat in tandem with the Lord's heart. A resurrection of meaning and purpose and desire was dawning on my horizon.

SECRET SERVICE

All along this ministry journey, I kept thinking God was looking for me to do great things for Him. But now I am convinced the Lord isn't looking for a bestselling author or an arena speaker. He isn't looking for people to dance in the limelight. He is looking for those souls who are willing to press close to His heart and hear the cries of the forgotten. He wants us to do great things with Him to reach "the least of these." Ministry that makes the biggest impact is that which is done in the secret places, the hard stuff that is void of glory but full of guts. Theodore Roosevelt spoke of this kind of service:

> It is not the critic who counts: not the man who points out how the strong man stumbles or where the doer of deeds could have done better. The credit belongs to the man who is actually in the arena, whose face is marred by dust and sweat and blood, who strives valiantly...who knows the great enthusiasms, the great devotions, who spends himself for a worthy cause; who, at the best, knows, in the end, the triumph of high achievement, and who, at the worst, if he fails, at least fails while daring greatly, so that his place shall never be with those cold and timid souls who knew neither victory nor defeat.[1]

A PROMISE MADE...

I knew in my heart that to try adopting Sergei would be costly, extremely time-consuming, and risky. By this time, we'd already started adoption proceedings for our two sons from Africa. My face was already "marred by dust and sweat and blood," so to speak. Were we to take on this too?

As crazy as most of our family and friends thought we were, we decided to march on with all three adoptions—our two boys from Libera and now Sergei. Sergei's would be much more complicated than the other two, but God kept opening the doors, so we kept walking through them. The same weekend our boys from Africa came to live in our home permanently, Sergei arrived for his five-week Christmas visit. Life was loud and crazy and messy and more wonderful than ever before. As a matter of fact, Art and I never opened our presents. They seemed a little insignificant when we had more joy than we could contain just watching kids who'd never had anything experience the love of a family at Christmas.

Sergei's visit flew by, and before we knew it, the time had come for him to return to his orphanage halfway across the world. The day before he left, we asked an interpreter to help us discuss with Sergei the possibility of adopting him. He said he loved our family and wanted to be a part of it. We promised him we'd do everything in our power to complete the necessary paperwork to bring him home quickly, never dreaming it could take years.

"HE WILL UNDERSTAND"

At the writing of this book, the process has already taken more than a year, and we still don't have him home. It has been a hard year of wanting and waiting, feeling hopeful and at the same time quite helpless. We've only been able to get a couple of packages to him, a few e-mails, and one phone call.

When we were working on arranging the phone call with Sergei, I asked some of the officials to please provide an interpreter to help facilitate our discussion. I wanted Sergei to know the adoption was being delayed not by us but rather by the red tape of two very different governments. When no interpreter was available, my heart sank. So much time had passed since Sergei had communicated in English with us, I doubted he would remember enough to make the conversation meaningful.

The lady helping to arrange the call, one of the few Christians involved on their end, knew I was disappointed with the news. So the day before the call was to take place, she sent me an e-mail to encourage me: "There will be no interpreter as nobody knows English at Ryasno. But you will tell him that you love him, and that he will understand."

What a beautiful truth. Yes, I believe Sergei did remember my voice and understand that his mommy loves him. One of the first sentences Sergei spoke to me in English was "I love you, Mommy." The conversation was shorter than I would have liked and void of all the explanations I wanted to give him, but it was good. It was just the way God planned and probably all Sergei needed.

The Belarussian lady's comment reminds me so much of what God continues to teach me about trusting Him. When I grieve over the bummer things in life and cry out to God, I can imagine God instructing the Holy Spirit to say something similar to me. There is no way to interpret this event in a way she can comprehend, but tell her that I love her, and that she will understand.

Isn't God amazing? Yes indeed, God is good. Even when I can't understand His timing and His ways, I do fully understand His love, and that is enough.

A PROMISE KEPT

No, God has not yet resurrected this situation the way I hope He will. But He has resurrected the way I now look at it. We may have to pass through the stages of faith many times before our sweet Sergei comes home, but the dream is worth the price. And what if God's final answer is no? With tears in my eyes I will say, like the hymn so beautifully states, it is still well with my soul. I will not see this as a waste of time and money. I will refuse to get bogged down in bitterness. I will feel privileged that I can know and love and pray for this boy. This boy, with whom I share no biological connection but who has captured my heart and tapped into my maternal instincts. This boy, whom I will forever love as I treasure our five short weeks together.

My favorite time with Sergei was at night after his bath, when I would come into his room and put him to bed. I would say prayers and tuck the blankets the way he liked, tight all around his small body with only the top of his head and eyes peeking out. Then I would sing him into dreamland and watch peace envelop this little life.

This is a picture I treasure. I feel certain that Sergei's soul was forever impacted by his time with us, and Jesus will someday come to be Lord of his life. Though he may not have the home here on earth I want him to, I'm convinced he'll have something far better: an eternal home with no more tears, no more hunger, no more lonely nights, no more uncertain days, no more dashed hopes, and no more unanswered questions.

Regardless of what happens, I've found peace in knowing that God has promised in Psalm 68:5 to be "a father to the fatherless." Even though the best answer seems to me to be having Sergei with us, truly the best place for him is where he can come to know God. Though a forgotten orphanage seems like an unlikely place, God is there. I can picture choirs of angels singing him to sleep and his heavenly Father tucking him into bed. As his eyes peek over the tightly wound covers, the last sight he'll see each night is his heavenly Daddy's smiling face.

And what about my promise to Sergei? My promise to come and get him will not be broken even if I never physically get to bring him home. For I taught Sergei about Jesus, the one his soul really longs for even more than a mommy and daddy. The most glorious part of the resurrection is the promise Jesus gave us that He will return. "Behold, I am coming soon!...Behold, I am coming soon! My reward is with me, and I will give to everyone according to what he has done. I am the Alpha and Omega, the First and the Last, the Beginning and the End...Yes, I am coming soon!" (Revelation 22:7, 12, 20).

I would be remiss if I led you to believe that on this faith journey, the resurrection phase always ends with "happily ever after." We live in a fallen world with gaps and gut-wrenching injustices. But our souls can rise above the dusty roads of this earth into the victorious heavenly realm that is our real home. We must always remember this place is but a stop along the way, not our real destination.

A Bible teacher once shared that FAITH stands for Forsaking All, I Trust Him. Numbers 23:19-20 says, "God is not a man, that he should lie, nor a son of man, that he should change his mind. Does he speak and then not act? Does

We must always remember this place is but a stop along the way, not our real destination.

he promise and not fulfill? I have received a command to bless; he has blessed, and I cannot change it."

He may not resurrect all of the circumstances in your life, but He will resurrect a deeper and more secure trust of Him if you will let Him.

BIBLE STUDY

Read Luke 1:5-25; 18:1-8.

Zechariah was a very old man when an angel told him, "Do not be afraid…your prayer has been heard." By the time the angel appeared, Zechariah had probably given up on ever having his prayer for a child answered by God. He had gone on with his life, accepting God's silence as a no and continuing to serve the Lord. Luke 1:6 tells us both Zechariah and his wife, Elizabeth, were "upright in the sight of God, observing all the Lord's commandments and regulations blamelessly." They chose to continue to honor God and placed their relationship with Him above their need to have children. They chose not to become bitter and did not turn away from the Lord. Yet God, in His timing, chose to answer their prayers long after they expected Him to. Sometimes we stop praying, throw our hands up, and assume that our prayers will be forgotten just because we've stopped asking. This story shows us that God answers prayers according to His timing, not ours. May we not forget that essential element in our prayer life.

Jesus uses the parable of the widow and the judge to show us that we should always pray and not give up. Just as the widow eventually "wore out" the judge, so we can prevail upon God by persevering in our prayer life. Luke 18:7 says, "And will not God bring about justice for His chosen ones, who cry out to Him day and night? Will He keep putting them off?" Don't let worldly wisdom keep you from going before God continually with your needs. I have learned this as I have felt that I must be wearing God out with my continued prayers for Sergei. I will continue to pray expectantly and will only stop when I feel God answer. Galatians 4:18 says, "It is fine to be zealous, provided the purpose is good." May we all be zealous in our prayer life! Write down an area you may have given up on that you need to recommit to pray for.

Read Psalm 56:8; Isaiah 25:8; Revelation 7:17.

The night I woke up crying for Sergei, God brought these verses to mind. Though I took Sergei's tears on that one amazing night, God shows us in His Word that He takes our tears every day. How amazing to me that the God of the universe pauses in the midst of all His creation to wipe away our tears and save them in a bottle. The next time I cry, I plan to thank God through my tears that He cares about me that way—and He cares about you that way too! Record what these verses mean to you personally.

Read Romans 8:23-25.

As I've experienced the miracle of adoption firsthand, I've learned what a gift from God it is to be grafted into His family. Every soul longs to feel at home, and we are all groaning inwardly for our real home, heaven. There we will experience resurrection unlike any form of resurrection we have experienced on earth. We will take part in God's family in God's house. As the song goes, "What a day of rejoicing that will be." Thank God that He has adopted you into His family today.

NINETEEN

GOD BRINGS DREAMS TO LIFE

As the lady made her way toward me, I knew exactly what she was thinking and feeling. She felt so insignificant. So small. She made her way to me in the front of the room. I was surrounded by women of all ages. Some just wanted to give me a tearful hug. Others held my book in their hands, looking for a note of encouragement and an autograph. She just wanted to ask me how? How could she take a broken life and allow God to use it for His glory? Is it possible that a girl rejected by her earthly father could actually be chosen and set apart for a divine calling? How could she get past the place of not being able to make it through the day to proclaiming God's love from the podium?

She waited in line for her turn. Then, as she opened her mouth to speak, her throat tightened, her eyes filled with tears, and all she could squeak out was an emotional "how?" She wanted me to take her home with me and teach her. She wanted me to pack her in my suitcase and whisk her away from her life and into the life of one making a difference. She wanted me to share some quick and easy answer, three easy steps to the life you dream of, all for the low price of attending the seminar. But I wasn't a magician, a slick salesman, or a woman looking for a new houseguest. I was a woman who had experienced deep hurts and bitter disappointments, and who had chosen to surrender her life to God and was now being used by Him.

I did not give her the quick and easy answer she was looking for. I didn't give her any profound wisdom or direction. We only had time for me to simply tell her how I got started, and then she found herself making her way back to her seat. But she wasn't heading back empty and without hope.

I pray what I lacked in words, I made up for in example. I pray she had seen Jesus in me. I pray she had seen living proof of God's redemption. I pray she thought to herself, *If God could do that with her, I think there's hope for me after all.* And I pray something new and big and God-directed was born in her and confirmed in her heart in an undeniable way that day.

Though she still didn't know how, I pray she knew God could find a way. Though she didn't know when, I pray she now knew the timing was in His hands. Though she didn't even think she had much to offer, I knew God would fill in her gaps. I pray she simply knew God was calling her, inviting her, wooing her to something with His fingerprints all over it, and that would be enough.

EXPERIENCING GOD

Remember the first chapter of the book? The same scene had happened many years before, only now I was the speaker. I could hardly believe it. God does bring dreams to life! I had just spoken to an auditorium filled with women and to more than 100,000 via simulcast. My book table was stacked high with my books, and now women were lining up to meet me. That's when it hit me.

This is not what fills my heart with joy. I was humbled to be a vessel through which other women could be touched. I was thankful to be able to experience all this. But it simply was not the pinnacle experience I always thought it would be. It didn't make me feel more significant or less insecure. It was fleeting, and the glimmer of limelight was quite empty. The realization hit me hard: The joy of the journey is not simply reaching the promised land. The real joy was experiencing God throughout all the phases of faith. I closed my eyes and drank in this moment of truth.

We are amazingly similar to the children of Israel. We spend half our lives looking back at our own Egypt with selective memories, longing to have our comfort zone back. Then we spend the other half wishing our days away for a dreamy future in our own promised land. The short time we actually focus on today's journey is often wasted on complaining, grumbling, wishing to be in a different place, or simply and mindlessly going through the motions of life. Why do we struggle with embracing the moment we've been given and experiencing God in the here and now?

Regardless of where you are today, God is with you. God is wooing you. God wants you to experience Him. Whatever you are going through today, you can find His joy and peace. However distant your dreams may seem, God is working things out, and today is an important part of that process. Remember your experiences with God. Write them down. Ponder them often. Treasure them in your heart. And vow to make experiencing God the highest goal of your faith journey.

SHORTCUTS

Neither the journey nor the promised land will give my heart what it truly desires. I have to walk with God daily and let Him have His way in my heart. I have to embrace the struggles as well as the triumphs, the joys and the sorrows, the deaths and the resurrections. No shortcut or quick fix will help me become the woman God wants me to become.

Some time ago, Art thought he would take a shortcut of sorts. Through the wonders of modern technology, the wonderful LASIK eye surgery held great promise to rid Art of his dreaded contacts and glasses. But he wanted to get it done cheaper and faster than most of the doctors in our area could promise, so he put the surgery off. Then one day, he spotted a coupon in our paper for a superfast, supercheap LASIK surgery, and he jumped at the opportunity.

I was a bit concerned the day of the surgery when I arrived at the medical facility. Whoever heard of having surgery on your eyes done in the back of a truck parked on the side of a shopping center near the dumpster! But the lure of saving a few bucks and getting a quick fix negated the doubts Art might have been having, and he walked up the wobbly stairs and disappeared into the truck.

At first, the surgery seemed to have worked. But as the months wore on, Art's eyesight went right back to being as bad as before, if not a little worse. He eventually had to drive out of town to a specialist to get his eyes worked on again, which wound up costing him more time and money than if he'd just had it done right in the first place.

But I can't fault Art for his medical escapade because I've made the same mistake in my spiritual walk so many times. You know about many of my experiences because you've read about them in this book. My times of running ahead of God, making suggestions to Him, manipulating circumstances, and feeling frustrated when my shortcuts...well, fell short! I get a vision for something, make a beeline toward making it happen, and request that God would bless my plans. How that must break His heart.

OUR DRIVING FORCE

There is an eternal purpose to all of this that cannot be left out.

> There dwells inside you, deep within, a tiny whippoorwill. Listen. You will hear him sing...We forget he is there, so easy he is to ignore. Other animals of the heart are larger, noisier, more demanding, more imposing. But none is so constant. Other creatures are more quickly fed. More simply satisfied. We feed the lion who growls for power. We stroke the tiger who demands affection. We bridle the stallion who bucks control. But what do we do with the whippoorwill that yearns for eternity?[1]

Have you heard this constant chirping in your soul? Little reminders that this place is not all there is? I'm so thankful the earth will always produce discontentments and shortcomings. I'm so grateful that speaking before crowds of people isn't all that it's cracked up to be. I'm thrilled to get to know other speakers I've long admired and realize they don't really have it any more together than I do. Because all this keeps my heart centered and grounded on God alone. We

Walking closely with God gives us a more keen insight of our desperate need for Him.

must learn to long for the one who holds our eternity and let His song be the driving force in our heart.

HALL OF FAME

Pursuing a deeper faith isn't about playing the spiritual game of keeping up with the Joneses, being admired and commended for our great spiritual acquisitions. No, quite the opposite. Walking closely with God gives us a more keen insight of our desperate need for Him.

Think for just a minute about the person who has been the greatest spiritual influence on your life. She could be a well-known Bible teacher or a lady in your church. Whoever it is, let me let you in on a little secret. She still struggles with insecurity every now and then. There are things about her life she has tried for years to change and still can't. She has people in her life who bug her and rub her the wrong way. God has even hurt her feelings a time or two. Oh, gasp! She is so human.

Hebrews 11, faith's hall of fame, commends many people for the way they walked with God. But as I scan these verses, I can't help but be struck by the reality that each and every person listed had some faults. None of them lived perfect lives, but they did live lives worthy of being mentioned in God's Word. Why? Well, it had very little to do with them at all. They were listed simply because they believed God is who He said He is, and they trusted He would do what He said He would do. "Faith is being sure of what we hope for and certain of what we do not see. This is what the ancients were commended for" (Hebrews 11:1-2).

As I've said over and over, the important thing is not what you do for God but rather that you come to know and believe Him along the way.

BIBLE STUDY

Read Acts 7:44-50.

As we've gone through this story of God's people from Abraham to Joshua, we have continually seen God in the midst of His people. Does He need a tabernacle or sanctuary on earth? No. As these verses tell us, He has all of heaven as His throne, and the earth is merely His footstool. He does not need us to build Him a place to rest. But He knew that we would need a place to meet with Him—a visual reminder that He is in our midst.

Our creator knows what we need. In His mercy, He gave the Israelites that visual reminder by instructing them to build the tabernacle. Today, the church, the Bible, and even our own homes can serve as visual reminders of God's presence. Jesus is accessible to us at all times. He came as Emmanuel, God with us. He tore the veil that separates us from God. Through His death, He is always in our midst, and we are never alone. Praise the Lord today for being Emmanuel in your life—and don't forget that He is there for you always. Write down ways that you can make your home a sanctuary.

Go back through this book and pick out Scriptures that have impacted you. Write them on index cards and place them around your home. Deuteronomy 6:9 says, "Write them on the doorframes of your houses and on your gates."

Read Psalm 78:4-7; 79:13.

This chapter is called "God Brings Dreams to Life." As you have taken the journey through this book and the Bible study, you have undoubtedly had some amazing encounters with the Lord. You have seen God bring dreams to life regardless of what point of the journey you are in. Be careful to remember your experiences with God and pass them along to the next generation as these verses describe.

In the days and weeks to come, make an effort to share some part of your story with someone. If you have children, share with them, in a way that they can understand, what you have been learning about God. Tell them about the dreams that God has planted in your heart and how God is working them out in your life. Reassure them that they are part of your dreams. By doing this, you make God real to them. They learn by example that they too can have a relationship with God. When Moses handed down the Ten Commandments to the Israelites, he told the people, "These commands that I give to you today are to be upon your hearts. Impress them on your children. Talk about them when you sit at home and when you walk along the road, when you lie down and when you get up" (Deuteronomy 6:6-7). Talk to your kids and to your loved ones about God. Make His name famous in your home. Write down some ideas of specific stories you can share with others about God's work in your life. Ask God to bring some to mind if you are struggling with this.

Read Exodus 17:14-15; Joshua 4:1-9.

Both of these passages talk about setting up some sort of memorial to what God has done in our lives. Whether we write it down as a remembrance, make a banner, or build an altar, we are memorializing God's work in our lives for all to see. God obviously feels that this is important for us to do because He included these and other examples in the Bible. How can you create a remembrance of what God has done in your life? Ask Him to reveal a way that perfectly suits your unique personality and giftedness. Write down some ideas in your notebook.

TWENTY

EVERY PROMISE
FULFILLED

W hat an adventure we've been on—and what unlikely people we've seen rise to be the starring members of the cast for this show. God first planted the dream of a chosen nation of people coming from a childless man named Abraham. Then on to Joseph, who spent a good bit of his life being betrayed and living in prison but then rose to be the second most powerful man in the world. And we must not forget Moses, who not only saw some of the most amazing miracles ever performed by the hand of God but also saw God Himself! Then it was on to the children of Israel, whose cycles of disobedience proved to be rich training ground for us. Now, finally, the moment we've all been waiting for—Joshua and the promised land!

Joshua inspires me like no other character in the Bible because of his determination to be absolutely obedient to God. He threw aside all his human reservations and followed hard after God. He was with Moses in Egypt through all the ups and downs of wandering in the desert, and saw his beloved leader die before reaching the promised land. He observed and learned well. Now his time to lead had come. But he did not hesitate like Moses. He did not question God as Moses did. God said it, Joshua believed it, and the promised land was conquered.

Look at the profoundly different ways Moses and Joshua approached the tasks set before them.

THEIR CONFIDENCE

When God told Moses he'd be the leader, Moses looked at all the reasons he couldn't do it. We see no similar record of Joshua hesitating. Joshua must have known his calling had very little to do with his qualifications. God would be the deliverer. Joshua understood and walked confidently in that knowledge.

God had said, "No one will be able to stand up against you all the days of your life. As I was with Moses, so I will be with you; I will never leave you nor forsake you. Be strong and courageous, because you will lead these people to inherit the land I swore to their forefathers to give them" (Joshua 1:5-6). What a confidence-building statement from God!

God went on to tell him to be "strong and courageous" two more times in this chapter. God even had the Israelites reassure him the same way, "Whatever you have commanded us we will do, and wherever you send us we will go. Just as we fully obeyed Moses, so we will obey you. Only may the LORD your God be with us as he was with Moses. Whoever rebels against your word and does not obey your words, whatever you command them, will be put to death. Only be strong and courageous!" (Joshua 1:16-18).

Did Joshua's confidence come as a natural by-product of his personality? I don't think so. If confidence came naturally to Joshua, I don't think God would have had to tell him to be strong and courageous over and over again. No, Joshua's confidence was steadfast because he was confident in God's promises.

THEIR BOLDNESS

Israel fled from Egypt under Moses' lead, but they panicked when they reached the Red Sea. They were trapped between a deadly army and a dangerous sea. Moses cried out to the Lord on their behalf and told the people to just stand still. God seemed frustrated when He replied, "Why are you crying out to me? Tell the Israelites to move on. Raise your staff and stretch out your hand over the sea to divide the water so that the Israelites can go through the sea on dry ground." Perhaps God had already said to move on and no one moved. Not even a toe was put into the water until the waters parted first and the ground was dry.

In contrast, when God instructed Joshua to tell the priests to go into the Jordan River, they did so without hesitation. Under Joshua's leadership they were willing to get wet and trust God to part the water before they saw dry land. "Yet as soon as the priests who carried the ark reached the Jordan and their feet touched the water's edge, the water from upstream stopped flowing...the priests who carried the ark of the covenant of the LORD stood firm on dry ground in the middle of the Jordan, while all Israel passed by until the whole nation had completed the crossing on dry ground" (Joshua 3:15-17).

This illustration challenges me. Am I the kind of leader who has to see the dry ground first? Or am I willing to get a little wet and a little dirty, to step into uncertainty and trust Him? How bold for God am I really?

THEIR COURAGE

The way they handled the giants in their lives was vastly different as well. When the Israelite spies explored the promised land and gave a report, Moses allowed the negative views of ten men to impact the opinions of the whole nation. God gave the assurance that He would go before them. The victory was certain. Caleb, one of the spies who held fast to God's promises, confirmed they should go by saying, "We should go up and take possession of the land, for we can certainly do it" (Numbers 13:30). But the people would not listen. The negativity grew and spread like wildfire throughout the camp. Moses was grieved when the people would not listen, but instead of standing strong, he threw himself down in front of them and pleaded. God was greatly displeased and thus started the 40-year period of wandering in the desert.

Joshua's courage and the Israelites' courage under his leadership were very different from that earlier generation's. Instead of focusing on fearing their enemy, they focused on purifying themselves, freeing their hearts from sin. Then they boldly went where God told them to go, did exactly as they were instructed, and conquered the promised land God's way.

Then Joshua went a step further. He wanted to put into perspective the fear that had kept the Israelites from the promised land for 40 years. So he made an example of their enemies' kings. Joshua 10:24 records a glorious moment for the children of Israel, "When they brought these kings to Joshua, he summoned all the men of Israel and said to the army commanders who had come with him, 'Come here and put your feet on the necks of these kings.' So, they came forward and placed their feet on their necks."

Henry and Richard Blackaby make this observation:

> The young Israelite soldiers had grown up in abject fear of these kings. They spent year after year squandering their youth in a barren desert while their aging parents feebly justified their disobedience to God by explaining that Canaan was populated with fierce, undefeatable giants. But now they'd seen these "giants" up close. Even their kings were ordinary men who could be humbled by God. Joshua wanted to remove any question from his soldiers' minds that when they walked obediently with God they were invincible. Throughout the remainder of Joshua's leadership there is no mention of his soldiers ever fearing their enemies.[1]

God gave the children of Israel victory and placed their fears under their feet. Joshua's quick, obedient heart inspired his followers to become quick, obedient people. In Moses' defense, Joshua had the advantage of learning from Moses' mistakes. Joshua saw Moses in his moments of complete obedience and God's blessing. He saw Moses in times of disobedience and God's punishment. He saw Moses die before getting to the promised land just as God said. Joshua saw Moses' great faith lived out, and despite Moses' mistakes, Joshua saw a hero. Joshua not only saw but he learned. He let what he saw have a profound effect on his life.

We have the same advantage that Joshua had. We have now seen these great heroes of faith who walked before us. We've observed, we've studied, we've pondered, we've learned. Now, what kind of difference will their lives have on the way we walk?

The story crescendos as God's people under Joshua's leadership take possession of the land. The long-awaited, promised land. The time has come for us to take possession of something as well. We must cross the river, shout the shouts, watch the walls tumble, and take possession of the promises of God.

Did you catch that theme in the background throughout this whole book? We've been in preparation to fully possess all the promises of God for ourselves. *Webster's New World Dictionary* defines possess as "(1) to have as belonging to one, to own; (2) to have as an attribute, quality; (3) to gain control over."

Isn't that a revealing definition? How applicable it is to our possession of the promises of God. We must first learn to take them as our own. Not that we own them exclusively but that we own them personally. We come to depend on God and His promises to instruct us, teach us, and lead us. Secondly, our possession of God's promises affects us. He shapes and molds our character. He redefines who we are and what we are about.

And lastly, God and His promises gain control over our lives. Our relationship with Him so profoundly changes us that we live completely different lives as a result. We truly become the new creation God intends for us to become. "Therefore, if anyone is in Christ, he is a new creation; the old has gone, the new has come!" (2 Corinthians 5:17). In order to possess God's promises in this way, we must surrender our old dependencies. What else or who else rivals God for your dependence?

Is it your parents? Your spouse? Your children? Your career? Your lifestyle? Your past accomplishments? Whatever or whoever it is, let me encourage you to surrender these false props and depend on God alone to empower you. Andy Stanley gives us this challenge:

> Your primary goal should be to live in an ongoing state of surrender, acknowledging that without the intervention of the Holy Spirit you will be defeated by the power of sin. If there is a singular theme that emerges from the entirety of Scripture, it is this: Through relationship with God, man is finally capable of doing that which he was incapable of doing on his own. That's what walking in the Spirit is all about. And that's what character is all about...Character is the

by-product of dependency…Character is the will to do what is right, as defined by God, regardless of personal cost.[2]

Joshua was indeed a man of character. When the Israelites finally possessed the promised land and divided it among the tribes, Joshua was the last to receive his allotted portion. He made sure everyone got what they deserved before himself. He possessed his promised land, but even more importantly, he possessed God's promises.

I pray this is true for you as well. Walking with God takes you to amazing places, but even more importantly, it allows you to experience Him in amazing ways. We have not only experienced Him but hopefully we have also been transformed by Him. I feel it only appropriate to leave you with a part of Joshua's final speech to the people he loved so much. They had journeyed together. They had triumphed together. They had fallen deeply in love with God together. May it be so for us as well!

> You yourselves have seen everything the LORD your God has done to all these nations for your sake; it was the LORD who fought for you…Be very strong; be careful to obey all that is written in the Book of the Law of Moses, without turning aside to the right or to the left… You know with all your heart and soul that not one of these good promises the LORD your God gave you has failed. Every promise has been fulfilled; not one has failed (Joshua 23:3, 6, 14).

What happens when women walk in faith? Well, now you know my story.

Oh, sweet friend, what a privilege it has been to walk this part of your journey with you. My prayer is that you have a clearer vision of where you are in the phases of faith and that this knowledge will give you courage to press on. Though the adventure is harder and grander than we ever imagined, I hope you can now say without a doubt that walking with God does indeed take you to amazing places. Continue striving to become a woman who looks back on her walk with God with no regrets. For that, my friend, is the real dream.

Walking with God

takes you to amazing places,

but even more importantly,

it allows you to experience

Him in amazing ways.

BIBLE STUDY

As we finish the book and Bible study, I would like to close with my prayer for you, my friend. Please look up these verses as I reference them, meditate on them, and make them your prayer for yourself as well. I pray that you would continually pray this prayer as you go forward in your walk with God.

I pray that when you hear His voice, you will not harden your hearts (Psalm 95:7-8; Hebrews 4:7-8).

I pray that you will live by faith and not by sight (2 Corinthians 5:7).

I pray that you will continue to grow in spiritual maturity (Colossians 4:12).

I pray that you will be able to understand the length, width, depth, and breadth of Christ's love for you (Ephesians 3:18-19).

I pray that you will always be eager to do the right thing (Hebrews 13:21).

I pray that the God of hope will fill you with much joy and peace while you trust in Him (Romans 15:13).

I pray that God would give you a spirit of wisdom and revelation (Ephesians 1:17).

I pray that you will be as loving as God and as patient as Christ (2 Thessalonians 3:5).

I pray that God will strengthen you with power through His Spirit (Ephesians 3:16).

I pray that you will get along with each other as well as Jesus got along with us all (Romans 15:5).

I pray that you will be on your face before the Lord, admitting your dependence on Him (James 4:10).

I pray that you will continue training for a godly life (1 Timothy 4:7).

And finally, I pray that you will continue to live in Christ, rooted and built up in Him, strengthened in the faith as you were taught and overflowing with thankfulness (Colossians 2:6).

Pray these prayers throughout your week and experience the power of praying God's Word. May your life be forever changed by your amazing walk with God. Amen and amen.

NOTES

WHAT HAPPENS WHEN WOMEN SAY YES TO GOD

Chapter Two: Hearing God's Voice
1. *Life Application Study Bible* (NIV) (Wheaton, IL: Tyndale House Publishers, 1988), p. 2125.
2. Rick Warren, *The Purpose-Driven Life* (Grand Rapids, MI: Zondervan Publishing House, 2002), p. 233.
3. A.J. Russell, ed., *God Calling* (Grand Rapids, MI: Spire Books, 2005), p. 113.

Chapter Three: When Obedience Becomes Radical
1. *Life Application Study Bible* (NIV) (Wheaton, IL: Tyndale House Publishers, 1988), p. 1632.

Chapter Four: You Never Know How God Will Use You Until You Let Him
1. *Life Application Study Bible* (NIV) (Wheaton, IL: Tyndale House Publishers, 1998), p. 2277.
2. A.J. Russell, ed., *God Calling*, May 19.
3. "I Wonder Why," blog entry, July 18, 2006, written by Beverly Daffron. Used with permission.

Chapter Five: What Keeps Us from Saying Yes to God
1. Rick Warren, *The Purpose-Driven Life* (Grand Rapids, MI: Zondervan Publishing House, 2002), p. 254.
2. Beth Moore, *Living Free* (Nashville, TN: LifeWay Press, 2001), p. 82.
3. Ibid., p. 77.

Chapter Six: If It Were Easy, It Wouldn't Be Worth Doing
1. Brent Curtis and John Eldredge, *The Sacred Romance* (Nashville, TN: Thomas Nelson, 1997), pp. 137-38.

Chapter Seven: Keeping Our Vision Clear
1. C.S. Lewis, *Mere Christianity* (San Francisco, CA: HarperCollins Publishers, 1952), pp. 149-50.
2. Max Lucado, *No Wonder They Call Him the Savior* (Sisters, OR: Multnomah Publishers, 1986), p. 126.

Chapter Eight: Giving Up What Was Never Ours
1. Randy Alcorn, *The Treasure Principle* (Sisters, OR: Multnomah Publishers, 2001), p. 57.
2. Elizabeth George, *A Woman's Walk with God* (Eugene, OR: Harvest House Publishers, 2000), p. 172.

Chapter Nine: Radically Blessed
1. Bruce Wilkinson, *Set Apart* (Sisters, OR: Multnomah Publishers, 1998), p. 175

Chapter Nine: A Most Unlikely Path

1. Phillip Keller, *A Shepherd Looks at Psalm 23* (Grand Rapids, MI: Zondervan, 1970), 26-27.

Chapter Twelve: Learning to Lead

1. *Life Application Study Bible*, NIV (Wheaton, IL: Tyndale House Publishers, 1988), 269-97.
2. Ibid., p. 127.

Chapter Fifteen: God Isn't Surprised by Death

1. With thanks to Mark Hamby, whose sermon inspired these thoughts.

Chapter Sixteen: God's Portion, Position, and Promise

1. Max Lucado, *Come Thirsty* (Nashville, TN: W Publishing Group, 2004), 121-22.

Chapter Eighteen: A Promise Made is a Promise Kept

1. Quoted in Bob Buford, *Finishing Well* (Nashville, TN: Integrity Publishers, 2004), 171.

Chapter Nineteen: God Brings Dreams to Life

1. Max Lucado, *When God Whispers Your Name* (Nashville, TN: W Publishing Group, 1994), 165-66.

Chapter Twenty: Every Promise Fulfilled

1. Henry Blackaby and Richard Blackaby, *Called to Be God's Leader: Lessons from the Life of Joshua* (Nashville, TN: Thomas Nelson Publishers, 2004), 182-83.
2. Andy Stanley, *Louder than Words* (Sisters, OR: Multnomah, 2004), 35, 174-75.

ABOUT THE AUTHOR

Lysa TerKeurst is the president of Proverbs 31 Ministries and author of 21 books, including the *New York Times* bestsellers *Uninvited* and *The Best Yes*. Additionally, Lysa has been featured on *Focus on the Family, The Today Show, Good Morning America,* and more. Lysa speaks nationwide at Catalyst, Lifeway Abundance Conference, Women of Joy, and various church events. She deeply loves her family and lives with them in Charlotte, North Carolina. Connect with Lysa on social media @LysaTerKeurst or on her blog at www.lysaterkeurst.com.

ABOUT PROVERBS 31 MINISTRIES

If you were inspired by *What Happens When Women Say Yes to God and Walk in Faith* and desire to deepen your own personal relationship with Jesus Christ, we have just what you're looking for. Proverbs 31 Ministries exists to be a trusted friend who will take you by the hand and walk by your side, leading you one step closer to the heart of God through:

Free First 5 app

Free online daily devotions

Online Bible studies

Writer and speaker training

Daily radio programs

Books and resources

For more information about Proverbs 31 Ministries,
visit www.Proverbs31.org

To learn more about Harvest House books and
to read sample chapters, visit our website:

www.HarvestHousePublishers.com

HARVEST HOUSE PUBLISHERS
EUGENE, OREGON